INSIGHTS
ON MANAGEMENT

ADDITIONAL BOOKS BY THE AUTHOR

Insights On Policy, 2011

How to Manage in Times of Crisis, 2009

The Ideal Executive: Why You Cannot Be One and What to Do About It
LEADERSHIP TRILOGY, VOL. 1, 2004

Management/Mismanagement Styles:
How to Identify a Style and What to Do About It:
LEADERSHIP TRILOGY, VOL. 2, 2004

Leading the Leaders: How to Enrich Your Style of Management
and Handle People Whose Style is Different from Yours:
LEADERSHIP TRILOGY, VOL. 3, 2004

Managing Corporate Lifecycles: An Updated and
Expanded Look at the Classic Work,
CORPORATE LIFECYCLES, 2004

The Pursuit of Prime, 1996

Mastering Change: The Power of Mutual Trust and Respect, 1992

Corporate Lifecycles: How and Why Corporations Grow and Die
and What to Do About It, 1988

How to Solve the Mismanagement Crisis, 1979

Self-Management: New Dimensions to Democracy,
with Elisabeth M. Borgese, 1975

Industrial Democracy: Yugoslav Style, 1971

To place an order or see a full list of Adizes publications,
including books and DVDs, visit us online at www.adizes.com/store.

INSIGHTS
ON MANAGEMENT

ICHAK KALDERON ADIZES
Founder, Adizes Institute
Santa Barbara, California

Library of Congress Cataloging-in-Publication Data

Adizes, Ichak.
Insights on Management

Library of Congress Control Number Pending

ISBN: 978-0-937120-24-8

Published by
Adizes Institute Publications
1212 Mark Avenue
Carpinteria
Santa Barbara County, California, USA 93013
805-565-2901; Fax 805-565-0741
Website: www.adizes.com

Design and layout by RJ Communications LLC, New York
Printed in the United States of America

Additional copies may be ordered from www.adizes.com/store

*To Irene and Bob Cortinovis, whose hospitality
and friendship brought me to where I am today*

ACKNOWLEDGMENTS

I want to thank my editor, Nan Goldberg, whose editing has helped me sharpen my thinking.

CONTENTS

Part 7: Management Education

Conclusion: The Adizes Methodology

PREFACE

The Adizes blog, which is posted at least once a week on the Adizes Institute website (http://www.adizes.com/blog/?cat=1) and sent by e-mail to thousands of subscribers, began life in 2003 as a monthly column called "Insights."

They were, literally, *insights*, rather than the products of scientific research. I dared to say what I thought. In doing so, I opened myself up to criticism.

And that is what I got: Many people wrote to say they disagreed with one or more of my observations or conclusions. But they kept reading, because what I wrote made them think. And that is exactly what I set out to achieve.

Recently, I decided to publish the essays in book form. I cherish books; I suppose in that way I will always belong to the pre-Internet generation. The Internet, blogs, and tweets are great for speed and mass distribution, but to me they seem temporary, perishable, while a book has permanency.

In this book—the second of a series of Insights collections—all of the essays deal with managing organizations. The ideas for the columns often evolved out of something I saw, heard, or felt as I traveled around the world, consulting to hundreds of companies, governments, and other organizations. Then, in light of the response from readers, I often rethought my Insights, re-edited, rewrote, or updated them.

In their new, book-length form, I believe these Insights will continue to stir thought and debate.

Contact me with your reactions at ichak@adizes.com.

– Ichak Kalderon Adizes, Ph.D.

INTRODUCTION:
DEFINING OUR TERMS[1]

IN 1969, I started the first training program in the world on how to manage artistic organizations: opera, dance, symphonic orchestras, etc. It began when I realized that you cannot manage artists as you manage other workers. Why not? What was going on?

WHAT DEFINES MANAGEMENT?

I found out that the word "management" cannot be precisely translated into any other language I have looked at (and I have lectured in fifty-two countries so far). Even the French, who are meticulous about using their own language, use the English word "management." In Spanish, the word "management" (*manejar*) is used only for horses.

So, what does "management" mean?

Do you agree with me that an organization is very well managed if it is effective and efficient in the short run, and effective and efficient in the long run? This is a functional definition: Basically, I am defining the role by describing the output it is supposed to produce. If the organization is ineffective or inefficient, now or in the future, the organization is mismanaged.

Please realize that this definition is value-free. Whether you are managing a prison or Mother Teresa's order, the definition is the same—although what it means to be effective or efficient may vary. The definition is also free of cultural or industry bias. It applies to organizations in any industry, in any culture, with any goals, whether macro- or micro-, for- or not-for-profit. And it applies not only to organizations, but also to countries. Some people even use it for family therapy. It is universal.

---

[1] Adizes Insights, November 2005. This essay is revised from the speech given at the annual convention of the Central and East European Management Association (CEEMAN), which encompasses business schools in that region and beyond, held in Kiev, Ukraine, in September 2005.

Many years ago I got lucky. I suppose I was also smart enough to realize I was lucky. I was like that British doctor who discovered the relationship between vitamin C and scurvy when he went out to sea for an extended period, during which he was deprived of vitamin C.

My luck was in discovering that there are four managerial "vitamins" that are essential for good management:

"Vitamin" (P) makes the organization effective in the short run.

"Vitamin" (A) makes the organization efficient in the short run.

"Vitamin" (E) makes the organization effective in the long run.

"Vitamin" (I) makes the organization efficient in the long run.[2]

Each time one of these roles is not performed, or is performed badly, the organization will be ineffective and/or inefficient, now and/or in the future. In a word, it will be mismanaged.[3]

This model, which I and my certified associates have spent more than forty years developing and applying all over the world, enables management or consultants to predict and diagnose organizational problems, determine whether they are normal or abnormal, analyze what is causing them, and decide in what sequence to solve them.

Let us discuss what those (PAEI) roles are.

(P) for Short-Term Effectiveness

What does it mean for an organization to be effective?

Every organization has its purpose, a reason that it exists. When a system is able to (P)roduce that which it exists to do, it is effective. Look at the pen you are holding. Does it write? If it does, it is effective. If it does not write it is not effective, even though you can still use it to scratch your head. It is ineffective because scratching a head was not the purpose for which the pen was designed.

The producer's focus is on satisfying the current needs of its clients: What do they want? An organization that serves its market well by providing for its clients' present needs is effective in the *short* run.

---

[2] For a more in-depth discussion of the four managerial "vitamins," see the chapter in this section titled "(PAEI): The Organizational DNA Code for Managing Change," which begins on page 37.

[3] For more information on diagnosing mismanagement, see Ichak Adizes, *Management/Mismanagement Styles: How to Identify a Style and What to Do About It* (Santa Barbara, CA: Adizes Institute Publications, 2004).

(A) for Short-Term Efficiency

First, let's define organizational efficiency. To be efficient means that the system uses the least input to produce an output. It is the role of (A)dministration to focus on how to streamline a system to use minimum resources to produce what is needed. The (A) role makes an organization efficient by systematizing, organizing, and programming tasks and functions—whenever possible—into manuals, rules, policies, and standard operating procedures.

Now let's look at what will make the organization effective in the *long* run.

(E) for Long-Term Effectiveness

What do you need to do to be effective in the long run? Let's use a tennis analogy: Simply hitting the ball over the net is not sufficient to win the game. To win the game—to be profitable in the long run—what do you need to do? While you are hitting the ball, you need to think about where the next ball might come from and where it might arrive on your side of the net. Then you have to position yourself so that when the ball arrives you are ready to hit it. In the marketplace, this is called planning.

How do we do that? We need to be creative, because no one knows for sure what is going to happen tomorrow. We need to imagine where the next ball (our client's future need) is going to land. And then what do we need to do? We have to take risks—because if we have to act today to prepare for the unknown tomorrow, we could make mistakes: In other words, what we anticipate will happen might *not* happen, and all that preparation will have been a waste.

An (E)ntrepreneur is someone who visualizes the future needs of the market and takes the necessary but risky steps today to satisfy those future needs. In the Adizes code, this is the (E) role.

(I) for Long-Term Efficiency

What I have learned during the past forty years is that the (I) "vitamin" is the most important. What makes the organization efficient in the long run is fostering a climate of open communication based on respect for each other's differences of opinion and judgment; and of cooperation based on perceived common interests.

When there is a culture of interdependency, mutual support, and teamwork, the system will survive longer than a system in which a failure in any of its components causes the whole organization to malfunction.

My name for the role that creates this consciousness of being organically interdependent is (I)ntegration.

AND THAT SPELLS 'PRIME'

If the (PAEI) roles are performed well, the organization will be effective and efficient in both the long and short term. It will be well managed. The organization will be in Prime.

Role	Makes the organization:		
(P)roduce or (P)rovide for the expected needs	functional	effective	in the short run
(A)dminister	systematized	efficient	in the short run
(E)ntrepreneur	pro-active	effective	in the long run
(I)ntegrate the	organic	efficient	in the long run

USES OF THE CODE

The Adizes (PAEI) code has many applications. It can be used to analyze the lifecycles of organizations; to explore which organizational problems are normal and which pathological; to evaluate decision-making; to evaluate the functionality of organizational structures; etc.

If a certain (PAEI) role of management is not performed or is performed badly, I can predict the organizational illness that will develop as a result. Thus, studying the four roles, and when, how, whether, and by whom they are being performed, can be a significant tool in treating the "disease" of mismanagement: If, for example, the organization is losing market share, it is being ineffective in the short term. Once you know that producing provides short-term effectiveness, if you know how to improve your (P), you can regain that market share.

If I see that the company is not profitable—whether it is losing money or its expenses are wasteful—then "vitamin" (A) is needed. If the organization is not effective in the long run—if it is not adapting, not changing, not flexible, or if it is bringing new products to the market too late and sacrificing its window of opportunity—then we need "vitamin" (E).

And if I see that the organization would be vulnerable if key people left, which happens in many businesses, then I know that "vitamin" (I) is missing.

This knowledge gives us a diagnostic tool. And, if we know how to "inject" the missing or weak "vitamin," or managerial role, we have a thera-peutic methodology, too.

What I have developed for forty years, what my books cover, and what I am still writing about, is how to insert the missing role in order to make the organization healthy; in other words, to be effective and efficient in the long and in the short run. And this methodology has been tested.[4]

THE IMPOSSIBLE DREAM

In order to be an excellent manager, ensuring that my organization is effi-cient and effective, now and forever, I need to do all the (PAEI) roles well: I must satisfy clients' needs efficiently; adapt and pro-act to their changing needs; and make no one indispensable. In other words, I should be results-oriented, client-oriented, and at the same time organized and efficient; also, I must be creative and a risk-taker; while, at the same time, I must be a people-oriented team-builder who tries to make myself dispensable.

What is the problem?

Not too many like us left around! Right?

THE MYTHICAL IDEAL MANAGER

Joking aside, in thousands of books on management, and in our business schools, we have been trying to create an animal that cannot be created. Why? Because we are all human beings. We have our strengths and weaknesses. We will never be perfect.

This reminds me of a joke: In church, a priest is talking about sin and perfection. "Have you ever met a perfect human being?" he asks. "Have you ever *known* a perfect human being?" And a voice calls out from the back of the church: "I haven't met a perfect human being, but I do know of one: my wife's late husband."

You know where you can really find a perfect human being? In manage-ment education books, where the good manager performs all four roles efficiently and effectively.[5]

In reality, however, we know that this ideal executive does not exist. The

---

[4] See the testimonials on www.adizes.com.

[5] For more information, see Ichak Adizes, *The Ideal Executive—Why You Cannot Be One and What to Do About It* (Santa Barbara, CA: Adizes Institute Publications, 2004).

perfect executive of these management textbooks is, in fact, a collage, created by pulling together the ideal characteristics of several different people and combining them into a mythical human being—who does not and never will exist.

Does this mean that by definition all organizations must be badly managed? No! Then what do we need? A complementary team with a leader.

Look at your hand. Which is the most important finger? The thumb, because it works with the other four fingers. Without the thumb, there is no hand.

Many people believe that a leader is a pointing finger, directing: Do this, do that, etc. This is true for a company that's just starting up, but as the organization grows, leadership must move from being the pointing finger to becoming the thumb, and those leaders who cannot change their style usually have to be replaced.

I am teaching nothing you do not know already. Look at the person you married. Together, you are a complementary team, right? If you are creative and bursting with ideas, you are probably married to a person who pours cold water on your head every morning and calms you down. Why do we marry our complements? Because children need both parents to grow up healthy and happy. Raising a child is like raising a company. And for that you need a complementary team. Think about a mom-and-pop store. Pop usually does the (PE) role and Mom the (AI) role.

> *If I ask managers how their company is doing, and hear, "Fine; we never disagree," I know the place is dead.*

If you know the history of management theory and how it was developed, you can trace how the (PAEI) roles were discovered and emphasized over time.

The grandpa of management theory was Frederic Taylor, who focused on efficiency and productivity, or (PA), in the 1940s. Then Henri Fayol came along, with his theory on organizational structure, followed by L.F. Urwick, with his work on staff line relationships. That is (A) for you.

Then strategic planning and the role of the CEO took center stage in management theory. That is (E). Today, the central role is thought to be people relations, conflict resolutions. That is (I).

It was Peter Drucker who first combined all of these roles into one theoretical person, claiming that a manager should do all of them. Drucker's thinking was characteristically American: American culture worships the individual, not the team.

But it's wrong. The managerial process is too complex for a single manager to perform. Just as it is not easy to raise a child alone, the same is true of organizations. We need a complementary team.

THE INEVITABILITY OF CONFLICT

What will happen when you get that complementary team? Conflict. Why? Because all four roles must be present, and the roles are incompatible. Too much of one will threaten another. For example, managers often say: "I am working so hard, I do not have time to get organized." That tells me that the (P) role is threatening the (A) role. Or they may say: "I am perfectly organized, and I will not sacrifice that by changing." That is (A) threatening (E). Or, "There is so much change going on that I cannot get the job done": (E) is undermining (P). Or, "Integration suffocates entrepreneurs. They like to be independent." That would be (E) threatening (I), or the reverse, (I) threatening (E).

If all four roles are necessary for good management, then conflict must also be necessary. That means that if I ask managers how their company is doing, and hear, "Fine; we never disagree," I know the place is dead.

Conflict is necessary, but it can be dangerous, because it can be destructive. Differences can destroy; they destroy companies, marriages, and countries. Because people are afraid of that destructive force, they try to avoid conflicts by creating teams of people who work well together: managers who have the same style, think the same way, and hire the same people. And that is a death sentence.

The trick is to *embrace* conflict by converting it into a positive force. That's a major role of management: to build a complementary team and create an environment of mutual trust and respect (MT&R), in which conflict is legitimate and constructive. We all know people who *agree* in such a disagreeable way that afterwards we don't want anything to do with them. A good manager is someone who knows how to disagree without being disagreeable.

It took me many years to understand what MT&R really means, so let me share it with you.

Mutual respect is *not* just how politely you speak. Respect is also recognizing that the other party has the undeniable right to think differently. It is the essence of democracy. When do people feel disrespected? Not when we disagree with them, but when we don't let them state their arguments or say why they disagree.

And, when you are confronted with a disagreement you can learn from, you have grown.

What is trust? Many people believe that trust and respect are synonymous. They are not.

Trust exists when there is common interest. Why do you say, "I can trust this person; I can turn my back on her"? Because you understand that if she stabs you in the back, she is also stabbing herself. Why? Because the two of you have common interests.

When there is mutual trust and respect, there is very little internal disintegration.

BODY LANGUAGE TELLS THE STORY

How can you tell if your organization operates with MT&R? By watching people's body language. If there is respect, then to make a decision they face each other and talk to each other. To implement the decision, if there is mutual trust, they are not afraid to turn their backs to each other and get to work.

Conversely, if there is *no* respect, they turn their backs to each other when making a decision, and when the time comes to implement, they keep their eyes on each other, because there is no trust. If you tell me which way you're facing and what your back is turned to when you are making and implementing decisions, I'll tell you how successful your company is.

When there is no trust and no respect, there is lots of wasted energy. But show me a system with MT&R and I'll show you a successful system.

When is a marriage over? Not when the divorce papers are signed. It is over when there is no trust and respect left. The same is true with countries. Which countries are considered to be successful? Japan, for instance, used to be. Have you ever seen a sign of disagreement in Japanese people? Even if they disagree with you, you might not know it. They simply don't do business with you until they trust you. That's tremendous internal integration! Because they do not waste energy internally, all the energy goes outside to competing in the marketplace.

What is the most important asset for an organization? It is not money; if there is a market, the money will come. It is not a market: If you have a technology, you will find the market. It is not technology: If you have money, you will find the technology. No, a company's most important potential asset is its culture.

It is the same with people. Imagine a young man who has money, good looks, and a premium education. He has all the ingredients for success—except that he lacks self-trust and self-respect. As a result, he spends most of his energy wondering, "Who am I? What am I doing? What do people think about me?" He cannot be successful. All that money and energy is wasted.

Now, what is the role of management? To build a complementary team and to create a climate of mutual trust and respect.

What makes a good manager is not what you *know*. It is what you *are*. It is easier to hire somebody who *is* and teach her to *know* than to hire somebody who *knows* and teach her how *to be*.

What does this mean for management education?

I believe that the role of management education is to teach people humility, to teach them how to work as a team, to work with MT&R, and to practice constructive conflict. That is the necessary platform. The rest is constantly changing anyway. In our schools, we are teaching too much *to know*, and not enough *to be*.[6]

PREDICTING ORGANIZATIONAL PROBLEMS

Here is another application of the (PAEI) code that has ramifications for management education: After consulting to many different organizations, I started to see that the problems were similar. It is like becoming a parent to many children: With the first child, each problem is a crisis; the fifth child grows by herself. Working with companies, I started to feel that I had seen their predicaments before, in the same pattern.

That was when I realized that these four (PAEI) roles develop in a predictable sequence. No company is born with all of them developed in full. Life is a university: You live and you learn. Organizational development, like child development, happens in a certain order. If the company has problems developing one specific role, it gets "stuck" and cannot go any further. That is when I know it is experiencing abnormal problems.

---

[6] For more detail about management education, see the essays in Part 7 of this book, "Management Education," beginning on page 239.

Another name for the sequence by which an organization's (PAEI) roles develop, as well as the predictable sequence in which its problems emerge, is its "lifecycle." Every lifecycle experiences predictable stages that I will write about in more detail later in this book: Courtship, Infancy, Go-Go, Adolescence, Prime, and often the stages of aging: Aristocracy, Witch-hunt, Bureaucracy, and Death.

Why do organizations die? Because as the organization passes through its lifecycle, its style of management has to change. It is like parenting children: With a little baby, you have to be very strict. But you can no longer treat your daughter like a child when she is 30 years old.

And it isn't only the leadership style that has to change; the organizational structure, the rewards system, the strategy, and many more variables need to be changed according to where the organization is on the lifecycle. You should not manage all organizations as if they were already in Prime. That was the mistake of the bestseller *In Search of Excellence.*[7]

You need to build your organization's culture by recognizing differences and respecting them, training for humility, always knowing that what is the right thing to do at one time can be absolutely the wrong thing at another time. So what you do, how you behave, what (PAEI) role you accentuate, will also need to change, along with the organization.

This, I believe, is the new paradigm of management that we need to teach.

---

[7] Tom Peters and Robert H. Waterman, Jr., *In Search of Excellence* (New York: Harper & Row, 1982).

PART 1

THE ROLES OF MANAGERS/LEADERS

On Effectiveness
and Efficiency
and Their Repercussions[1]

I have said that a well-managed organization is effective and efficient, in both the short and the long term.

It is interesting to note that some languages do not have a literal translation for the words "effectiveness," "efficiency," or both. Hebrew, for example, has a word for "efficiency," but to communicate "effectiveness" they use the word "purposeful," which, as I will explain below, is not literally accurate because not all purposeful systems are necessarily effective.

Russian, on the other hand, has a word for "effectiveness," but not for "efficiency"; to communicate "efficiency," Russian translators use the words "organized" or "productive" instead. Neither is truly accurate, because getting organized is only one means of becoming efficient, and not all productive systems are necessarily efficient.

> To be effective ... means to produce that for which the system was established.

To add to the confusion, it seems to me that the meaning of these words is not even clear in English. At least not to me.

If we want organizations to be effective and efficient, we must first clearly define what that means.

What Is 'Efficiency'?

"Efficiency" is the way in which you carry out a process. It is measured by how many units of input are needed to produce one unit of output. A system is efficient if it can carry out its process with the minimum energy possible. To become efficient, you need to get organized, systematized, and programmed.

---

[1] Adizes Insights, July 2010.

To be efficient means to follow a process that uses the minimum energy and minimizes the waste of energy. Efficiency is the result of following the right *form*. There is no room for mistakes. When you use a system that was designed for efficiency, there is no learning process involved. You just have to follow the programmed, prescribed system, which tells you in detail where, when, how, and with whom to do what. You do not have to think or innovate or make choices. As a matter of fact, the more efficient you want to be, the more you must avoid making choices and innovating.

Thus, the more efficient you try to be, the less you will innovate and the less effective you will be in the long run.

What Is 'Effectiveness'?

To be "effective," on the other hand, means to produce that for which the system was established. It means to provide the desired *function*. To become effective, you need to try out different solutions until you find the right one. Thus, by definition, you have to make what most people consider "mistakes," but what I consider to be a necessary step in becoming effective. Nevertheless, making choices involves making mistakes, and mistakes do waste energy.

Furthermore, for effectiveness in the long run, you must innovate, because clients' needs change over time.

Can you measure an organization's effectiveness? Many people believe that sales are an accurate gauge. Not true. The correct measurement is: Are the clients coming back? This applies to anything. It even refers to monopolistic organizations where people do not have a choice—although in that case, the question should be: If the clients had a choice, *would* they come back? If the answer is no, then the organization is not effective. Clients are like intelligent animals who know where the watering hole is. They are not going to come back to a dry watering hole.

The Efficiency/Effectiveness Trade-Off

Can a system be effective without being efficient?

Yes, it can: The organization reaches its goals—but uses excessive resources and/or energy in order to do it.

Can a system be efficient and not effective? Sure. I can practice hitting a tennis ball from one spot on the tennis court until my movements are perfect. Now that I am so efficient, I tell my opponent: "Send me the ball *right here!*" and I hit only the balls that come to my racquet; if they do not arrive in precisely the right place, they are missed.

For example, take a company in which everything is well organized and documented into manuals and standard operating procedures so that everyone knows what to do and when and how to do it. The system is fully in control of everything so that there is no waste of energy.

The organization follows its rules and policies religiously, but it satisfies few needs—because the needs have changed over time, while the operating systems have not. The result is that clients are made to fill out useless forms and to wait a very long time for products or services.

> The higher the rate of change, the more efficiency organizations have to sacrifice in order to be effective.

In this example, the organization is not serving its clients well. The organization is ineffective, even though it is following the procedures as designed for efficiency.

That is called a bureaucracy.

How does this happen? How could an organization become efficient and lose its effectiveness?

To be effective, the organization needs to satisfy its clients' needs—*which change frequently*, much faster than the time it takes for the company to reorganize itself to satisfy those needs efficiently. By the time the organization has reorganized to stay efficient, its clients' needs will have changed again.

The higher the rate of change, the smaller the chance that effectiveness and efficiency will be synchronized.

In a changing environment, the needs will either be satisfied but inefficiently, or the organization will try to preserve its efficiency by refusing to change its products or services—which will make it efficient, all right, but not effective.

The higher the rate of change, the more efficiency organizations have to sacrifice in order to be effective. If they are not willing to sacrifice efficiency, they will have to sacrifice effectiveness.

It is easier to sacrifice effectiveness than efficiency. Why? Because reorganizing a company to remain effective in a changed environment means making structural changes—and that means stepping on some people's toes. As Machiavelli said (I am paraphrasing): If you want to be hated, try changing people. In other words, it is easier to sacrifice clients' needs than to get into intra-organizational political battles.

So, the faster the rate of change, the greater the chance that the world we live in will become more and more bureaucratized. Doesn't that make you optimistic about the future?

MORE ON EFFECTIVENESS[1]

L ET us say that you manage an organization. Where should your focus be? What is your priority? Do you know for whom or for what you are managing? How can you be most effective?

An economist will tell you that you are managing for profits. A sociologist will tell you it is for organizational survival.

My answer to this question is that for an organization to be effective, its goal should be to satisfy its clients' needs.

If it does that efficiently, it will be profitable. Thus, profit, the outcome of a well-managed company, is actually a measurement of how well the organization manages to produce that which it exists to produce.

For long-term survival, an organization needs to constantly reinvent and re-engineer itself, because the needs of its clients, and thus the purpose of its existence, continually change.

But either way, the focal point is to satisfy clients' needs. Without that, profitability is either the exploitation of some monopolistic opportunity, or the result of short-term maneuvers to cut costs at the expense of satisfying client needs. In the long run, it cannot work. Nor will a strategy of avoiding the costs of re-engineering, even though that may ensure survival in the short run. In the long run, the organization will be doomed.

ELEMENTS OF EFFECTIVENESS

Let me suggest that a system is effective if it functions and if, in doing so, it produces the desired results.

I am making this distinction because not all functioning systems are effective. Any part of a system can be functioning and still, the total system might not be producing results. For instance, the engine in my car is func-

[1] Excerpted and revised from Adizes Insights, May 2004.

tioning—I can hear it running—but the car is not producing results, i.e., it is not moving.

Producing any results, however, is not sufficient for being effective, either. For instance, let us say that the car in our example moves, but only in reverse. That is ineffective. To be effective, the system has to produce the desired results—in other words, go forward.

> A system is effective if it functions and if, in doing so, it produces the desired results.

Consider the mug I am drinking my coffee from. It is serving its purpose because it contains the coffee, and it has a handle so I can hold it comfortably without burning my hand.

The light bulb above my desk is producing the desired results because it lights the desk.

The clothes I wear are effective if they keep me warm.

What is the common denominator in the above examples? What are the desired results?

The results are desired if they serve the purpose for which they were intended.

And what is that purpose?

It is not any purpose. The purpose must be to serve someone else's needs—not just one's own. The coffee mug, for instance, does not exist for itself. It exists to serve those who are drinking from it. The clothing exists to keep me warm.

Everything in this world is designed with a purpose in mind, and that purpose is to serve something else. The light fixture over your head was put there to illuminate your space. The purpose of your car is to transport you somewhere. The only entity that serves no one else is cancer. It serves only itself. (Some people are "cancerous"; we call them "takers." And some governments are "cancerous," too: They take rather than serve.)

Thus, not all systems that function or produce results or serve a purpose are necessarily effective. They are only effective if: a) they function; b) they produce the results for which they were designed; and c) those results serve something or someone else.

In my lectures, I dramatically ask: "Who will cry if your company dies?" In other words: Whose needs will no longer be met if you perish? If the answer is, "No one"—if no one will cry, if no one needs your company—

then although the company might be functioning and even producing results, it is not being effective.

So why does your organization exist? This is not an easy question to answer. In fact, since everything functional exists in order to serve something else, the question "Why do we exist?" can be answered only after we know for whom we exist: Who will cry if we die? If nobody will cry, then we are merely wasting energy.

For whom do you exist? For your clients? (Please note that I deliberately do not use the word "customer"; I use the word "client" instead. Why? Because when I use the word "customer," only the sales department wakes up. Accounting's reaction is: "Thank God he's not talking to me!")

Every manager, no matter what she manages, must ask herself for what and for whom she exists. Just as the sales department does research to find out what its customers want, the accounting and production departments should do the same, asking their clients—the departments they serve inside the company—what they must do in order to be effective.

THE PROBLEM WITH SHORT-TERM PROFITS

Economic theory says that organizations should focus on the long-term profitability of the company; thus, a CEO who aims for short-term profits at the expense of undermining her clients' satisfaction is not an effective leader. But "long-term" and "profits" are both elusive terms. How much should the profits be? And how long is long? As Keynes once said: "In the long run we are all dead."

And how should management produce long-term profits? Here is my answer: Never lose sight of your customers' changing needs; and always treat short-term profits as a limitation, not as a goal that should be maximized per se.

In other words, sacrifice owners' interests for customers' interests; treat owners as stakeholders, not as clients. Meet their demands; do not maximize them.

The goal that management should maximize is customer satisfaction; that is what the organization exists for. That is the source of revenues, without which the organization will die; without revenues there are no profits, and without profits there are no investors.

It all starts with revenues—and thus, with customer satisfaction.

What happens when management focuses on short-term profits to meet their quarterly earnings-per-share goals? In effect, it is maximizing owners' interests: The owners are now the clients and the customers become mere stakeholders, for whom the company should do better than what the competition does for them, but no more and no less. By undermining customer satisfaction in that way, management could destroy the company.

As an analogy to companies that focus on profits at the expense of serving their clients, think of a family with little children. Who are the clients? For whom does the family exist if not to raise the children healthy in body and spirit? Now, imagine that the parents are so dedicated to building their careers and making money that they are often absent from their children's lives. True, those careers provide vast income, vast enough to exceed what the children need for their education and healthy maintenance. But what is the outcome? What is the result? "Latch-key kids," growing up rich but badly. Hello! The parents have forgotten the purpose of being parents. Right?

You are effective as a father or mother if you raise healthy children in body and spirit, assuming that the children are one of the

> Why does your organization exist? This is not an easy question to answer.

main purposes of having a family. In the same way, your company is effective if it serves its clients well, if it satisfies their needs as measured by the fact that those clients come back to be served by you even when they have other choices. Profits should be only as much as is necessary to attract the capital you need to be able to serve the clients well. It is a limitation to be met, not a goal to be maximized.

Why Maximizing Profit Is Bad

Imagine a family that has made a budget for a certain standard of living they want to have. No more, no less. And that is all they have to earn. No more, no less. All the remaining time left in the day or year is used to focus on the children, on the family as a unit, and on the community they live in.

Would you not say this is a healthy family?

I suggest that this is also how a company should be run. Decide how much profit you should make in order to competitively attract and keep capital. Pick a salary range that is competitive with the salary ranges in the market. Now focus on customers, on your clients and their changing needs.

That is where your focus should be. The investors/owners and employees are the constraint, not the goal.

But that is not how we usually manage our families or businesses in Western society, and that is not the message and theory we are spreading around the world through our business schools and schools of economics. In a company, we recommend growing earnings per share—which means more and more return to the owners—as if that defines how well the company is doing. And as we maximize profits and ignore the constraints by community stakeholders, we are destroying our planet.

In personal life, we work harder and harder to improve our standard of living, as if that increases our quality of life. In reality, as we work night and day to increase our standard of living, our quality of life goes down: no time for our children or spouse or extended family or the community at large. Not even time for ourselves. …

Materialistic goals should be treated as limitations that need to be honored, not as goals to be maximized. Stockholders should be treated as bondholders. Give them the return that keeps them investing. No more. And no less.

Focus on your clients.

In order to stay focused on this invisible, uncommunicative client who may not even exist yet, you have to ask an almost spiritual question: "Why do I exist? For whom do I really care?"

Every leader, every manager, and every parent should regularly stop and ask herself, "Why am I on this earth? Who needs me? If I die, who will cry? And what needs am I here to satisfy, so that I can fulfill the purpose of my existence?"

When you succeed at fulfilling the purpose of your existence, you will feel elated and inspired.

As a matter of fact, hard work will not kill you. What will kill you is abusing your life by wasting it on what you were not born to serve.

WHICH HAS PRIORITY:
EFFECTIVENESS OR EFFICIENCY?[1]

IN previous chapters, we discussed the meaning of the words "effectiveness" and "efficiency."

Let us now discuss which is more important: effectiveness or efficiency?

The intuitive answer is: effectiveness. It is more important to do something, even if it is done badly, than to do the wrong thing very well and miss the purpose. Right?

Wrong!

That is how children behave. Give them a task and they will do it; but when you analyze *how* they did it, you wish you'd never asked them to do it in the first place, right?

As I get older, I am starting to appreciate the importance of form over function. Quality over quantity.

True, in the short run effectiveness *is* more important than efficiency: Get it done, even if it is not perfect. But in the long run, if you repeat this behavior, you risk creating a disaster. Without efficiency, we will eventually run out of energy and collapse—and the functionality of effectiveness will end.

TAKING THE LONG VIEW

Look at yoga or any other sport as an example: First, you learn to do the posture correctly. Then you start building endurance—holding the posture longer and stretching more. You see? Efficiency (form) first; *then* effectiveness.

To continue the yoga analogy: If you stretch using the wrong posture (form), you could easily tear a muscle. The same should be true for learning: First we must learn *how* to learn. Then we can apply what we've learned to discover the content. Form first; functionality later.

---

[1] Adizes Insights, July 2006.

I've observed that we do not do this in our educational institutions. We teach students *what* to know. If they manage to learn *how* to learn, it is only by happenstance. If they do not learn *how* to learn, so that learning can become a lifelong, continuous process, they will eventually become ignorant people with impressive degrees, because what they *did* learn, content-wise, will have become obsolete over time.

This same analysis applies to management: In their rush to achieve results (especially if the Infant organization[2] is starving for cash), efficiency suffers. Form suffers. It is analogous to ignoring how children behave as long as they bring good marks home from school. But if they are ill-behaved, it won't surprise anyone when in spite of their good grades they are not successful in life.

How we do things is extremely important. Doing it right, then applying what we know to achieve results, is better than achieving the results and then trying to correct the process. It is like letting a tree grow untrimmed and then trying to straighten its crooked trunk.

The principle that form should precede function also applies to *how* we should manage conflict. Many people will say or do whatever it takes to win an argument. But, having won the battle, they might end up losing the war. Years later, we probably won't remember what the argument or conflict was all about; but we will never, ever forget *how* it was conducted. If it caused us to lose trust in our opponents, then even though we do not remember the details of what happened, our blood still boils remembering how the conflict was dealt with. We will never work with that person again.

So, the *how* is more important than the *what*. Pay attention not only to winning the war, but to *how* you are winning it. Take the long view. Form first, function later.

But, wait, there is a problem.

> Form over function. Quality over quantity.

How do you know the correct form unless you have a good idea of the necessary function? You would not go and build a dam unless you have a well-articulated idea of what that dam is supposed to do.

The answer is to distinguish between a purpose and the fulfillment of that purpose. You must have an *idea* of what you want. Many people (and I am no exception) get an idea and jump right into implementation. No!

---

[2] For more information on the various stages in the lifecycle of an organization, see Part 2 of this book, "Lifecycles," beginning on page 77.

Stop there. Start with the idea, but do not immediately start to implement it. Articulate and develop the form to fulfill the idea. Work out the details. Then—and only then—go and do it.

In (PAEI) terms, for those of you who know the code: (E) first, then (A), and only *then*, (P).[3]

---

[3] For a more in-depth discussion of the (PAEI) code, see the next chapter in this section, "(PAEI): The Organizational DNA Code for Managing Change," beginning on p. 37.

(PAEI): The Organizational DNA Code for Managing Change[1]

FIRST, let us define what I mean by the term "organizational DNA." About forty years ago I made a discovery: that there are four roles that management, as a team of people, must perform in order for an organization to be effective and efficient in the short and long run. Each time a role is not performed, or is performed badly, the organization will be ineffective and/or inefficient, now and/or in the future. In a word, it will be mismanaged.

This model, which I have been developing and applying with my certified associates worldwide (in more than fifty countries so far), enables management or consultants to predict and diagnose organizational problems, whether they are normal or abnormal, analyze what causes them, and decide in what sequence to solve them.

What are those roles?

(P) FOR (P)RODUCING

For an organization to be effective in the *short* run, management must see to it that the organization serves the needs of its market, of its clients. I call this role the (P)roducer role.

The producer drives performance and delivers results. Producers are defined by their desire to see tangible outcomes. Archetypal producers focus on what's happening at the moment, respond to immediate needs, and tend to make snap judgments. For the (P) role to be performed well, there are two requirements: (P) managers have to know the needs of the market that the organization is designed to fulfill; and they must also have what David

---

[1] Excerpted and revised from an article published in the *Harvard Business Review*, Russian edition, 2006.

McClelland, the Harvard professor of psychology, has called "the achieve-ment motivation": They cannot rest till the task is complete.[2]

(A) FOR *(A)*DMINISTRATION

The role of (A)dministration is to make an organization efficient by organizing tasks and functions into systems, routines, and manuals so that we do not waste energy. Whether you're talking about supply chain manage-ment, inventory management, or production management, you don't want to have to reinvent a wheel each time you have to wheel something around.

The (A) role learns what works, then analyzes successes and programs them so that they can be repeated. It moves the organization up the learning curve so it can capitalize on its memory and experience.

> By "planning," I do not mean deciding what to do tomorrow. That is dreaming. Planning is deciding what to do <u>today</u> in light of what we predict tomorrow will be.

To fulfill the (A) role, managers need to be detail-oriented, linear thinkers. Rather than thinking out of the box, the administrator tries to put things *into* a box, where they can be organized and systematized. An (A)-type manager's need, in McClelland psychological typology, is for control.

If you are effective and efficient, you can be profitable in the short run. Why? Because every need has its price. People are willing to pay a price to satisfy their need. And if you can satisfy this need at a lower cost, you make a profit, which I interpret as adding value. If you are willing to pay $10, and I can satisfy your need for $8, then I am making a profit and both of us are happy.

(E) FOR *(E)*NTREPRENEURSHIP

For an organization to be effective in the *long* run, management has to pro-act: It has to predict the newly emerging needs that it believes it will have to satisfy in the future; and then it must prepare the organization to fulfill them. That is the purpose of planning.

---

[2] D.C. McClelland and D.G. Winter, *Motivating Economic Achievement* (New York: The Free Press, 1969), and *The Achieving Society* (Princeton: Van Nostrand, 1961) are representative of McClelland's pioneering research in synthesizing economic activity and motivation, which he published in many studies in the 1950s and 1960s.

Please realize that by "planning" I do not mean deciding what to do tomorrow. That is dreaming. Planning is deciding what to do *today* in light of what we predict tomorrow will be; when tomorrow's needs emerge, the organization will be ready to satisfy them.

How can an organization be proactive when no one knows for sure what the future will be? In order to pro-act, the organization needs to be creative and imagine that future.

Creativity is necessary, but not sufficient, for successful pro-acting: Taking action today to prepare for the uncertain future means that the organization also needs to take risks, because the future might not happen as predicted.

Who is creative and takes risks? It is the (E)ntrepreneur. Thus, the third role necessary, which will make organizations effective in the long run, is the entrepreneurial role.

(I) FOR (I)NTEGRATION

The role that makes an organization efficient in the long run—where mutual interests are nurtured, and where a culture of mutual learning from differences in perceptions and judgments is fostered, molding individuals into a team—is called (I)ntegration.

What makes an organization efficient in the long run? It must develop and maintain an organic organizational consciousness, which is very different from a mechanistic consciousness.

For example, look at a chair. You can sit on it; it is effective. It serves the function for which it was created. It is perfectly efficient, too; there is no waste of material. But what would happen to it if one leg broke down? It would be a broken chair. Somebody from outside would have to come and fix it. In a mechanistic system of consciousness, as in any machine, there is no consciousness of internal interdependence among the parts.

Let's say I go to a company that is losing sales, and the production department says that it is not their problem, it is the sales department's problem. In other words, it is as if the left leg of a broken chair pointed to the right leg and claimed it was the right leg's problem. Why doesn't the left leg move into the center of the chair and create a tripod? Because there is no interdependency.

Now look at your hand. It has five fingers. Even when three fingers are broken, your hand is still a hand. Why? Because there is interdependency. It is as if every finger thinks like a hand. The fingers cooperate. They support each other. In sports that is called team play.

In an organic, integrated organization, the problem of falling sales is *everyone's* problem—even the messenger boy, not to speak of production.

EVERY MANAGER'S STYLE IS UNIQUE

Among its other applications, the (PAEI) code can be used to analyze a person's typical style of managing. The code has thousands of permutations, depending on an individual's managerial strengths and weaknesses (designated in the code by either an upper-case or lower-case letter) and sometimes even a complete lack of ability (designated by a -) in each of the four roles. It's important that a manager maintain at least a minimal, "threshold" level of competence in all four roles, no matter which one is her particular strength. If a manager completely lacks the ability to perform any of the roles, she will mismanage.

In order to introduce you to these roles and dramatize how each of them affects a manager's style (as well as how it should affect management education), I am going to create four archetypes of profound *mis*management. Let us imagine some extreme situations, in which only one role is being performed to the exclusion of all others.

(P---): 'The Lone Ranger'

This person is the best engineer you have: productive, hard-working, so good at his job that we promote him to a management position. But he has no (A)—no skills at administration, paperwork, and control. He has no (E)—no new ideas; and no (I)—no ability to promote teamwork. His style is (P--): Show me the tracks, give me the train, and let me go.

So how does he manage? He works hard: He comes to work first and leaves last. He has so much to do that he has no time for meetings.

Does he delegate? No, because his subordinates "are not ready yet." How long have they worked for him? "Twenty years." Why doesn't he train them? "Because I do not have time." Why not? "Because there is nobody to delegate to." I call this type of manager the Lone Ranger. He might have people working for him, but they function merely as errand boys.

What is he most interested in? *What* we do. Never mind how. Do! Shoot first, ask questions later.

(-A--): 'The Bureaucrat'

The next archetype, the exclusive (A) who totally lacks (P), (E), and (I), is not interested in *what* we do. She is completely focused on *how* we do it.

She and her subordinates arrive at work on time and leave on time. What they do in between is not important—as long as they arrive on time and leave on time. The company could be going bankrupt—but on time.

This is the type of manager who would rather be precisely wrong than approximately right. She gives you a precise budget, but in the wrong direction. Does she have meetings? Every Monday, Tuesday, and Friday at 9 a.m. on the dot, with a detailed agenda. This is the Bureaucrat. How does she manage? By the book.

(--E-): 'The Arsonist'

The third archetype, the exclusively (E) manager, is interested in *ideas*. He has a vision. His attitude toward change is, "Why not? Let's do it!"— whatever it is! He is most dangerous on the Monday mornings after a long weekend or vacation, or after being on a plane for three hours. Why? Because this is when he accumulates new ideas, new possibilities.

Does he have meetings? Yes, but no one knows when they are going to be. He just calls a meeting on the spot. But his staff doesn't really have to prepare for it anyway, because he does all the talking. I call this type of manager the Arsonist. He likes to start fires.

(---I): 'The Superfollower'

The exclusive (I) is a political animal who spends most of her energy watching the political climate. But she keeps this information to herself. She wants to know what others think first, and thus to gauge which way the political stream is going, before committing herself in any direction.

IT'S ALL ABOUT PERCEPTION

Here is another analogy about the typical perspective of each organizational role: Let's say there are four people in a room, with one window.

One, looking through the window, sees sky, birds, mountains, and clouds. Another one only sees the dirty window frame.

Who sees the whole world? The (E).

Who sees that the frame is dirty? The (A).

That's why (E) and (A) do not like each other and are often in conflict. (E) has ideas and plans, and (A) sees there is a comma missing somewhere and draws the conclusion that (E) is going to bring the company down because she is not paying attention to the details. What does the (E) think? That (A) is stupid.

The (P) style sees neither the dirty frame nor the clouds. He's busy wondering: How do they open this window? Is there a cross-breeze?

And the (I) type is not even looking at the window. She is watching the other three people and trying to figure out what they're looking at.

These are all bad managers, because we need all four roles to be performed if the organization is going to be well managed: in other words, effective and efficient in the short and long run.

Conscious Management of Change

A problem that indicates that an organization is deficient in a certain role—not developing, but deficient—is an abnormal problem. For example, a common abnormal problem in an aging organization is the loss of its entrepreneurial spirit. Without entrepreneurship, the organization does not innovate, does not change as market needs continue to change.

What I have found, working as a consultant to corporations worldwide, is that the four roles develop and are nurtured in an organization in a predictable sequence. And if we know that sequence—if we know which role will develop next—we can predict the next generation of normal problems that the organization will face.

Conversely, if a role is not developed properly and at the appropriate time, there will be abnormal problems, which, if not treated, will become fatal to the organization. As Henry Kissinger once said: "An untreated problem is a crisis in waiting."

The Difference Between Clients and Stakeholders[1]

EVERY organization exists, or should exist, to satisfy its clients' needs first and above all. It is the necessary, although not the sufficient, condition for being profitable as well as for surviving in the long run.

Who are the clients?

I am using the word "client" in a generic sense, to mean those for whose satisfaction the organization exists.

But who, exactly, are those clients whose needs an organization should satisfy?

Every organization exists to do something, to serve someone. Those "someones" are called "clients."

For instance, who are the clients of the accounting department? Leaving aside the tax authorities and the investors, their clients are whoever inside the company needs information from accounting.

Who are the clients of the human resources department? Whoever needs them to provide services.

Thus, there is no organization that does not have clients. Without clients, it would not have any reason to exist.

Who Are the Stakeholders?

But clients can easily be confused with stakeholders; after all, stakeholders will also cry if an organization perishes.

So how do we distinguish between stakeholders and clients?

A stakeholder is anyone who has a stake in what the organization does. Stakeholders provide either the resources or the cooperation needed for the company to serve its clients well.

---

[1] Excerpted and revised from Adizes Insights, May 2004.

Investors, the owners, are stakeholders because they put their money or lives into the endeavor. Banks, bondholders, or other entities to whom the organization owes money are also stakeholders, because their money is at risk.

How about employees? They are definitely stakeholders, because their employment and thus their livelihood is at risk if the company folds. The same holds true for management of any rank.

How about the community where the company resides? They, too, are stakeholders, because the company might pollute the air or the water or cause too much traffic on surrounding roads.

Whoever has anything at stake is a stakeholder.

Focusing on capital, on owners' needs first and above all, makes sense only in a company that is privately owned, where the owners have a long-term as well as a short-term interest in the company.

Stakeholders are all those interests, internal and external, that are brought together for the purpose of satisfying client needs. And they justifiably expect a return for their contribution. But they are not the driving force. They are not the purpose for which the organization exists; the *clients* are the purpose for which the organization exists. Rather, the stakeholders are a constraint management must honor; the company has to meet their demands, no more and no less— like paying interest on a loan.

A Customer Is a Client Who Pays

Now, who are the customers? Those are the paying clients, who pay for the services or products they get. Without customers, the company would go bankrupt.

But even the parts of an organization that do not have paying customers still have clients—those who need that unit's services. If no one needs its services, then a unit is useless and has no reason to exist. If it serves only its own needs, it is cancerous.

When each department serves its internal clients well, the organization as a whole can serve its customers well. When departments do not serve their internal clients well, it becomes a losing battle for the organization to serve its customers well.

This is quite confusing, is it not? But the distinction is significant, because not understanding the difference causes organizations to be ineffective. How can an organization be effective when it does not know who its clients are?

Let me give you an example from my professional experience. Many years ago, I was working with the Los Angeles County Department of Children and Family Services. This is one of the country's largest organizations specializing in the needs of children who have been abused, psychologically, economically, emotionally, or physically.

I asked the employees, who were almost all social workers, "Who are your clients?" In response, I got a startling number of answers, including:

- the newspapers who write about the department (the department was obsessed with what the media said);
- the court system, which decides what to do with the endangered children;
- foster families;
- the politicians and bureaucrats, in Sacramento and Washington, D.C., who control the department's budget.

Somewhere on that list were the words "abused children," but it took some time to make the social workers understand and focus on the fact that all the others on the list were stakeholders, while the purpose of the organization's existence was, in fact, the children themselves. The children were, and are, the department's clients.

Now Test Yourself ...

Who are the clients of a private equity firm: the company it just bought and took over, or the investors who put their money into the private equity fund?

I have worked with several PEFs, and my conclusion is that the customers for which it exists and who pay them for their services are the investors.

The company they took over is the means of satisfying the investors.

The PEF is not there to improve the health of the organization it has taken over. It is there to maximize a fast return on investment, and if that has a negative effect on the acquired company's long-term ability to function, that is of less concern. The PEF's goal is the return on investment. Period.

In other words, the talk you often hear about PEFs—that they serve a purpose by improving the functionality of firms they take over—is based on misunderstanding this important distinction: Who is the client? For whom does the PEF exist?

Some PEFs, if they find it profitable, will actually destroy the long-term functionality of the companies they buy. Their clients, however, the investors, smile all the way to the bank.

Is this what we want?

THE OBSTETRICIAN'S CLIENT

Let me use my own organization, the Adizes Institute, as an example. Who is our client?

It isn't the organization's CEO, because sometimes we have to tell the CEO that he is dysfunctional according to the needs of the organization.

It isn't the organization's employees, because sometimes the employees are destructive to the organization. They may be asking for concessions the organization cannot afford.

It isn't management, because sometimes management actually robs the organization of its resources for its own self-gratification. Nor is it the investors, whose demands for short-term returns can potentially destroy a company.

> Your question is not, "Whom am I trying to please in order to protect myself?" The question is, "Whom am I trying to serve?"

Not even the organization's current customers are the Adizes Institute's clients; those customers might be asking for all kinds of benefits, concessions, and discounts that could be ruinous.

Our client is the organization. But what does this mean? Who is the organization, if not its customers, its investors, or its employees?

The answer is: The organization is none of them alone, but all of them together. It is an amalgam of all the ingredients necessary to satisfy the needs of its present and future clients. In other words, the client of an Adizes Symbergetic™ consultant (that is the new "breed" of consultant I have developed and trained) is the health of the organization.

I like to compare Adizes' services to those of an obstetrician. We worry about the health of the mother, so that many healthy babies will be born. In other words, the Adizes Institute concerns itself with an organization's ability to satisfy the needs of present and future clients—who may not even exist yet! We want to ensure that the organizations we consult to are proactively capable of changing and adapting to satisfy the needs of their clients, in the present and in the future.

WHAT ABOUT NON-PROFITS?

This confusion about who is a stakeholder and who is a client or customer is even more pronounced in not-for-profit organizations. In a business organization, clients are easier to identify because they are the source of the company's revenue. They provide money—the organization's lifeblood—which ensures that the organization will survive and flourish. Without clients, the organization would perish.

But at non-profit organizations, the financial resources do not come from the customer base. The funds are allocated by state or federal budgets or solicited from donors. Predictably, then, many not-for-profit organizations tend to focus on their funding source as the group most needing to be satisfied, rather than on their clients—the ones for whom they should provide services.

Take classical music orchestras as an example. When their administrators plan the next season's programming, they often take the path of least resistance and choose to play what their major donors want to hear, rather than what inner-city youth might want or need to hear. But this approach hinders audience development, which may be more important for the orchestra's long-term success as an agent of social change, education, and social enrichment.

In order to avoid confusing stakeholders and clients, organizational leaders should try to elevate themselves spiritually and ask the question, "Who really needs my services?"—or, even better, "Who *should* need my services?"—and focus on the future. Those who need your services are the clients.

The next question should be: "Whom does the organization need in order to satisfy the clients' needs?" Those are the stakeholders.

And finally, "How can the organization satisfy the stakeholders' needs without sacrificing the needs of its clients?" This is the most difficult question, because often there is a real conflict of interest between stakeholders' and clients' needs: In order to give higher returns on investment to its investors, management could decide to cut client services drastically, or shy away from performing controversial social services, even if those services are critical for the clients it serves.

WHERE IS YOUR FOCUS?

Think of yourself as a camera lens. Should you focus sharply on owners and have customers in the background, or focus directly on the clients/customers, even if that means the owners are a little blurry in the background?

I am suggesting the latter.

Why would anyone disagree with what I am saying? Because in effect, my arguments challenge the property rights of owners—and that, in a capitalist system, is a sacred cow. I am contradicting Milton Friedman, a Nobel Prize-winner in economics, who claimed over and over again that "the purpose of business is business," i.e., to serve the owners and nothing else. Owners put their money into something, he argued. They should have the right to use that money as they see fit and maximize the returns on that investment.

But focusing on capital, on owners' needs first and above all, makes sense only in a company that is privately owned, where the owners have a long-term as well as a short-term interest in the company, and will automatically focus on clients and their changing needs to be sure the company survives and even flourishes in the long run.

That is not the case when a company goes public or is bought out by a private equity fund. When that happens, there is a separation of ownership from management. In a public company, capital does not have the loyalty and long-term commitment that an owner of a privately owned company has. Stockholders move from one company to another in a heartbeat. They do not behave like owners who dedicate their lives to building the company. They are investors who are loyal only to one thing: their return on investment. Thus, they are stakeholders only. They are not the purpose for which the organization exists.

It reminds me of the transition from being single to having a family. As long as you are single, you can focus on your needs exclusively. Once you get married and especially once there are children, the focus has to change. You cannot behave as if you are single anymore.

Or look at it another way. When a company goes public and management gets separated from ownership, the interests of owners and of the company also get bifurcated. And the non-owner managers have to refocus.

Now, the owners are stakeholders—because their long-term commitment is no longer there. The company's purpose of existence is to satisfy the clients, because the company needs their long-term loyalty to remain viable.

The stockholders can move their money around instantly. The company does not have the luxury of that flexibility. It has to worry about its clients, whose loyalty secures the long-term survivability of the organization.

This argument, if valid, has many repercussions. One of them is that the composition of the board of directors has to be re-evaluated. It should represent the clients and the stakeholders as well as the owners—like in Israel, where each board of directors of a public company includes a representative of the community at large and is appointed by the stock exchange, not elected by the stockholders.

Are They Coming Back?

To be effective as a manager, ask yourself why the organization you manage exists. Who are the stakeholders, whose resources or cooperation you need to satisfy and whose interests you must deal with in order to maximize your goals? And who are the real clients or customers, whose needs you are supposed to satisfy? That is your goal, and you can measure it by repetitive sales: Are they coming back or not? Or, in the case of a non-profit where the clients may not have a choice: Would they come back if they didn't have to?

You have to carefully watch all the stakeholders to make sure they don't impair your ability to serve that group. Remember that the stakeholders are more of a constraint than a client base. Your question is not, "Whom am I trying to please in order to protect myself?" The question is, "Whom am I trying to serve?" That is the purpose of your business.

Now, focus on maximizing the changing needs of your clients/customers.

Measuring Success[1]

ONE of the distinctions typically made between for-profit and not-for-profit organizations is that the latter lack profit as a metric for success, and thus are unable to take advantage of a tool that is routinely utilized by for-profits. According to the conventional wisdom, this puts them at a disadvantage.

I take issue with this reasoning. In fact, I regard it as a total misunderstanding of the process of managing the dynamics of organizations.

Whether it happens to be a for-profit or a not-for-profit, the well-managed organization must be effective and efficient in both the short and long run. This holds true even for a family or society. Thus, profit does not necessarily provide an accurate measure of either effectiveness or efficiency, and sometimes does not come into the picture at all.

In terms of the roles that management and leadership need to provide, there are many other similarities to be found between for-profits and not-for-profits—provided we understand what constitutes a healthy managerial process.

THE CASE OF FOR-PROFITS

First, let's look at measuring success at a for-profit organization.

When you ask leaders of for-profit organizations why they exist, the typical response is "profit." But we should all know that "profit" is not the correct answer. Profit is like the scoreboard in a tennis match: You can't win the game by watching the scoreboard instead of the ball. (Many managers have climbed to top executive positions by learning finance or accounting, while knowing nothing of management. It is very dangerous for management when leaders only watch the numbers.)

Then what is "the ball"? The ball is satisfying your clients' needs. If you

---

[1] Adizes Insights, December 2003.

satisfy your clients' needs repeatedly, you are effective. If the organization satisfies its clients' needs in an efficient manner by being well administered, which is the (A) role, then the organization will also be profitable in the short run.

Why? In a competitive market, if the company can satisfy a need at a cost to itself that is less than the perceived value of that need, as measured by what people are willing to pay, then the organization has added value to society, measured by the profits the company has generated.

In other words, profit in a market economy is added value. People are willing to pay a certain price to have their needs satisfied. When those needs are satisfied efficiently—that is, at a cost that is lower than the price people are willing to pay—it means the company has added value. And the difference between that price and the cost is profit.

THE CASE OF NON-PROFITS

How does this apply to non-profit organizations?

Not-for-profits also have a client base, in this case the community for whom they provide services, and they need to satisfy those clients' needs. The question is: What is the price that people are willing to pay to have those needs satisfied?

In a non-profit organization, the question of what price people are willing to pay to have their needs satisfied is more difficult to discern; still, there is a price for everything. For example: How long are people willing to wait in line to be treated at a particular hospital?

When I did the health planning for Ghana, I looked at how many miles people were willing to walk in order to be treated at a clinic—because that was the price they were willing to pay.

All non-profit organizations should ask themselves: What community do we serve, and what price are people in that community willing to pay to satisfy their needs? Price does not necessarily mean money. It can be cash equivalents, such as time, effort, hardship, or pain. It could be the length of time people have to wait to learn whether their application for funding has been approved. Rather than saying, "We don't have profitability as a metric," non-profits should ask themselves:

1) "Whom do we serve?"
2) "What is the price our clients are paying to be served?"

3) "Are we assisting them, and in the most efficient manner (i.e., are we both effective and efficient)?"

4) "Are we adding value?"

SHORT-TERM VS. LONG-TERM VALUE

For-profit businesses measure themselves by short-term profitability, a measure of added value. The non-profit organization should measure itself against something more intangible, yet still real, by asking if it is adding value in the best possible manner.

These are hard questions to answer, and it often requires more self-discipline, honesty, and integrity to measure price equivalents than it does to measure profit. Does the non-profit organization truly understand the needs of the community it serves? Does it recognize what the people in the community must endure in order to be helped? Is the organization doing its best to satisfy those needs in the most efficient manner?

> In comparison to leaders of for-profits, leaders of not-for-profits have to be much more self-governing and honest with themselves.

There is an added complication: Many not-for-profits—especially government agencies—have a monopoly over what they provide. So their clients can and often do incur much higher "costs," in terms of time wasted or pain endured, than they would have incurred if that service had been privatized and had to compete with other service providers.

In comparison to leaders of for-profits, leaders of not-for-profits have to be much more self-governing and honest with themselves; their measurement of success ultimately is based on how honestly they evaluate their own work.

LONG-TERM ISSUES IN COMMON

In order to be effective and efficient in the long run, a for-profit organization has to identify the future needs of its clients, and it has to be structured in an organic manner so that no one is indispensable and so that the entire organization is not harmed if a part of it runs into trouble.

This applies to non-profit organizations as well. Non-profits must address long-term issues: Can we identify the future needs of our community? Are we proactive or are we stuck in historical patterns? Are we organized organically, so that if the organization's founding executive director leaves, we are capable of surviving in the long run?

In summary, there are significant similarities between for-profit and not-for-profit organizations. The primary difference is in the interpretation of the various roles required for the organization to be effective and efficient in the short and the long run.

(I) Before (E): Second Thoughts on Integration[1]

THE myth of the American Way is that we can solve anything if we have innovative technology and let individual ingenuity have a go at it. Our heroes are those lonely geniuses who go their own way and find new ways of doing things: Henry Ford tinkering away by himself for years, late into the night, in his Dearborn garage; Thomas Edison, the "wizard of Menlo Park," knocking off invention after invention with one epiphany after another; the "rugged individualists" of the post-Civil War years, who created new forms of production and organization to make America an industrial giant in the 19th century.

In recent times, we've had new heroes and villains—Steve Jobs, Bill Gates, Michael Milken—who developed innovative products, marketing schemes, and financial instruments, and whom we have mythologized as part of this tradition.

As the rate of change has increased exponentially in the past few decades, so has our concern for finding creative ways to reorganize corporate energies and compete in the global marketplace.

American companies developed a craze for rediscovering the "spirit of entrepreneurship" in their corporate roots. We began to extol "intrapreneurs"—employees within the organization who wanted to try out their own entrepreneurial ideas—and attempted to create an environment in which they could flourish. The "Masters of the Universe" ran free on Wall Street, and boutique investment firms invented new rules for playing with risk and debt. In the Silicon Valley, California, young people started up high-tech companies in informal, late-night discussions around tables

---

[1] Originally published in somewhat different form in *Executive Excellence* (now *Leadership Excellence*) magazine, November 1994; reprinted with permission.

littered with Coke bottles and overflowing ashtrays. The start-up mentality was mythologized as a new kind of "California Dreaming."

It was as if, somehow, we could again bring about corporate health and profits through our national traditions of individualism, innovation, and business creativity.

But are our myths accurate? Do we have the right take on innovation and creativity? Is individual genius really enough?

THE ELEMENTS OF SUCCESSFUL CREATIVITY

It has long been accepted in economic theory that entrepreneurship is a primary factor causing economic growth. The modern proponent of this theory was J.A. Schumpeter, who argued in 1913 that innovation and enterprise were the critical factors in the growth and development of capitalism.[2]

In the 1950s, D.C. McClelland looked at the issue from the angle of psychology, in his studies of how entrepreneurship in villages in India affected their economic vitality. His findings confirmed Schumpeter's theory: that entrepreneurship is of major significance in economic growth and success.[3]

> Are our myths accurate? Is individual genius really enough?

In my own book on corporate lifecycles, *Corporate Lifecycles: How and Why Corporations Grow and Die and What to Do About It*,[4] I, too, asserted that what causes the growth of a company is entrepreneurship, and what causes a company's decline is the lack of it.

But after it was published, I had second thoughts.

In wrestling with these questions, another answer began to occur to me, and it was surprising. It has to do, not with individualism, but with integration.

We know that every system has a lifecycle. It is born, grows, ages, and dies. That's true for people, for trees, for cars, and even stars. A "system" does not have to breathe to have a lifecycle.

---

[2] Schumpeter's ideas were first published in 1912 as *Theorie der wirtschaftlichen Entwickelung* and first translated into English as *Theory of Economic Development* (Cambridge: Harvard Economic Studies, 1934). In *Business Cycles* (New York: McGraw Hill, 1939), pp. 102-109, is found his most popular discussion of the entrepreneur and entrepreneurship.

[3] D.C. McClelland and D.G. Winter, *Motivating Economic Achievement* (New York: The Free Press, 1969) and *The Achieving Society* (Princeton, N.J.: Van Nostrand, 1961).

[4] Ichak Adizes, (New Jersey: Prentice Hall, 1988).

What that means is that systems change in a predictable pattern. And there is a typical behavior for each stage of its lifecycle.

Thus, a new car has the typical problems of a new (i.e., young) car: parts that aren't successfully integrated need fixing; a new software system might need debugging.

Old cars, on the other hand, have different typical problems; they are usually falling apart. The same goes for an old house, an old person, or an old computer system that is incompatible with newly developed software.

PROBLEMS OF INTEGRATION

What is the common denominator? Growing systems struggle to get integrated with their market—externally, in other words—while disintegrating internally, because keeping up with the rapid changes leaves no energy for creating or maintaining internal integration.

And aging systems are the opposite. In order to maintain internal integration—that is, peaceful internal politics—they increasingly lose focus on their market integration.

Only when a company is in Prime is it integrated both externally and internally, and the challenge of a Prime company is to stay that way, despite the rapid changes that it will continue to experience.

Growing and aging both pose problems of integration: What makes a company achieve balanced growth is integration, and what retards aging is also integration. (Have you noticed that people in love look younger and people who hate look old? Love is the ultimate integration.) So the way to get to Prime and stay in Prime is to work on and maintain integration.

In India, I have observed that yogis who have spent years doing yoga and meditation look ageless; it is difficult even for a native Indian to tell their age. This makes sense, because both meditation and yoga are ways to become more "centered"—achieve personal integration.

But what does "integration" really mean? How does it influence growth, or lack of growth (aging), and how does that relate to entrepreneurship?

There are both psychological and organizational dimensions to these questions.

Artists and scientists as diverse as Van Gogh, Paul Klee, and Albert Einstein have all described the creative process as one of integration rather than pure illumination. Great artists are integrated with their art to such an extent that that they sometimes experience it as an extension of themselves. They were inspired—and please notice that the word "inspired" comes from the root "to be in the spirit."[5] When you are in the spirit, inspired, you are integrated with something larger than you are. You transcend yourself, as if you are communicating with something beyond yourself. (Many sacred books, including the Torah and the Koran, were "dictated" by a holy presence, according to their authors.)

In a broader sense, this sensation belongs to all creative effort—including business. The more innovative an engineer is, the more she feels a part of the mechanism. Henry Ford, the "tinkerer," had that quality in relating to engines. When Edsel Ford came up with a splashy design for a new car (the later Model A), his father had a "feel" both for making the engine efficient and for making the car a marketable product with a good margin of profit.

Steve Jobs also illustrates, in both his career and public comments, this sense of integration—of being one with his product. He has said he sees the computer as a collective work of art and that "sharing its creativity" is what gets him so excited.

Calvin Klein, the famous fashion designer, has said he started losing his touch when he became too involved with manufacturing. He was no longer integrating with the market, thus he was not innovating with a market touch. Eventually he decided to switch to subcontracting his manufacturing, to be more available to "feel" the market.

Thus, *integration precedes entrepreneurship*, because this consciousness, feeling, and awareness of what we are innovating is necessary if we are going to come up with something new that works.

While integration is not the *cause* of growth, it is a necessary condition within which the factors exist that will cause this constructive growth to occur. And what we often mean by being "entrepreneurial" is really the ability to integrate. I once read, in an advertisement: "What is a new idea? It is when two old ideas meet for the first time." That is another way of saying that innovation, new ideas, are created by combining and integrating existing ideas. They do not come from nowhere.

The Japanese are not known to be extremely entrepreneurial as individ-

---

[5] I thank Wayne Dwyer for making this point.

uals. Nevertheless, "Japan, Inc." has been dominating the world economic scene for quite a long time.

In Japan, both the hard-edged business sense and innovative instinct rest on traditional cultural and social codes that stress the integrative functions of mutual trust and respect (MT&R): The leader should foster trust, but is dependent on those beneath her. Both *shinyo* (mutual respect) and *wa* (social harmony), which simultaneously satisfy corporate, personal, and social goals, need to be nurtured.

These paradigms are behind the Japanese success in team production and in their *keiretsu* (networks) of producers and suppliers, and they are the source of Japan's innovation and creativity. They make the coalescing of power, authority, and influence (CAPI) a highly efficient process in the execution of decisions. And as operating codes, they make the cascading and decentralizing of entrepreneurial activity a workable process.

THE HISTORICAL YANKEE MODEL

We don't have to look overseas to find a model for integration as a source of business creativity and innovation. We customarily think of Yankee know-how and individualism when we look at the beginnings of our manufacturing legacy in 19th-century New England. The Yankees had a knack for developing resources for worldwide commerce—ginseng to China, cod to Europe, slaves to America, even ice for India and granite stones for building American public architecture—and this commerce released capital for take-off industries.

> Have you noticed that people in love look younger and people who hate look old? Love is the ultimate integration.

But as historian Daniel Boorstin has pointed out,[6] the technology that made the factories possible was not invented in New England. England already had the traditions of mechanized manufacturing. The French had the insights of cooperative production as envisioned by Saint-Simon and Fourier. What made Yankee industrial enterprises so original and successful was their genius for bringing together production processes and then separating them into discrete, team-produced parts.

---

[6] Daniel Boorstin, *The Americans: The National Experience* (New York, Random House, 1965), Chapter 4: "Organizing the American Factory."

Taking advantage of water as a source of cheap energy, and linking their factories through the new railroads to world markets, New England entrepreneurs such as Robert Lowell brought together manufacturing processes under one roof. The Waltham factory system established by Lowell in 1814 became a pioneering model for the development of industry. Later, the Whitney Uniformity System did the same for the production floor: Eli Whitney broke down the production of guns into a number of steps, each performed repetitively by one person (a harbinger of Ford's assembly line), thus developing the process of component part-making.

This style of manufacturing required a relatively educated labor force, so that the individual laborer could easily move from one workplace to another within the production process. Workers had to be able to function as part of a team and participate in an organic process. So, ironically, it was not individuality or technology that was the key to America's stunning industrial success; it was the ability to creatively integrate processes. (Please note that it was not human integration. I am talking about a more mechanistic, systemic integration, more commonly associated with the (A) role. Nevertheless, it was this systemic thinking that made the system successful.)

BEHIND AND BEYOND ENTREPRENEURSHIP

Did the myths of individuality and technology actually lead us astray? What is it, exactly, that causes the entrepreneur to be entrepreneurial?

Is it "the unbridled appetite of greed," as Werner Sombart claimed in his classic studies on the rise of capitalism in Europe during the Renaissance?[7] Is it the childlike behavior that somehow continues into adulthood—dreaming, taking chances—ultimately a cluster of fixations and obsessional neuroses as described in the Freudian psychoanalytic tradition? Is it the rootlessness of someone who is trying to prove she is worthy of belonging? Or might it be a culturally learned capitalist ethic, derived in America from religious values, as Max Weber argued in *The Protestant Ethic and the Spirit of Capitalism*?[8]

---

[7] In *Luxury and Capitalism* (first English translation: Ann Arbor: University of Michigan Press, 1967), Sombart described the new risk-taking attitude throughout the culture and society of Renaissance Italy as the beginning of modern capitalism. Sombart pointed out that many business words are adapted from the vocabulary of gambling and risk, and they illustrate the special character of the new entrepreneurial spirit: *ratione, prudenza, fortuna, ventura, sicurta,* among them.

[8] New York: Charles Scribner's Sons, Inc., 1958. In this work, first translated into English in 1930, Weber sketched how religious values were sublimated into secular thinking. In American society,

In two surveys of its readers during the 1980s, *Inc.* magazine asked some five hundred CEOs of entrepreneurial companies what drove them. The results were at times contradictory, but several trends stood out. In the main, the executives who were surveyed had stereotypical American backgrounds and values. A significant number in both surveys shared a self-acknowledged "drive for power" and desire for "control over their lives."

But a second survey trend was the growth of "situational entrepreneurship"—individuals who were well experienced and integrated with their fields, who took advantage of "niche shifts" in the market to launch their entrepreneurial enterprises. They knew their industries and were "connected" with them.

THE 'BIG IDEA' AS AN ACT OF SYNTHESIS

Let's take a closer look at the act of entrepreneuring. When a company starts up, we tend to think of that launch as the act of an individual. Like an epiphany: A light bulb goes on and some brilliant idea appears that the entrepreneur will turn into a reality. We don't even think of the word integration. Maybe later, as a company starts to get larger, we see the need for "teams" and "integration for productivity." But at least at the beginning of a business, we usually don't think about entrepreneuring and integrating as being related to each other. We think of the new company as an extension of the founder/entrepreneur herself.

When a business idea first occurs to somebody, it is in reality an act of integrating. Light bulbs often go on; but the process of transforming that lit bulb into a start-up requires synthesis. These entrepreneurs have been in the market as consumers, as CEOs, as managers of other companies, and they've absorbed lots and lots of information about the market, its competitors, and market conditions.

Or maybe it's their technical "feel" for an enterprise: At some point, they begin to integrate all this information, and that's when a new idea is born. The act of coming up with the idea, testing the idea, and building the

---

Puritan values "shifted" into business values; e.g., in Ben Franklin's "Poor Richard" axioms: "Early to bed, early to rise, makes a man healthy, wealthy, and wise." See also McClelland's treatment of Weber's ideas in his comparison of economic motivation in Catholic and Protestant countries, especially in "Some social consequences of achievement motivation," in M.R. Jones (Ed.), *Nebraska Symposium on Motivation*, Vol. 3 (Lincoln, NE: University of Nebraska Press, 1955).

company around it is fundamentally tied—at least in its Infancy—with the process of integration: synthesizing functions, ideas, products and markets, people, and processes.

The Entrepreneur as Integrationist

As a company begins to mature, an entirely different level of integration is required. The challenge now for the entrepreneur is dramatic and immense: She has to perform the same act of integration she did before, but now the problem is that the information is coming to her second-hand.

At the start, the founder is close to the market, even out selling in that market. But more often than not, even the best-intentioned founders end up back in the office dealing with problems, dealing with bankers—becoming, to some extent, administrators, managers, and organizers. As a result, they have to hire managers who will become their hands, eyes, and ears. They must learn to coordinate and choreograph both the information and the actions of a group of people.

This is the first, real, significant managerial challenge that a founder faces: to make the transition from being the sole and principle integrator. And this is where "intrepreneurs" often hit the wall.

Avoiding the 'Founder's Trap'

This integration—the sensitivity and awareness—that the founder provides needs to be transferred to the organization as a whole if the founder is to avoid the founder's trap, my name for what happens when the organization is totally dependent on its founder for direction and, eventually, when the founder leaves or dies, the organization also "dies."

So, even before she transfers creativity and entrepreneurship, the founder has to make the transition from being the sole and principle initiator and integrator, who makes all decisions, to a higher-level integrator, whose role is to integrate those who will now provide the integration.

It is just at this point that many founders fall into the founder's trap.[9] Fearful of losing power, they resist transferring the integration functions. Even when they finally do it, they usually end up confusing delegation with

---

[9] For more information on the founder's trap, see "Potential Solutions for Getting Out of the 'Founder's Trap,'" beginning on page 105, in the "Lifecycles" section of this book.

decentralization—which, at this stage of the lifecycle, when organizations have few controls in place, is tantamount to abdication. There is too much to do, and the founder can't integrate the entire organization. But trying to delegate without first having established control systems, blind to the needs of integration, the founder will justifiably feel threatened when people begin to make decisions on their own.

The inevitable then occurs: The founder re-centralizes authority.

This cycle of "You are in charge"/"No, *I* am in charge" may repeat and repeat, putting the company on the end of a managerial yo-yo string and eating away at its employees' morale and its founder's authority.

The mistake the founder makes is to delegate authority for entrepreneurship without first providing integration. The founder is trying to find a substitute for herself, but of course she will never be perfectly satisfied.

Since integration should precede entrepreneurship, a better strategy would be to put together a team, rather than an individual, to make decisions and act.

For example, the second generation of managers, when they come on board, are usually professionals who specialize in marketing, R&D, and so on. In essence, they are taking on some of the founder/entrepreneur's role, to the extent that they are in the market and she is not. But that's just when the founder starts to fear that she is no longer indispensable—that the company is no longer "hers." She begins putting obstacles in the path of her subordinates and then complains that delegating her responsibilities is not working out. And as a result, the company begins to disintegrate.

Is your company like the universe, expanding at the margins and collapsing at the core?

Why do many organizations grow fast but become unhealthy? There can be any number of specific circumstances, but one underlying factor explains it. When there is change—and growing companies change a lot—not all sub-systems grow together, in a synchronized, integrated manner. Marketing pushes ahead, accounting lags behind, R&D needs to take a big leap forward; and so on. The totality does not directly develop together. The result is disintegration.

The act of integrating echoes throughout the lifecycle of corporations. The trick of healthy growth is balanced growth: paying attention to integration as you are growing, and paying attention to the growing process, which is the balancing act between internal and external orientations, your company, and your market. In a word, synchronicity.

If you want to rejuvenate an organization, make it more responsible to and dependent upon its franchise—its clients and customers. Integrate the organization with those it serves. Today's integration enables tomorrow's entrepreneurship. It is the balance between integration and entrepreneurship, between synchronicity and risk-taking, that causes long-term growth and enables an organization to reach Prime.

When are we in Prime? At a point of poised control and flexibility, when we are fully integrated, or, as we say in California, "when we have it all together." Whether it is a human being, a company, a marriage, or a country, we are getting to Prime when we have it all together.

When are we *not* getting to Prime? When we are all trying to run, but some people are holding hands, some are running faster, and others are going in a different direction. And when we get out of Prime, disintegration intensifies and speeds up the process of aging.

BARKING UP THE WRONG FOREST

What conclusion does all this lead to? That we are barking up the wrong tree, or perhaps I should say the wrong forest, as we search for growth factors both within the business world and within society as a whole.

What is hurting America is not a lack of entrepreneurs or a lack of economic rewards for entrepreneurs. The problem is that in recent years, the nation as a system—"United States, Inc."—has been falling apart just like an aging, Aristocratic corporation. Disintegrative forces have been accelerating: in the labor market, in the continuing adversarial positions of the labor force and management. In the destruction of the environment. Socially, in the continuing tragedy of drug use, community and school violence—and, in the background, the falling apart of our families. Politically, in the lack of confidence in and respect for our governmental institutions and the rapport between government and society. Economically, in the growing anomie in our work force and apparent lack of direction for our productive capacities.

In addition, the higher the rate and intensity of change, the stronger the intervention of legal institutions to regulate it. As a result, more and more external rules regulate our behavior, which feeds the sense of disempowerment and is a source of further disintegration in society and business.

We need to encourage and foster a creative environment for both business and society. That does not mean, necessarily, more economic incentives for entrepreneurial individualism. Government policy needs to look at other social, political, and economic areas where highly integrative processes can be shaped. That includes the relationships between Congress and the President, business and labor, business and government, and especially government and society. This may mean new ways of looking at how we measure national and industrial growth, including factors such as quality of life and environment, so that we are encouraging quality rather than exclusively quantity.

THE CHALLENGES AHEAD

Because we have encouraged and mythologized entrepreneurship as an individual act, we will have trouble making the transition toward team entrepreneurship. We need to develop the attitudes toward business that have been common in Japan. We have to develop a culture and habit of teamwork and of viable and realistic mutual trust and respect. This requires a sublimation of the ego. It will be difficult. But if we don't do it, then whatever kinds of "team management" and "team production" we put into effect will be superficial and without a solid basis in reality.

CEOs of growing companies, ask yourselves: Is your economic success manifested in the growth of your company at the expense of your personal physical disintegration? Is your own family falling apart under the pressures of modern work and society? Is your company like the universe, expanding at the margins and collapsing at the core?

The more entrepreneurial you are, the more attention you should give to corporate integration. The more energy and resources you spend on external expansion, the more you need to spend on internal integration. Your centrifugal forces should be countered by centripetal forces, or you will make it big and lose it all.

Peter Drucker has written eloquently of the emerging "society of organizations."[10] If we are to keep our corporations innovative and creative, we must do more than increase R&D budgets or clone production-floor forms of team production and management. We also have to develop atti-

---

[10] Peter Drucker, *Post-Capitalist Society* (New York, HarperCollins, 1993); Chapter 2, "The Society of Organizations," beginning on page 48.

tudes that encourage integration as a condition for creative business activity, specifically by creating truly complementary teams built on mutual trust and respect. In this way, we will be creating a predisposition to an organic consciousness within corporations, rather than a mechanistic consciousness in which groups and individuals remain isolated although inter-related.

SEEING THE BIG PICTURE

There is an old story about three men who were laying bricks for a new building. An onlooker asked the first person, "What are you doing?" and he replied, "I'm laying bricks." Then she asked the second person, who was doing the same thing, "What are you are doing?" He replied, "I'm building a wall." Finally, the third person was asked: "What are you doing?" He replied, "We are building a temple to worship God." He understood what creativity and innovation are all about.

An Analysis of President Obama's Inaugural Address[1]

ASSOCIATES Nebojsa Caric of Adizes South East Europe, Sunil Dovedy of Adizes USA, Carlos Valdesuso of Adizes Brazil, and Ichak Adizes of the Adizes Institute performed a content analysis of President Barack Obama's inauguration speech, in order to diagnose his (PAEI) style.

Below is the entire speech, each sentence or clause labeled as a function of one of the four essential management tools. You will find our conclusions after the speech.

President Obama's Inaugural Address[2]

I stand here today humbled by the task before us (I), grateful for the trust you've bestowed (I), mindful of the sacrifices borne by our ancestors (I).

I thank President Bush for his service to our nation (I), as well as the generosity and cooperation he has shown throughout this transition (I).

Forty-four Americans have now taken the presidential oath. The words have been spoken during the rising tides of prosperity and the still waters of peace. Yet, every so often, the oath is taken amidst gathering clouds and raging storms. At these moments, America has carried on not simply because of the skill (P) or vision (E) of those in high office, but because we, the people, have remained faithful to the ideals (I) of our forebears and true to our founding documents (A).

So it has been; so it must be with this generation of Americans.

That we are in the midst of crisis is now well understood. Our nation is at war against a far-reaching network of violence and hatred. Our economy is badly weakened, a consequence of greed and irresponsibility on the part of

[1] Adizes Insights, January 2009; by Ichak Kalderon Adizes, Ph.D., Nebojsa Caric, Sunil Dovedy, and Carlos Valdesuso.

[2] Presidential inaugural address, given by Barack Obama in Washington, D.C., on January 20, 2009.

some, but also our collective failure (I) to make hard choices (P) and prepare the nation for a new age (E). Homes have been lost, jobs shed, businesses shuttered. Our health care is too costly, our schools fail too many—and each day brings further evidence that the ways we use energy strengthen our adversaries and threaten our planet.

These are the indicators of crisis, subject to data and statistics. Less measurable, but no less profound, is a sapping of confidence across our land (I); a nagging fear that America's decline is inevitable, that the next generation must lower its sights.

Today I say to you that the challenges we face are real (P). They are serious and they are many. They will not be met easily or in a short span of time (A). But know this, America: They will be met (P).

On this day, we gather because we have chosen hope over fear (E), unity of purpose over conflict and discord (I).

On this day, we come to proclaim an end to the petty grievances and false promises, the recriminations and worn-out dogmas that for far too long have strangled our politics (P).

We remain a young nation. But in the words of Scripture, the time has come to set aside childish things. The time has come to reaffirm our enduring spirit (I); to choose our better history (E); to carry forward that precious gift, that noble idea passed on from generation to generation (P): the God-given promise that all are equal (A), all are free, and all deserve a chance to pursue their full measure of happiness (E).

In reaffirming the greatness of our nation we understand that greatness is never a given (P). It must be earned (P). Our journey has never been one of shortcuts or settling for less (P). It has not been the path for the faint-hearted, for those that prefer leisure over work, or seek only the pleasures of riches and fame (P). Rather, it has been the risk-takers (E), the doers (P), the makers of things (P)—some celebrated, but more often men and women obscure in their labor (P)—who have carried us up the long rugged path towards prosperity and freedom (P).

For us, they packed up their few worldly possessions and traveled across oceans in search of a new life (E).

For us, they toiled in sweatshops, and settled the West; endured the lash of the whip, and plowed the hard earth (P).

For us, they fought and died in places like Concord and Gettysburg, Normandy and Khe Sanh (P).

Time and again these men and women struggled and sacrificed and worked till their hands were raw so that we might live a better life (P). They saw America as bigger than the sum of our individual ambitions (E), greater than all the differences of birth or wealth or faction (I).

This is the journey we continue today (P). We remain the most prosperous, powerful nation on Earth. Our workers are no less productive than when this crisis began (P). Our minds are no less inventive (E), our goods and services no less needed than they were last week, or last month, or last year (P). Our capacity remains undiminished (A). But our time of standing pat, of protecting narrow interests and putting off unpleasant decisions— that time has surely passed (E). Starting today, we must pick ourselves up, dust ourselves off, and begin again the work (P) of remaking America (E).

For everywhere we look, there is work to be done (P). The state of the economy calls for action, bold and swift. And we will act (P), not only to create new jobs (E), but to lay a new foundation for growth (E). We will build the roads and bridges, the electric grids and digital lines that feed our commerce and bind us together (P). We'll restore science to its rightful place, and wield technology's wonders to raise health care's quality and lower its cost (E). We will harness the sun and the winds and the soil to fuel our cars and run our factories (E). And we will transform our schools and colleges and universities to meet the demands of a new age (E). All this we can do (P). All this we will do (P).

Now, there are some who question the scale of our ambitions, who suggest that our system cannot tolerate too many big plans. Their memories are short, for they have forgotten what this country has already done (P), what free men and women can achieve (P) when imagination (E) is joined to common purpose (I), and necessity to courage.

What the cynics fail to understand is that the ground has shifted beneath them (E), that the stale political arguments that have consumed us for so long no longer apply (E).

The question we ask today is not whether our government is too big or too small, but whether it works (P)—whether it helps families find jobs at a decent wage (P), [health] care they can afford (P), a retirement that is dignified (P). Where the answer is yes, we intend to move forward (P). Where the answer is no, programs will end (P). And those of us who manage the public's dollars will be held to account (A), to spend wisely (A), reform bad habits (E), and do our business in the light of day (A), because only then can we restore the vital trust between a people and their government (I).

Nor is the question before us whether the market is a force for good or ill. Its power to generate wealth and expand freedom is unmatched. But this crisis has reminded us that without a watchful eye, the market can spin out of control (A). The nation cannot prosper long when it favors only the prosperous (I). The success of our economy has always depended not just on the size of our gross domestic product, but on the reach of our prosperity, on the ability to extend opportunity to every willing heart (I)—not out of charity, but because it is the surest route to our common good (I).

As for our common defense, we reject as false the choice between our safety and our ideals (I). Our Founding Fathers, faced with perils that we can scarcely imagine, drafted a charter to assure the rule of law and the rights of man (A)—a charter expanded by the blood of generations. Those ideals still light the world (E), and we will not give them up for expedience's sake (E).

And so, to all the other peoples and governments who are watching today, from the grandest capitals to the small village where my father was born, know that America is a friend of each nation, and every man, woman, and child who seeks a future of peace and dignity (I), and we are ready to lead once more (E).

Recall that earlier generations faced down fascism and communism not just with missiles and tanks, but with sturdy alliances and enduring convictions (I). They understood that our power alone cannot protect us, nor does it entitle us to do as we please. Instead they knew that our power grows through its prudent use (A); our security emanates from the justness of our cause (A), the force of our example (P), the tempering qualities of humility and restraint (I).

We are the keepers of this legacy (A). Guided by these principles once more we can meet those new threats that demand even greater effort (P), even greater cooperation and understanding between nations (I). We will begin (E) to responsibly (I) leave Iraq to its people (P) and forge a hard-earned peace in Afghanistan (P). With old friends and former foes (I), we'll work tirelessly (P) to lessen the nuclear threat, roll back the specter of a warming planet (E).

We will not apologize for our way of life, nor will we waver in its defense. And for those who seek to advance their aims by inducing terror and slaughtering innocents, we say to you now that our spirit is stronger and cannot be broken (P)—you cannot outlast us (P), and we will defeat you (P).

For we know that our patchwork heritage is a strength, not a weakness (I). We are a nation of Christians and Muslims, Jews and Hindus, and non-believers (I). We are shaped by every language and culture, drawn from every end of this Earth (I); and because we have tasted the bitter swill of civil war and segregation, and emerged from that dark chapter stronger and more united (I), we cannot help but believe that the old hatreds shall someday pass (I); that the lines of tribe shall soon dissolve (I); that as the world grows smaller, our common humanity shall reveal itself (I); and that America must play its role (P) in ushering in a new era of peace (E).

> "[Some] have forgotten … what free men and women can achieve (P) when imagination (E) is joined to common purpose (I), and necessity to courage."

To the Muslim world, we seek a new way forward (E), based on mutual interest and mutual respect (I). To those leaders around the globe who seek to sow conflict, or blame their society's ills on the West, know that your people will judge (A) you on what you can build, not what you destroy (P).

To those who cling to power through corruption and deceit and the silencing of dissent, know that you are on the wrong side of history, but that we will extend a hand if you are willing to unclench your fist (I).

To the people of poor nations, we pledge to work alongside you (I) to make your farms flourish and let clean waters flow (P); to nourish starved bodies and feed hungry minds (P). And to those nations like ours that enjoy relative plenty, we say we can no longer afford indifference to the suffering outside our borders (I), nor can we consume the world's resources without regard to effect (A). For the world has changed, and we must change with it (E).

As we consider the road that unfolds before us (E), we remember with humble gratitude those brave Americans (I) who at this very hour patrol far-off deserts and distant mountains (P). They have something to tell us, just as the fallen heroes who lie in Arlington whisper through the ages.

We honor them (I) not only because they are guardians of our liberty

(A), but because they embody the spirit of service (I)—a willingness to find meaning in something greater than themselves (E).

And yet, at this moment, a moment that will define a generation, it is precisely this spirit that must inhabit us all (I).

For as much as government can do and must do (P), it is ultimately the faith and determination of the American people upon which this nation relies (I). It is the kindness to take in a stranger when the levees break (I), the selflessness of workers who would rather cut their hours than see a friend lose their job (I) which sees us through our darkest hours. It is the firefighter's courage to storm a stairway filled with smoke (P), but also a parent's willingness to nurture a child (I) that finally decides our fate.

Our challenges may be new (E). The instruments with which we meet them may be new (E). But those values upon which our success depends— honesty (A) and hard work (P), courage (P) and fair play (A), tolerance (I) and curiosity (E), loyalty (P) and patriotism (I)—these things are old. These things are true. They have been the quiet force of progress throughout our history (E).

What is demanded, then, is a return to these truths (A). What is required of us now is a new era of responsibility (A)—a recognition on the part of every American that we have duties to ourselves, our nation and the world; duties (P) that we do not grudgingly accept, but rather seize gladly (P), firm in the knowledge that there is nothing so satisfying to the spirit, so defining of our character than giving our all to a difficult task (P).

This is the price and the promise of citizenship (A).

This is the source of our confidence—the knowledge that God calls on us to shape an uncertain destiny (E).

This is the meaning of our liberty and our creed, why men and women and children of every race and every faith can join in celebration (I) across this magnificent Mall; and why a man whose father less than sixty years ago might not have been served at a local restaurant can now stand before you to take a most sacred oath.

So let us mark this day with remembrance of who we are (I) and how far we have traveled. (P) In the year of America's birth, in the coldest of months, a small band of patriots huddled by dying campfires on the shores of an icy river. The capital was abandoned. The enemy was advancing. The snow was stained with blood. At a moment when the outcome of our Revolution was most in doubt, the father of our nation ordered these words to be read to the people:

"Let it be told to the future world ... that in the depth of winter, when nothing but hope and virtue could survive ... that the city and the country, alarmed at one common danger, came forth to meet (it)." (P)

America, in the face of our common dangers, in this winter of our hardship, let us remember these timeless words. With hope (E) and virtue, let us brave once more the icy currents (P), and endure what storms may come (P). Let it be said by our children's children that when we were tested we refused to let this journey end (P), that we did not turn back nor did we falter (P); and with eyes fixed on the horizon (E) and God's grace upon us (I), we carried forth (P) that great gift of freedom and delivered (P) it safely to future generations (E).

Thank you. God bless you. And God bless the United States of America.

ANALYSIS

It emerges, if the content analysis is correct, that Obama's style is first (P), then (I), then (E), and last (A).

We attribute the (P) content of his speech to the situation the United States is in: He had to refer to the crisis and what needs to be done. Thus, it is possible that the (P) characteristic is more indicative of a situational imperative than of a style.

We believe—which did not come as a surprise—that he is mostly (I) and then (E).

That makes him a statesman.

GETTING STARTED ON THE PATH TO GOOD MANAGEMENT[1]

I N the past decade, management theory and practice from Japan has led the way, with its axioms of team management and team production. Now, team thinking is trendy and has become part of the American corporate scene.

But if we only borrow the organizational formula of team management, without understanding what really drives it, where are we really heading?

Change means conflict. For good managers and good management, we need a working process of mutual trust and respect (MT&R). Good managers are people who can command MT&R, and good managers know themselves.

It's not unlike handling a horse or a racing car. If you want to train or ride a horse—or even stay on it—the horse has to trust you, and you have to "feel" the horse. Race-car drivers tell us that the difference between winning and losing is how well you "feel" the machine as you handle it. You can't drive the car to pieces; you have to "listen" to its engine and operation.

A good manager cannot possibly be an accumulation of all the virtues we would wish to ascribe to management. However, there are some ways to get started on the path to becoming a good manager:

1) *Who is perfect?* Some managers are good administrators, others excel in entrepreneuring or integrating. Some are superb producers. Not everyone is born with natural skills in all aspects of the (PAEI) code—(P)roducing, (A)dministrating, (E)ntrepreneuring, and (I)ntegrating. But that doesn't mean we are stuck for life with only one capability. That starting place gives us our first way of

---

[1] Adizes Insights, August 2009. Originally published in *Manage* magazine, July 1993; reprinted with permission.

perceiving things and is the most natural way for us to look at the world. But it is also possible to learn how to perceive from other perspectives. We should aim at improving our perceptions and performance in areas that don't come as naturally to us, while at the same time accepting the fact that we can't be perfect.

2) *Getting in touch:* Be in tune with your social environment. Accept feedback from others in order to determine who you are. Realize that you are what you do, and learn how to learn from the feedback of others. If managers can accept their own weaknesses as well as their strengths, they will be able to deal with the conflicts that stem from differences in managerial styles. As poet Robert Burns wrote:

> *And would some Power the small gift give us,*
> *To see ourselves as others see us!*[2]

3) *This business of self-actualization:* Have a balanced view of yourself. Come to a realization of both your strengths and weaknesses. In the words of Miguel de Cervantes, "Make it thy business to know thyself, which is the most difficult lesson in the world."[3]

In the past, social thinkers including Abraham Maslow and Carl Rogers have written of the "self-actualized personality." Now, others are sounding the same theme. The names may change but the idea is the same: Self-actualized people are action-oriented, march to a different drummer, and are willing to learn from anyone. They are the meat and potatoes of an effective, participative management team.

4) *Getting out of boxes:* Good managers are people who hear, listen, and feel. They do not just hear without listening, or listen without feeling. That isn't easy these days: Modern technology boxes us in and closes off our sensibilities. But good managers are sensitive to the impact they have on others and the impact of others on them.

---

[2] Robert Burns, "To a Louse, On Seeing One On A Lady's Bonnet At Church," 1786.

[3] Miguel de Cervantes Saavedra, *Don Quixote*, part II, first published in 1615.

5) *Really seeing:* We have one word for "snow." The Eskimos have many. We need to stretch our capabilities in dealing with others, learning to identify excellence in others—especially in areas where we ourselves do not excel. Recognizing others' skills that complement our own is another big step toward creating a working team.

6) *And really listening:* The good manager accepts the opinions of others in areas where their judgments are likely to be better than his own. It's a mistake to characterize people as subordinates or superiors because it breeds a cult of personality and assumes that the manager is superior to his subordinates in everything.

7) *Handling conflict:* We have to recognize that conflicts are the order of the day. Conflicts are inevitable for growth. The high-achieving manager can resolve the conflicts that necessarily arise when people with different needs and styles have to work together to create an effective managerial mix. You are courting disaster if you walk away from battles of managerial styles, or seek instant and permanent harmony. The goal is to work toward creating a supportive learning environment—one in which conflict is perceived not as a threat but an opportunity to learn and develop as a team.

> In the words of Miguel de Cervantes, "Make it thy business to know thyself, which is the most difficult lesson in the world."

8) *Knowing how "to be":* If we rush pell-mell into the 21st century with new forms of participative and team management without developing techniques for handling others, we may be inviting managerial and organizational disaster. In modern society, we often overemphasize the having of information—the *how to*—and almost ignore the critical importance of *how to be*. Management is about listening, feeling, and knowing yourself—the hardest lesson in the world. Success is not easy to achieve, but that is the role management has to produce.

PART 2

LIFECYCLES

THE 'ROAD MAP' OF ORGANIZATIONAL LIFECYCLES[1]

NO organization is "born" effective and efficient in the short and long run, with all four of the essential (PAEI) roles already fully developed. Organizations gradually develop each of the roles over time. Even if the organization hires someone who excels in any of the roles, it takes time for the organization to co-opt the role, to develop this DNA.

A role does not develop in a vacuum. It develops as we solve problems. Thus, problems that force us to develop the role are normal. Think of a baby falling as it learns to walk, or a start-up company learning to control its cash diligently.

How the roles develop, age, and die over time provides a road map that predicts problems the organization will have to deal with and whether they are normal, abnormal, or fatal. That road map is the lifecycle of an organization,[2] which enables us to manage change proactively and consciously—in other words, to make decisions that will transform the organization to become effective and efficient, both now and in the future.

The following chapters summarize a typical organization's life stages, beginning when it is a mere idea in the founder's brain, and ending when the organization dies or falls apart.

COURTSHIP (paEi)

In the Courtship stage, the organization does not even exist yet! The founder is dreaming of what the organization can be or should be or what he wants it to be, and in doing so the first role—the (E)ntrepreneurial

---

[1] Excerpted and revised from an article published in the *Harvard Business Review*, Russian edition, 2006.

[2] For more detail, see Ichak Adizes, *Managing Corporate Lifecycles* (Upper Saddle River, NJ: Prentice Hall, 1999).

role—begins to develop: The founder is imagining the future and is willing to take risks to create that future.

What's normal at this stage is a lot of noise in the system: The founder of the company is constantly telling everyone how great his business is going to be. He is excited, full of passion. Ironically, the person he is trying hardest to convince is himself, because he is building up commitment, which he needs in order to take the risk of starting a company.

This commitment to the project or organization should be institutionalized over time and shared by as many people in the organization as possible, because without universal commitment, when the founder dies, the company will die, too. The organization is only as viable as the commitment of its members. (Take political systems, for example. During the Communist era, getting into the USSR was very easy; getting out, very difficult. Conversely, to get into the United States is very difficult, but it's very easy to get out. What does that tell you about which system is more viable?)

If *only* (E) gets developed during this phase, it is an unhealthy Courtship. The other essential roles must also develop to their threshold level—signified by lower-case letters, such as (p), (a), and (i)—otherwise the organization will be unable to move on to its next stage, when the next role develops. Think of a rosebud: It has all the ingredients of a full-blown rose in it.

The (pai) roles evolve during the development of a business plan, which should articulate the exact needs that the organization is going to satisfy, who the clients will be, and why. That develops the (p) role to the necessary threshold level, in addition to serving as a test of the founder's vision. When the business plan addresses *how* the organization is going to satisfy those needs, the (a) role is developing; and when the plan includes the values system that will lead the organization, like a constitution that will govern its behavior (rarely done, unfortunately), it is addressing the (i) role.

All organizations, including not-for-profits, should make a business plan because all organizations, in order to be managed well, need all four roles to be performed well. In my work with presidents of nations, I have noticed that the same principles also apply to countries. Nations that have been colonized, for instance, are usually deficient in the (A) and (E) roles. These were the roles that the colonialists performed, and when they left the colonies, those roles had not developed indigenously.

Characteristics of a healthy Courtship: lots of passion and excitement and willingness to take risks—but with attention to reality and specifics; it is not just dreaming. The commitment has been tested by a reality check: the business plan, which specifies the (p), (a), and (i) roles. The healthy code of the Courtship stage is (paEi).

In unhealthy Courtship, whenever the founder is confronted by an obstacle, usually generated by the requirements of implementing his idea, he jumps from that idea to the next, aborting one brainstorm for another. All motion with no progress. Lots of noise—in neutral. Its code is (--E-).

All organizations, of any kind, have a finite amount of energy at any given moment. Once the (E) role is stabilized and articulated well and has survived the reality test of the business plan specifying the (p), (a), and (i) roles, the healthy organization can turn its energy away from (E) to the next role—(P). It is as if the system has a brain. It has a fixed amount of energy that needs to be utilized effectively and efficiently. First it dedicates that energy to developing (E), then it redirects that energy away from (E) and dedicates it to (P). The organization enters the Infancy stage, (Paei).

An organization moves from Courtship to Infancy when risk is taken: Contracts are signed, people hired, loans taken, investments made, money spent. The organization stops planning and starts acting.

INFANCY (PAEI)

At this point, the (P) role is developed. Now comes the time to *do*, not to dream. The time for talking is over; now you need do-ers, people who can produce. Good founders combine (E) and (P): They have ideas and they know how to work hard.

An Infant organization, characterized by the (Paei) code, is busy, busy, busy—*doing*. There's no time to dream anymore. The founder controls all decisions and usually is very authoritarian, with very low (I). The organization has little (A), either. Whatever (A) there is, is written down on the back of an old envelope stuffed into the founder's pocket. But watch it: If (E) is neglected because of all the focused hard work for survival—the organization will lose its vision, its purpose. The dream will become a nightmare: work, work, work—with no sense of a mission or goal.

By the same token, if the (A) role in an Infant organization is below the necessary threshold, then although it might be working hard and earning revenues, without coherent developed systems the organization will be effective but inefficient. The result could be high sales with high losses and maybe even a bankruptcy.

Too much (A) or (E) is not desirable, either. It is normal for an Infant organization to lack detailed job descriptions. If the start-up Infant insists on detailed organizational charts and job descriptions, as major bureaucracies do with their own start-ups, that organization may be stifled by too much (A) too early. It's like a child trying to play soccer in black tie attire. In Infancy, it is OK to be a little dirty or muddy and to break a bone or two. One learns from early mistakes. In fact, it is essential to make the mistakes in order to learn from them. The organization needs to accumulate experience.

Too much (E) can also destroy an Infant organization. The founder might be constantly reinventing and tinkering with the technology, instead of turning his energy to selling and generating revenue. He is internally oriented, toward the product and its technology, while the clients' needs are dismissed or overlooked. An Infant organization has to switch its orientation from (E) to (P).

Normal Infancy should be (Paei). Abnormal Infancies commonly look like this, (P---)—or, reverting back to Courtship, (paEi), or even worse, to (--E-).

The transition to the next stage of the lifecycle happens when the organization has proven to itself that the vision can be commercialized; it can count on repeat clients, and its cash flow is positive. The two roles—the (E) role that developed in Courtship by providing a vision, and the (P) role that developed in Infancy by being task-oriented, making the vision a reality—now need to be synchronized to work well together.

That takes energy, because the (E) and (P) roles are not compatible: The growth of one comes at the expense of the other. The harder you work at satisfying current needs—(P)—the less time you have to pay attention to the future—(E). Thus, the organization needs to dedicate energy to making the two roles work together.

Eventually "the baby" sleeps through the night, and starts watching its fingers, looking around the crib, and turning around to explore. When a company experiences positive cash flow, some consistency in sales and some control of expenses, it moves to the next stage of the lifecycle.

Go-Go (PaEi)

The company is successful, active, and arrogant, growing by leaps and bounds, rapidly, like a bush in the spring—and here is where it can get into trouble. The organization looks like a mini-conglomerate. Management dreams and then works on realizing its dreams, and usually there are too many dreams simultaneously.

When an organization reaches this level of success—especially if its founder's style is strong in (E) and (P) but lacks (A) and (I)—the founder may become so excited by his dream-come-true that he feels omnipotent. He dares to take bigger and bigger risks. He is like a baby who is beginning to crawl: Just about everything looks exciting and needs to be explored. He might decide, "What we did with shoes we can do with real estate, and why not start a trading company as well?"

The Go-Go company is opportunity-*driven* rather than opportunity-*driving*. It has many, many priorities, more than it can address in a reasonable period of time. It hires tomorrow the people it needed yesterday, and it can easily run out of cash.

A healthy Go-Go's code is (PaEi). It is all about dreaming and doing, but it has at least enough (A) and (I) to set some limits to (P) and (E). It has in top management (or in a spouse) someone who performs a harnessing function that provides some boundaries, some reality considerations, to the hyperventilating founder.

When (A) and (I) are far too small in relation to (E) and (P), an abnormal Go-Go code will be (P-E-). One manifestation of this imbalance is the extreme arrogance of the entrepreneuring founder. He starts believing that he is indestructible; that there is nothing he cannot do, so he takes more and more risks. He listens to no voices of dissension. He challenges the establishment and even common logic. His early success has made him a hero whom no one dares to question, and he could actually take the company over the edge of a cliff.

> [The Go-Go organization] is like a baby who is beginning to crawl: Just about everything looks exciting and needs to be explored.

Another manifestation of the imbalance between (A) and (E) is that the company lacks clear accountability: Who is responsible for what? This happens because the company is growing faster than it can define and implement a workable structure. So people wear multiple hats and have multiple bosses—and increasingly it is not clear who is truly accountable. The organization functions nevertheless, because it is and always has been highly centralized—and guess who keeps all the authority? The founder.

This dependency on the founder has repercussions. When he dies, the organization, too, is dead in the water: no rudder and no sails. I call this syndrome the "founder's trap."[3] The second generation of leadership has the founder's aspirations but lacks the founder's capabilities. On average, it takes three generations for a family business to fail.

There are other consequences as well. The exceptional growth in several directions at once, without discipline, systems, and order, even in a healthy Go-Go, will not go unpunished. The company will inevitably make a mistake: It might introduce the wrong product into the wrong market, make promises and not be able to deliver, or any of a thousand other mistakes. When a crisis finally emerges—which it will, because of this uncontrolled rate of change—it will not be clear who created it or who is responsible for dealing with it, except for the founder. The centralization of authority makes him responsible for all crises. So when a catastrophe occurs, all searchlights turn to him; and now, instead of being perceived as a genius, he is seen as dangerous.

If he loses control of the board, the founder will probably be fired. Even if he stays in control and cannot be fired, he might eventually lose his self-confidence. These crises are repetitive, and he cannot solve them alone, so eventually he starts entertaining the idea of selling the company, or else he starts looking for a "savior," a chief operating officer (COO) who knows how to manage. "I only know how to build companies, not manage them," the founder tells himself.

Usually, such transitions do not happen without trouble. If he sells, it could be to another Go-Go leader who is just as disorganized as he is but has not hit his crisis point yet; or to a cash-rich, aging organization that is looking to buy the Go-Go's entrepreneurial spirit—only to end up stifling it with excessive (A).

Predictably, if the Go-Go leader brings in a COO to manage the company, it will only be on paper: In reality, the founder will constantly

---

[3] For more information on the founder's trap, see the chapter in this section titled: "Potential Solutions for Getting Out of the 'Founder's Trap,'" beginning on page 105.

interfere in daily decisions until, eventually, there will be a clash of personalities between the founder, whose style is mostly (E), and the newcomer COO, whose style should be (A), for that is what the organization needs. The harder the new COO tries to insert order into the chaos, the worse her political standing becomes within the organization, and who is her biggest enemy? The founder, who cannot abide her management style, which is 180 degrees different from his own. Eventually, if the founder is still in control, the COO will be fired. If the founder is no longer in control, the COO will build an alliance with the board, and the board will fire the "out-of-control" founder.

In summary, the relatively disorganized growth of a typical Go-Go creates (A) problems. The company will lose on a deal or a new product that was inadequately analyzed; it might be sued by the government, by the franchises, or by labor for some violation. It will probably encounter cash problems, because its information system is not equipped to provide quick, accurate information about the company's state of affairs. All because the company has grown too fast and in too many directions, and the accounting system could not catch up.

When that crisis occurs, the company will make its transition to the Adolescent stage of the lifecycle. Now, it's time for (A) to develop: The company needs administrators to introduce some order, some organization, some rules.

ADOLESCENCE (pAEi)

Now we have new challenges. (A) threatens (E): (E) needs flexibility, while (A) wants to minimize flexibility in order to attain the standardization and predictability that is necessary for efficiency.

In a healthy Adolescent organization, as (A) develops it works to stabilize (E), instead of working to *reduce* (E). The energy needed for (A) is taken from (P), not from (E). Developing (A) at the expense of (P) means that it is normal for an organization to turn inward at this stage; thus, revenues will not grow at the same rate as during the Go-Go phase. An external board of directors takes more control of the high-flying organization, providing some brakes and discipline. The CFO, who has been ignored during the Go-Go phase, is now a voice the entrepreneur listens to. The organization becomes more controllable, more predictable. But the entrepreneuring leader is not squeezed out. He just takes another role—perhaps chairman or president—and appoints a COO to perform the needed (PA) role.

For this transition to occur smoothly, without the clashes or turnover I described above, the organization must first be structured correctly—*before* the new COO is brought in—otherwise she will fall into the abyss of the disorganized Go-Go and fail. When that happens, the Adolescent organization is experiencing an abnormal problem: (A) cannot grow; or else it grows at the expense of (E).

Here is the typical pattern: The board—intimidated by the founder's entrepreneurial style, which reminds them of an unguided missile—fires the founder and gives the reins to a CEO with a dominant (A) managerial style. As a result, the organization loses its creative, entrepreneurial element. In the short run, the organization will become stabilized and profitable, but it will lose its market position over the long term.

Another symptom of abnormal Adolescence is a burgeoning (A) that squeezes out not only the founder but all the other (E)s as well. This is a dangerous period, when fighting breaks out among the professional managers, or bureaucrats, and the start-up entrepreneurs, the partisans who made the revolution.

Usually the (A)s win and squeeze the (E)s out—but when you "kill" (E), the company suffers. The old-timers, the entrepreneurial types who were attracted to the Go-Go company, find the new (A) culture and its demands stifling and start leaving the company in hordes. The company will stabilize for a while and might even become more profitable. It will eliminate waste, and the quality of its products will improve. But without (E), innovation and plans for dealing with the future will be lacking. It will not be able to adapt to changes in the marketplace. The organization will lose its place in the market. This is called premature Bureaucratization.

Another manifestation of an abnormal Adolescence is the "divorce."

The need to draw energy from either the (P) or (E) roles as (A) tries to grow can produce internal political struggles. In Adolescence many partnerships break down. If a company is started by two partners, one is typically (PaEi) in style and is usually the one in charge of sales, marketing, technology, and product development. The other partner, with a (pAeI) style, is internally oriented, taking care of purchasing, finance administration, and operations. If the partners happen to be extreme in their styles, if there is no

(I) and no shared (E)—a partnership of a (P-E-) with a (PA--)—the partnership will break down, and it is time for a "divorce." Usually the (A) partner buys the (E) partner out.

Normal Adolescence is (pAEi). Sometimes, there may be a very short period of (PAei), but the healthy organization, after developing its (A), reverts right back to (E).

Abnormal is (PAei); or, the organization might revert back to the Go-Go stage, (PaEi).

What you *do not want* is (E) and (A) fighting. What you *do want* is (E) and (A) together. And that is very difficult to do. It requires (I): the ability to (I)ntegrate the conflicting roles.

But if you survive this transition, you will be in Prime of the lifecycle. In the next chapters, we will deal with Prime, as well as the potentially unnecessary stages of aging.

Prime, and the Preventable Stages of Aging[1]

I N the first chapter of this section, we discussed the necessary and predictable stages that any organization will experience as it starts up and begins to mature.

In this chapter, we deal with the stage that every organization aims for but may never achieve; and the aging stages, which organizations reach only if they fail to maintain the flexibility and self-control to stay in Prime.

The Prime Organization (PAEI)

Once (A) develops, the organization has three of its four essential "DNA" components. Now it can focus on (I). That is when the human factors come onto the radar screen in full force—when the organization starts paying attention to salary administration, performance reviews, training and development, and HRD in general. It's not that those problems and issues didn't exist before; the organization simply had bigger fish to fry and had put off focusing on these issues.

Please note that in Prime, you are still growing; you are not at the top of the lifecycle curve. Remember: When you are green, you are growing; when you are ripe, you are rotting. Getting to Prime (PAEI) does not mean that the company stays in Prime. As (I) grows, the relative power of the four roles starts to change. (P) and (E) are the functions, (A) and (I) are the form. In the developing stages, (P) and (E) were stronger than (A); thus function was driving the form. Now that (I) has also developed, form starts to dominate function. The first element to suffer is (E), and the decline of (E) is a predictor of the eventual decline of (P). The organization is starting to age.

---

[1] Excerpted and revised from an article published in the *Harvard Business Review*, Russian edition, 2006.

That brings me to a new point: Whether an organization is developing or decaying, growing or aging, does not depend on its size or its chronological age. Two factors determine location on the lifecycle: organizational flexibility and organizational self-control. Flexibility is a function of (E) and self-control of (A).

LOCATION ON THE LIFECYCLE

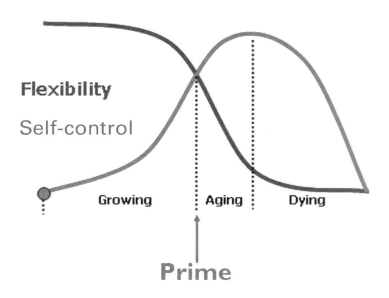

THE AGING PROCESS

I have found that the following factors cause (E) to decline, starting the aging process:

1) *Functionality of the leadership style:* How appropriate is the leadership style for what the organization needs? For instance, in Adolescence, (A) leadership is usually promoted to bring order to the chaotic Go-Go organization. However, quite often the (A) "forgets to leave" after her job is done, and this continuing (A)

stifles the Prime organization, which needs more (E) to continue to grow and change.

2) *Mental age of leadership:* When a person's desires exceed her expectations, she is mentally young and will work to make the desired become the expected. When a person looks into the future and perceives that what is expected is just what is desired and thus there is no need to change anything, that person has mentally aged. That will bring (E) down.

3) *Functionality of organizational structure:* The function of marketing is to focus on the future. Its role is to "make waves"—requiring the organization to change and react or pro-act to the changes in its markets. Thus, marketing's function is (E)-oriented.

   Sales, on the other hand, should be focused on current clients, seeing to it that purchase orders are signed. That is mostly a (P) function. Since the two roles, (E) and (P), are incompatible, and because in competition the odds tend to favor the role with the short-term orientation, whenever an organizational structure has marketing and sales under the same vice president, the marketing department ultimately is reduced to doing sales support.

   The same holds true for putting technology and new-product development together with manufacturing or production. Again, (P) and (E) are mixed, and invariably, technology and product development will suffer. The attention will be dedicated to the short-term function of maintenance, at the expense of the long-term function of technology development.

4) *Perceived relative market share:* If the company has a high market share and the competitor in second place has a significantly smaller share, the leading organization may become complacent. As in sports, if you want to improve you must engage in competitions you might lose. If you compete only with those you can easily defeat, you will become too confident and stop trying hard, and eventually you will lose your leadership position.

   As (E) decreases, innovation and planned change decrease.

Instead of building a new high-rise, the organization might spend money on polishing the doorknobs of the existing building. It engages, at best, in "continuous improvement," while in the meantime, in a garage somewhere, an as-yet-unknown entrepreneur is developing a disruptive technology that will soon displace the aging organization in the marketplace.

ARISTOCRACY (pAeI)

If (E) is low for a prolonged period of time, (P) will eventually also have to decline. When (A) and (I) are in the ascendant and (E) and (P) are low, the organization is in Aristocracy. The company motto becomes "Don't make waves." No one is willing to take risks, and it is the managers who take the least risk who get promoted.

Why? Because when we dream and change less and less, when we fail to prepare to serve future needs, we will be unprepared when those future needs arrive; we will still be selling what we used to sell in the past. Imagine selling horsewhips in Detroit.

The organizational code in Aristocracy is (pAeI): The company is dominated by (A) and (I). The climate now is one in which those who succeed in the organization are not the ones who know but the ones who know *whom* to know, those who are politically correct and do not make waves. "If you lay low long enough, you can become the president" is the message one gets in a (pAeI) company.

The organization has become a social club to which no new members are accepted. Innovators in such a company, the (E)s, are recognizable by the arrows in their backs. The company, to stay "successful," starts raising prices in order to keep revenues growing—but the absolute number of products sold or services rendered is declining.

Eventually the moment of reckoning will arrive: The company's products or services are obsolete, and, on top of that, they are overpriced. This will not go unpunished. The company will experience an abrupt decline in sales. Profits will go down, losses up. If it does not quickly cut costs (which it might not, because the culture of Aristocracy is the culture of a social club: "You scratch my back and I

> As in sports, if you want to improve you must engage in competitions you might lose.

scratch yours"), the company will start eating its cash reserves and soon have negative cash flow.

Often, organizations in this phase do a kind of organizational liposuction, putting the company on the scale and deciding it is overweight—then cutting one leg off. People are fired. Now the numbers are good, but the company is missing a leg.

At that point, (I) declines, the social club is disbanded, the knives come out, and the search for scapegoats—the Witch-hunt—begins.

THE WITCH-HUNT (pA-I)

The mutual-support club of yesterday now becomes a den of suspicion, back-stabbing, and paranoia. Who did it? Who is responsible for the losses and negative cash flow? The organization turns its energy inward, looking for villains, and (I) declines or disappears. Predictably, the scapegoat will turn out to be the remaining vestiges of (E): the product developers, the R&D people, the strategic planners, the marketing people. If the organization happens to be a country, the scapegoat will be those ethnic groups that have historically nurtured the entrepreneurial spirit: the Jews, the Indians, or the Chinese. Eventually the organization becomes a Bureaucracy, and if it does not receive external political support, it will soon be dead.

As the last islands of entrepreneurship are fired or exiled, the company accelerates its demise. It has lost its (P), (E), and (I) roles. Only the (A) is left standing. Like a dead tree, the structure is there—roots, trunk, and branches—but it is no longer a living organism. The (PAEI) code is now (--A-).

BUREAUCRACY (--A-)

In Bureaucracy, the organization is mostly form; it lacks the function that serves real needs. It has manuals, procedures, and rules, but its clients' needs are served ineffectively, if at all. The organization is a machine that appears to be functioning, but no product is coming out at the other end. There is motion and action without the desired results.

Bureaucracies do not depend on their clients to survive. They rely on external support, which may be political or social. But when the Bureaucracy becomes a political liability, that support disappears and the organization collapses. What appeared to be a monstrous machine turns out to be a heap of dead particles, and the organization is dead: (----).

AGING IS AVOIDABLE

My forty years of consulting experience has shown me that there are no normal problems in the aging stages of the lifecycle. That's because aging is an abnormal phenomenon. Organizations do not have to age. They can stay in Prime forever if they know how to maintain their position there. They need to nurture, stimulate, and maintain their (E), which is done by appropriate restructuring and decentralization.

Some aging companies, to avoid becoming obsolete, try to find and buy a company with the new, disruptive technology. The new company usually is in its Go-Go stage; thus it needs the deep pockets of the aging company and is willing to be acquired. Now we have a new set of cultural organizational problems: for example, how to integrate a Go-Go culture, (PaEi), with the aging culture of Aristocracy, (pAeI). Many such acquisitions fail to produce the desired results. Why? The Aristocracy kills the Go-Go initiatives, because its enormous (A) overwhelms and suffocates the Go-Go's (E).

How to overcome problems of any stage of the lifecycle, and how to either retard or successfully rejuvenate an aging organization, are subjects for further reading.[2]

---

[2] See Ichak Adizes, *Pursuit of Prime: Maximize Your Company's Success with the Adizes Program* (Santa Barbara, CA: Adizes Institute Publications, 2005).

A COMPANY IN PRIME[1]

THE editors of the magazine Agenda *recently talked with Dr. Ichak Adizes about what makes a company successful.*

AGENDA: *As the CEOs of growing companies, our readers want to know the key things they can do to make their company succeed. Tell us a little bit about your concept of companies in Prime, this optimal state of success.*

DR. ADIZES: A company is in Prime when form and function are in balance. The *what* and the *how* are in balance. Prior to Prime, function is more important than form. In other words, *what* we do is more important than *how* we do it. After Prime, *how* we do it is more important than *what* we do. That is why, after Prime, *how* you do something and *whom* you know is more important than *what* you do. In Prime, the *what* and *how* are in balance. In Prime, the company is both flexible and in control. Prior to Prime, the company is flexible, but not very much in control of itself. After Prime, control is very high, and the company loses flexibility. In Prime, flexibility and control are together.

However, in a company in Prime, the management is not as flexible as before Prime, because there is professional management: The tendency to depend on any single indispensable individual does not exist as it does in younger companies. On the other hand, in Prime, the organization has a strategic outlook without losing attention to detail. Furthermore, the organization does not look only at detail without losing its strategic outlook. So the company in Prime has controlled flexibility, and it doesn't depend on any single individual.

Q: *How do you get a company into this Prime shape? Of course, CEOs want to make their companies successful and avoid any pitfalls that will harm*

---

[1] Published in *Agenda* magazine, Fall 1993, by Ichak Adizes and the editors of *Agenda;* reprinted with permission.

their business. It would be interesting to know if there is any way that CEOs can develop themselves, in particular, to accomplish success. In your book Mastering Change[2] *you point out that there is no perfect manager. So how do we get to Prime?*

A: The obvious answer is very long and complicated, so let me just start with a tip.

If you look at systems, they have one thing in common. Look at an old car: It's falling apart. Look at an old house: It's falling apart. Look at an old person: He is falling apart. The common denominator is falling apart.

Look at a young company: It is not growing in a balanced way. Yet, it is also falling apart, however differently, because some parts of the organization, some systems of the organization, are growing faster than others. Think of a child. If you look at a child, especially an adolescent, he often looks as if his clothes do not fit. He has outgrown his clothes. His arms are too long. He is not in balance. He is growing helter-skelter.

When a company is in Prime, its main characteristic is that it has it "all together." That is why when we are really impressed with someone we say he has it all together. When we are impressed with a family, we say that family has it all together. A nation can have it all together. We are in Prime when we have it all together.

> There is no perfect manager. There is no perfect spouse; there is no perfect mother; there is no perfect father; there is no perfect child. There is nothing perfect in this world, because we are all subject to change.

Before Prime, we are struggling to keep it all together, and after Prime the organization is deteriorating rapidly and disintegrating rapidly. Diseases, in any organization or company, stem from disintegration, and the antidote, quite simply, is integration. So if somebody asks me to give a CEO one tip to bring his company to Prime, it would be to watch out for whatever is causing disintegration, and the solution is to provide integration.

Q: *Could you give us an example?*

A: For example, I might look at a company and ask: Is disintegration occurring within marketing and sales? Where exactly are the conflicts? Where is the disintegration occurring? Are you losing touch with the marketplace?

---

[2] Ichak Adizes, *Mastering Change* (Santa Monica, CA: Adizes Institute Publications, 1992).

Are you losing the portions between manufacturing, distribution, and servicing? Is there disintegration between finance and controls and budgets and what marketing does?

Q: *If we understand that disintegration is occurring, your immediate prescription is ...*

A: Continuously look for cracks in the system that are being caused by rapid growth and change, and close those gaps. And if you maintain continued integration, you *will* get to Prime, because Prime *is* being together.

Q: *Our Council members need to know what the optimal organizational structure might be that would support a company to get to and stay at Prime.*

A: The optimal structure in Prime has to reflect the diversity of styles that are necessary for complementary teams. Let me repeat that one important point: What we need for successful management is a complementary team. Nobody is the perfect manager, so we need a complementary team. But you will not get a complementary team unless you have a complementary structure. So we need that. Now, what does that mean to a CEO looking at his company? I would split the long-term orientations from the short-term orientations, so that the short-term orientation does not dominate the company's goals. For example, I always recommend splitting marketing from sales, because every time you put sales and marketing together under one vice president, the sales orientation (the short-term orientation) wins and dominates, and marketing becomes nothing more than a sales-support activity. The company has a marketing department that does not perform the marketing function.

By the same token, I do not like and I do not recommend having engineering reporting to production, because engineering will become merely a maintenance function, and technological innovation will be lost.

Let me just finish with one more pet project of mine, which has sometimes made me unpopular.

I always fight the practice of having a CFO, a chief financial officer. The chief financial officer unites short-term orientation, which is accounting, with long-term orientation, which is finance, and that makes the CFO far too powerful a figure in the company. That is why the numbers men will increasingly win the company's power struggles and the marketing people will lose. And that is also what is causing many organizations to become too short-term-oriented, concentrating on the quarterly results and forgetting their clients and the market. I usually recommend splitting finance from accounting: I think that is a good example of a workable structure for a company in Prime.

Q: In your books and speeches, you talk about the four roles an effective company must perform.

A: I'm suggesting that any organization, in order to be effective and efficient in the short run and in the long run, needs to perform four roles. To be effective in the short run, it has to have (P)—that is, it must (P)roduce, or provide for the needs of the clients for which the organization exists. In order to be efficient in the short run, it needs to systematize itself, which means it needs to (A)dminister itself correctly, which I call the (A) role.

In order to be effective in the long run, it has to be proactive. It has to position itself today to be able to deal with situations that will emerge tomorrow—which is (E)ntrepreneurship, which I call (E). Finally, in order to be efficient in the long run, the organization has to become organic, rather than mechanistic, which means that no single factor or component is so indispensable that if it breaks down, the rest of the organization will break down. In an organic system, there is such a level of internal interdependency that nobody is indispensable.

An example would be a hand. A hand is so organic that if any finger breaks, you still have a hand. In contrast, look at a chair: If a leg breaks, the whole chair collapses.

To become organic instead of mechanized, you need integration—the (I) role. Integrated systems are more efficient in the long run, because no component is indispensable.

Q: Who can perform these four functions?

A: Good question! It is impossible for any single individual to excel at all four roles simultaneously, in all situations, forever, because for one thing, no one is perfect, and for another, they are incompatible. So tell your readers that textbook managers, who can plan and organize and motivate and staff and control and lead and build a team and be sensitive to human needs, do not exist. There is no perfect manager. There is no perfect spouse; there is no perfect mother; there is no perfect father; there is no perfect child. There is nothing perfect in this world, because we are all subject to change. We might be perfect for fifteen minutes, to paraphrase Andy Warhol, but not before and not after. What we need is a complementary team, and that is also why a complementary husband-and-wife team is better for raising children.

Q: *You have done work in other cultures; what would you say are the particular strengths and weaknesses of the American approach to running businesses?*

A: To be quite honest, American management is not the best I have seen. I believe that American culture is very short-term oriented. It is excessively functionally oriented. It is not intellectual in its orientation. It tries to see what will work immediately and without too many facts or too many theories. It's a question of, "I don't want to understand the why, and I don't have the patience to go into the details." It is an instant society: instant management, the one-minute manager, one-minute coffee; everything is short and to the point, and that is very dangerous. Because, as the world is becoming more and more complicated, we need to think more and act less, rather than act more and think less. So my experience has been that when I work with American companies, my main role is to try to hold them back from jumping to conclusions and from acting prematurely and too hastily. They are too cowboyish in their orientation.

When I work abroad in other countries, there is time to contemplate— and "contemplate" is not a negative word. There is much more patience and much more intellectual orientation, which enables the organization to act much more wisely than I have seen American companies acting.

Q: *In light of what you are saying about the one-minute manager and one-minute everything, I can just picture a CEO wondering how he will find the time and the money to do the retraining and reorganizing and so forth that you recommend in your books. In the hundreds of companies and countries that you have worked with, how do they keep their businesses running while taking the time and money to evaluate and make the necessary changes?*

A: I really do not think it is a question of money. I've seen companies in the United States that have followed my philosophy intuitively and have done very, very well. And the same thing abroad. In the Far East, they are building incredible empires based on the structure of families: that same sense of belonging and commitment and loyalty to each other and to the company. And I think the same thing is true in the United States. Management needs to start thinking more about the *how* and less about the *what*. And pay attention to the *who*, the human element, and to creating the right structure in the organization. I don't think it is a question of money; it is more about providing leadership and the right values to the organization.

What costs money is our involvement, *my* involvement. That happens when companies cannot do it by themselves, because they are too big in size and in complexity, and now they need external intervention to make it happen.

> As the world is becoming more and more complicated, we need to think more and act less, rather than act more and think less.

But for a growing company, starting companies, the ones that I think are members of the Council, I believe CEOs can do it by themselves if they just pay attention to the right factors. And the right factors are not only market share and profit margins, but also how the market shares and profit margins are being achieved.

Q: I'm sure that our Council CEOs want to know, in short, what makes a company successful.

A: What makes a company successful is integration. Now, what does integration mean? Integration means a climate of mutual trust and respect.

If I were a CEO, how would I do that integration? You make a list: On one side of the page, write down any factors that increase mutual trust and respect. On the other side of the page, write down all the factors that hamper, hinder, and decrease mutual trust and respect. Your role is to increase the trust and respect side and to decrease the negative side. That is what is going to cut down on destructive conflict and increase constructive conflict. That is going to make your company grow in a balanced way rather than in a destructive way.

GENERAL MOTORS:
AN ANALYSIS[1]

G ENERAL Motors has gone bankrupt. Who could have imagined it? A company that was once the pride of American manufacturing; a company whose CEO, Charles Wilson, once said, "What's good for GM is good for America."

How did it happen?

First, let us clarify that the credit crisis did not cause the bankruptcy. It was only the last straw. GM has been aging (dying) for some time.

My consulting experience, from which I developed the Adizes theory and practice, has shown that aging is caused by the loss of the entrepreneurial spirit. Without entrepreneurial spirit, organizations turn inward and become more concerned with internal issues than with the external market. If this goes on, uncorrected, for a prolonged period of time, the company starts losing sales, and if expenses are not or cannot be cut to reflect the decline in revenues, over time the company becomes so weak that any abrupt change, such as a credit crisis, sends it into bankruptcy.

How did GM lose its entrepreneurial spirit?

In my book *Managing Corporate Lifecycles*,[2] I identified four causes for the loss of the entrepreneurial spirit:

- Perceived relative market share;
- Functionality of the organizational structure;
- Functionality of the leadership style; and
- Mental age of the leadership.

Let us examine each of these factors in relation to GM.

---

[1] Adizes Insights, June 2009.

[2] Santa Barbara, CA: Adizes Institute Publications, 2004.

PERCEIVED RELATIVE MARKET SHARE

First, let us discuss the meaning of the word "perceived."

Often, market share is accepted at face value because it is a mathematically generated percentage based on data, so it must be a "fact." Yet in my work, I have found that two companies, in the same industry, with the same sales revenues, can have drastically different perceptions of their market share.

I often joke that I can teach anyone how to get 100 percent market share in one minute. Interested? Simply redefine your market as exclusively those clients whom you are currently serving. Your market share depends entirely on how you define your market.

Why "relative" market share?

As a consultant, I am always wary of an organization that boasts about its market share. If there is a significant difference between your market share and your competitors'—if yours is way, *way* bigger—that can make you arrogant and complacent. What would happen if an Olympic runner competed only against weak competitors? Obviously, she isn't going to run faster and set new world records. She will only run faster, the best she can, if she is faced with stiff competition.

GM, twenty or thirty years ago, was big—*very* big, with a majority of the market share. Because it dominated the market, it was slow to accept new ideas and take risks. That is when it stopped "running" (competing effectively). The entrepreneurial spirit was driven out of the organization; one example was John Zachary DeLorean, a rising star who left in frustration to start his own car company.

FUNCTIONALITY OF THE ORGANIZATIONAL STRUCTURE

The functionality of the organization's structure refers to how responsibility—and even more important, authority—is assigned throughout the organization.

In growing organizations, a centralized organizational structure is common, because the systems and controls required for decentralization are insufficiently developed. If the organization continues to grow, then at some point it will have to decentralize; if it does not, management will be too far removed from the market—from where added value is created—and thus it will lose touch with the operations of the business. When a separation like this occurs, a loss of entrepreneurial spirit naturally follows.

The larger the organization, the more important it is that the organization decentralize authority and responsibility, allowing the burden of management to spread throughout the organization, and in doing so, increasing the leadership capabilities of additional managerial ranks. Decentralization increases organizational flexibility, which is essential in changing markets.

What happened at GM on this score?

> A gardener might say: "Don't treat the leaves. Treat the roots." In other words, "Don't treat the manifestations. Treat the causes."

About twenty years ago, while I was lecturing at the Columbia University Executive Program, I had the opportunity to meet GM's strategic planner, who was a visiting lecturer. He told me something very interesting that I would like to share with you: When, in the 1980s, the United States Department of Justice initiated its anti-trust suit against AT&T, which resulted in the mandated splitting of AT&T into seven separate, independently operating companies, GM became concerned that it would be next.

As it was one of the largest car manufacturers in the United States, its worries were not unfounded. GM decided to take defensive action to make sure that it could not be split apart. The company proceeded to restructure itself, becoming so integrated that it was impossible to split the whole into separate pieces.

However, the resulting organizational structure was top-heavy and overly centralized. This increased the need for top-down control systems, which further bureaucratized the organization.

When an organization the size of GM becomes heavily centralized, it will (no surprise here) be managed by the numbers. It is not strange, then, that the people who subsequently climbed to the company's CEO position advanced from the financial sector.

FUNCTIONALITY OF THE LEADERSHIP STYLE

This brings us to the third factor that causes aging.

A quick review of the last five CEOs at GM shows that all but Robert C. Stempel came from backgrounds in accounting and finance.

Managers coming from this field are typically not creative visionaries, but rather number-crunching administrators. They watch the dials rather than the road ahead.

The style of an organization's top leadership plays a part in defining that organization's culture. In order to maintain a culture of entrepreneurial spirit, it is important to have leaders who are creative and visionary and who drive the organization to push its boundaries and reinvent itself. That is not what happened at GM.

MENTAL AGE OF THE LEADERSHIP

The mental age of an organization's leadership is defined as the disparity between the desired and the expected. When I examine an organization, I try to assess the mental age of its leadership. Is it still ambitious? Is it stretching the organization, pushing it to take risks and try new things in order to get the results it wants—which *exceed* what it expects? If the leadership does not do that, I know I am dealing with an aging organization.

A few years ago I was consulting for an organization in the computerized die-casting business. Die-casting is one of the oldest technologies in the world and has not changed significantly for generations. This company had licensed a patented technology from MIT that drastically reduced the amount of time it takes to create a die cast. This new technology would allow a car manufacturer, such as GM, to design a new engine more quickly by months.

Clearly, this would have been a no-brainer, of tremendous benefit to GM. Yet GM has yet to adopt this new technology. In the culture of GM, apparently, what was desired was what was already expected. So why make waves? Why change?

YOU CAN'T BUY (E)

As we can see, GM has been affected, for many years, by all four causes of aging. As a predictable result, there was a loss of entrepreneurial spirit. Instead of trying to develop (E) internally, GM, like most aging companies, dealt with the problem by trying to buy (E) through acquisitions, such as Hughes Aircraft and EDS.

But mergers and acquisitions do not rejuvenate a company. At best, they make the numbers look better (which is why it is a popular strategy of financial people). Thus, the company looks as if it is growing, but in the meantime, top management's focus has been diverted from its core business. Instead of organic growth through innovation and following market preferences, these acquisitions only make the numbers *look* good enough.

When a company starts to age and die, what can be done about it? What should be done with GM?

A gardener might say: "Don't treat the leaves. Treat the roots." In other words, "Don't treat the manifestations. Treat the causes."

What is the manifestation of the problem? The losses. Thus, covering the losses with loans and investments will not solve the problem. GM needs to rejuvenate itself. It needs to renew the entrepreneurial spirit that it lost so long ago.

Changing the culture of an organization takes quite a bit longer than President Obama's projected time frame for GM to return to profitability.

In order to deal with the causes, we have to deal with the culture of the organization and its loss of entrepreneurial spirit.

GM has to reorganize itself and decentralize. Only that will create the necessary conditions for entrepreneurial management to re-emerge. GM will have to get organized around markets, split marketing from sales, and split engineering from production. It will need to bring new blood into the organization and free itself from domination by its financial division.

This might be very difficult—maybe even impossible—to do, given the financial crisis GM is in. But if marketing (not sales, *marketing*) and engineering (not production, *engineering*) do not take control of the company's power centers, the future will not be much different from the past.

POTENTIAL SOLUTIONS FOR GETTING OUT OF THE 'FOUNDER'S TRAP'[1]

MANY organizations have been started, grown to some point, gotten into a trap from which they could not find a way out, and disappeared.

There are many reasons why companies might fold. One of them is called the "founder's trap." Thousands of companies worldwide are currently struggling with this syndrome and looking for a solution.

THE TRAP

Let me describe the trap: Start-up companies need strong, opinionated leadership. But when the company reaches the Go-Go phase, when it is not a start-up anymore but is growing fast and usually in many directions, the founder (who doesn't have to be the initial founder; he could be the third or the fourth leader after the initial founder) starts to realize that he can't run the company as a one-man show anymore. It is too big or too complicated for him to handle.

This is the beginning of the next stage in the lifecycle, called Adolescence. In this transition, the company needs more order, discipline, systems, and predictability of behavior—none of which the entrepreneurial leader provides.

The transition between Go-Go and Adolescence is the most difficult transition in the corporate lifecycle. It is difficult both because the changes are fundamental and necessary, and because the leader in power at the time often appears to be an obstacle to making them. Some companies successfully pass this transition, but many of them get stuck in the founder's trap, where the founder is the biggest asset the company has and, at the same

---

[1] Adizes Insights, April 2007.

time, the biggest liability. He can't manage anymore with the same style that made the company grow, yet he can neither change his style nor let someone else with a different style take over. The company gets stuck in neutral, which in a changing environment can be fatal. If a founder is going to lose his company, it usually happens because of this syndrome.

THE TREATMENT

Unfortunately, there still are no clear prescriptions for how to get out of this trap. But frequently you will find the following on the treatment list: "Fire or buy out the founder and hire a professional manager from outside to head the company."

Will that work?

Well, let's look at what can often happen when the founder himself brings in a professional manager to head the company. That manager will usually be a "number-cruncher," an administrative type, because most of the obvious problems that arose during the founder's reign were of an administrative nature: insufficient order, discipline, information, etc.

But bringing in a new style of management that is almost 180 degrees the opposite of the entrepreneurial founder's style often causes widespread rejection by the organization, which resents the changes the newcomer brings in. And when the old-timers start resisting the new manager, the founder may side with them, fearing that the "number-cruncher" is worrying more about cutting costs than about increasing revenues, and that he might cut "muscle" along with the "fat."

Furthermore, the old-timers know the founder best and have learned how to accommodate his style. The new manager has a totally different style, which clashes with the founder's as well as the old-timers' styles. As a result, the place becomes riddled with conflicts.

Add to this the fact that, up to this point, the organization has been structured around people instead of around tasks, so who is accountable for what is not necessarily clear. The professional manager, in trying to establish order and discipline in such an "organic," messy organization, is going to make many unpopular decisions and will become ostracized in no time. The founder, if he is still around, will grow concerned, fire the newly appointed professional manager, and go back to managing the company himself—only to repeat the errors he has made in the past.

So it appears to be a no-win situation. Whether the founder is in or out, the company is in trouble. Often, in his despair, the founder sells the company and gets out.

Isn't there a way for the founder to remain in the company, to benefit from the years of sacrifices he made to build the company, and still make the desired transitions?

Yes, there is, and it is an intervention I have developed and tested now at more than one hundred companies of different sizes and all types of industries.

What the company needs is a new structure that is organized around the tasks to be performed and not around people. With a clearer mission, which the founder has to develop with his team, and a clear, well-designed structure, it is easier to develop budgeting systems and controls.

Once that is done, a new leader can be brought in.

If the new leader is brought in prematurely, he will have difficulties fitting in and will have to fire old-timers and bring in a new team. It is very radical surgery, which might take the organization years to deal with.

The solution, then, is to turn inward and get the place organized *first*, *before* a new manager is brought in, not *after*, which is the typical mistake I have encountered in my consulting work.

But the founder doesn't know how to do that. He probably finds it boring, maybe even threatening. He knows the company has to change, but he worries that all these new policies and rules and structures will cause the organization to lose the entrepreneurial spirit that got the company to where it is.

Despite his worries, there is no escaping from what needs to be done. At this point, the company needs clear responsibilities, clear authority, and a rewards system that makes sense. That means the company needs account-ability—which means structuring people around the organization.

THE ROLE OF THE CONSULTANT

In order to get out of the founder's trap, the founder should first restruc-ture the company with outside help. Preferably, this should be a consultant who will eventually take the founder's place as head of the company, but who acts only as a consultant at this point. This should happen slowly, care-fully, and in the right sequence.

Hiring a consultant to replace the founder is a smart decision, but founders have to do this properly. First of all, the founder has to precisely define the task of the consultant: to assist the company—including the founder—in defining the mission of the organization. Since its establishment, the company has taken many roads in many directions, and by now it has probably lost a clear vision of what the company is about. The founder needs to rearticulate the company's mission with the management team.

Then, in light of this redefined mission, the consultant can proceed to restructure the company to fulfill this mission. The existing management will not feel threatened by the consultant, since he is only there temporarily and is expected to leave when his task is completed.

However, while helping the founder to restate the mission, and then reorganizing the structure to correspond to that mission, the consultant will be "learning" the company. If the founder really likes the consultant, he could appoint him as the chief operating officer (COO), while the founder remains the chief executive officer (CEO).

So, the appropriate sequence is: Hire an external consultant; have him restructure the company; see how well he works with others; let him learn about the company; and then, when the company is structured properly, the founder could either hire him as a COO, or bring in some other professional to run the company.

Hiring an external consultant to be the COO is good, but the founder is still going to be too involved—and he *should* be. He is where the organization's entrepreneurial spirit is probably still located. Furthermore, the founder probably still controls the company, which means that without him, no decisions about change will be implemented.

So we want the founder "in," but not *too* "in." Because the founder was always closely involved, his involvement can become an addiction. Such involvement can stifle the team-building that needs to be done to free the executives from the founder's suffocating embrace.

RULES OF CONDUCT

The solution is to establish an executive committee (EC), composed of all the top managers of the company, with the COO—the newly appointed professional manager—as its chairman.

The key to the success of this body is: rules of conduct. The founder will be invited to all meetings if he wants to come. But if these rules are scrupulously followed, he will rarely come.

What are those rules?

The agenda of the meeting should be submitted to the founder at least 48 hours prior to the meeting. During those 48 hours, the founder can add subjects to be discussed, and also has the right to veto any subject he does *not* want to be discussed.

Next, the minutes of the meeting must be submitted to the founder not more than 48 hours after the meeting; then he has another 48 hours to veto any decision. If there is no veto of the agenda or of the decisions, they are accepted by default.

All decisions of the executive committee have to be agreed on unanimously by the EC. If there is a disagreement even by one person, the decision must go to the founder.

I have found from experience with companies all over the world that this process works. The rules allow the founder to feel that he remains in control, without micro-managing, and once this feeling is established, he rarely goes to meetings. And invariably, since the EC is required to decide unanimously or else cede the decision-making to the founder, the committee members will argue among themselves until they reach agreement, and will usually make very good decisions.

The benefits of the EC are obvious: The founder now has a complementary team that has to make decisions together. And if they decide together, they are likely to make even better decisions than the founder could have made alone. If they can't agree, the decision-making reverts to the founder; who is still in charge. He can also veto the decisions made by the EC.

> Somewhere between Go-Go and Adolescence, the company grows complicated for the founder to run by himself.

What happens in reality, however, is that after the first few meetings the founder realizes that the team is working very well together. The founder reads the agenda for the first meeting; maybe he reads the minutes from that meeting as well. But from then on, he doesn't pay much attention.

So what do you have? A company that no single individual can hijack. Everyone works together and makes decisions together.

Now, how much time does this take? That depends on (a) the founder's readiness to let go; and (b) the company's readiness to emancipate itself from the founder. It shouldn't take too long if all the steps are done properly; I would say months, not years.

SUMMING UP

The founder builds a company, and somewhere between the organizational stages of Go-Go and Adolescence, that company grows to the point where it becomes too big or too complicated for the founder to run by himself. He is overwhelmed and begins to want to separate himself from the company. Quickly bringing in someone to replace the founder usually does not work. It is too disruptive. The founder even feels as if someone has hijacked his company; someone has stolen his "baby." It is terribly painful.

Hiring a professional manager and giving him full authority to run the company cannot work because the company—its power structure, its tasks, its procedures—has been custom-built around the founder. The chances of a professional manager fitting into that custom-made structure are therefore slight.

Thus, the first thing the founder should do, *before* he brings in an outsider to run the company, is to restructure and re-systematize the organization so that anyone can run it. As I said earlier, the best way to do this is to hire a consultant and ask *him* to restructure the company. If during that process the consultant gains the trust and respect of both the founder and the organization, he can later be appointed COO; if not, after the company is structured and organized professionally, a professional manager can be brought in, minimizing the probability that he would have been rejected if he had been brought in to organize the company in the first place.

THE BERNIE EBBERS / KENNETH LAY PHENOMENON[1]

IN the wake of scandals involving top executives of some of the world's largest corporations, CEOs are becoming increasingly worried about their legal liabilities.

In May 2006, Enron founder Kenneth Lay was convicted on ten fraud and conspiracy charges[2] stemming from the company's bankruptcy. Former WorldCom CEO Bernie Ebbers was convicted on similar charges in March 2005,[3] and numerous other leading corporate executives have also been found guilty of unethical conduct.

Millions of dollars are being spent on lawyers and accountants—not to mention the time invested by executives—to bring corporations into compliance with the Sarbanes-Oxley Act of 2002, which requires public companies to disclose accurate and reliable accounting information.

What is going on? Have CEOs suddenly lost their ethical compass, or have government regulatory agencies simply become more eager and zealous?

I suggest that there are several reasons for the host of cases brought to trial and that there are some effective steps we can take to bring about changes in behavior.

LOST IN TRANSITION

Although many cases are clearly ethical in nature, involving executives who actually stole from the company, I submit that in a significant number

---

[1] Updated from Adizes Insights, April 2005.

[2] Lay died of a heart attack in July 2006, only months after his conviction. A federal judge revoked the conviction soon after his death, hewing to a legal precedent that reverses the conviction of a defendant who dies before he has the chance to appeal the verdict.

[3] Ebbers, convicted of defrauding WorldCom investors of $11 billion (the largest accounting fraud in history until Bernie Madoff's $50 billion Ponzi scheme came to light in 2008), began serving a 25-year sentence in federal prison in 2005.

of these cases, those who were brought to justice were not fully conscious of their breach of ethics; their behavior simply had not changed as it should have when their companies went public.

This does not mean that they are not liable. It means that their behavior had been allowed to exist, virtually condoned, by the organizational culture that is typical of companies at a particular stage of their lifecycles.

Just like human beings, organizations go through a lifecycle, with distinct stages and predictable transitional problems at each stage. I call these stages Courtship, Infancy, Go-Go, Adolescence, Prime, and the stages of aging: Aristocracy, Witch-hunt, Bureaucracy, and finally, Death.[4]

In Go-Go companies, when the company is not a start-up anymore and is growing rapidly, faster than its administrative infrastructure can keep up with, the founder usually believes that since she built the company, she must be entitled—*de facto* if not *de jure*—to control it. It is her "baby."

This perception does not necessarily change when the company becomes public and a board of directors is elected. You might compare it to the fight many mothers-in-law have with their daughters-in-law. The son, although now married, is subconsciously still considered his mother's "baby." She does not necessarily accept the daughter-in-law as her son's partner. She does not transform her behavior to adapt to the new circumstances.

THE ISSUE OF ACCOUNTABILITY

My experience is that the leaders of a Go-Go company, especially if they founded it, perceive public ownership as a debt obligation: They believe their job is to earn a fair return for investors, and if the stock appreciates significantly they believe they have satisfied that obligation. They do not perceive public stockholders as real owners and partners, nor do they regard the board that represents those owners as really entitled to manage the company. It is still the founders' baby, and what they do with their baby, they believe, is no one's business as long as the stock has appreciated.

At this stage of the lifecycle, the board is usually composed of fraternity brothers or golf club chums or family members—all of whom have made a fortune from the company going public. They do not feel the need, or

---

[4] For more information on lifecycles, see Ichak Adizes, *Managing Corporate Lifecycles* (Santa Barbara, CA: Adizes Institute Publications, 2004).

desire, to challenge the benefactor. I have seen many boards that had no real operational control over the usually charismatic CEO/founder of a company that went public. They were there mostly to clap their hands and shout "Bravo!" to the founder for the company's unbelievable rate of success. If the founder spends lavishly on herself, they turn a blind eye: They are making a fortune themselves on their stock options, and the stockholders are not doing badly either—so why complain?

To further aggravate the situation, many founders start behaving even more imperially when their companies go public than the way they behaved before. Going public means success. In capital letters. Financially and in terms of community status. The more successful the company is, the more imperial the founders tend to be and the sloppier their style of management becomes.

With their incredible success and the applause from everywhere, the founders believe they walk on water and have difficulty admitting that their feet, their knees, and eventually their necks are getting wet.

After going public, many of them are so full of themselves, their heads are in the clouds, and they refuse to come back to earth and face facts. The unexpected enormous success makes them feel omnipotent; thus they believe they can weather any problem. They have done it before; didn't they build this incredibly successful company in spite of all the obstacles and warnings?

I had an experience with the founder of a very successful company who was so successful that he lost touch with reality. He literally believed he could do no wrong. Whoever dared to disagree with him got fired or was ostracized.

Such founders take full personal credit for the company's success. It is as if it was their genius alone that was responsible for that success—and therefore, they, the geniuses, deserve to do as they like. These founders do not think twice about using company funds to buy a plane that they then use for their personal needs, or of spending a fortune to furnish an unnecessarily lavish office, stocked with lots of expensive art that might end up in their homes. They believe they are entitled to these fringe benefits, for the incredible success of their company, their intelligence, and their entrepreneurial leadership.

And it all feeds their egos, which are already ample or they would not have started the company in the first place.

Again, I am neither justifying nor supporting this behavior or belief system. I am just describing what I have noticed over forty years of working with founders and CEOs of Go-Go companies. I am hoping that explaining what I perceive to be their state of mind can help us find the right solution to this behavior.

After all, the behavior is not new. It began long before the company went public: The company paid many of the founder's personal expenses, and no one challenged it then. When the company goes public, the founder does not abruptly change her behavior; she continues doing what she has been doing for years. Nor does the company change its behavior and culture just because it's gone public. It allows the old behavior, and even condones it.

I suggest that the lavish way the founder treats herself at the expense of the public company is the result of a failure to make the necessary cultural and behavioral transitions from private to public ownership.

MANDATORY TRAINING FOR BOARDS AND CEOS

My solution would involve designing a training course that outlines the managerial, cultural, stylistic, legal, and ethical changes that become necessary when a company goes public—and making it mandatory for all officers of corporations that are about to make that transition. Beyond just financial listing on the stock market and the requirement for financial disclosure, there must also be a cultural transformation. All board members of the organization must be made aware of the managerial and behavioral pitfalls the company will face as it goes public. They should be certified as fully understanding the managerial and cultural changes that need to happen.

Going public is not just a task for lawyers. The transition to becoming a public company is not just a legal issue. It is also a behavioral issue, a managerial and ethical adjustment that needs to be explained and trained for.

To avoid fraternization of the board, where the board is composed of family and friends, I would even recommend that along with its approval to do the public listing, the SEC should appoint from the public at large a board member who is trained and certified to supervise the leadership and the ethical behavior of the company's leaders during the transition.

DANGERS OF AN INADEQUATE STRUCTURE

A second reason for the legal mess some executives are in is that the organization did not provide them with the right structural tools to make the right judgments.

Imagine a court in which only the prosecutor is allowed to present his case. The judge and jury will be at a tremendous disadvantage, and justice will not be served.

That is called single advocacy, and that is what is happening in many business organizations.

When the CFO controls the treasurer, the financial planning, and the controller of the company, the result is that the CEO has only one source of financial information: the CFO. The CEO gets only one interpretation of what is going on.

Auditing the company books is not sufficient as a quality-control mechanism, because by the time an audit finds something, it might be too late: The horse has already galloped out of the barn. Audits provide a post-mortem, while the CEO needs to decide upfront and in real time.

Accounting is not as simple as 2 + 2 = 4. True, it involves numbers, but accounting is the art and science of determining cost and value, and how to account for them can vary significantly. Anyone with even cursory knowledge of accounting knows that profit can vary depending on how inventory and depreciation are valued, not to mention more complicated items like cash equivalents, future contracts, etc.

The CEO should have the controller and the finance person report to him separately. The finance person will make recommendations designed to satisfy the investor community; these recommendations usually represent the liberal view. The accountants usually represent the conservative view and stick to a strict interpretation of the regulations. There will and should be professional conflict between the two, but now the CEO has a chance to really understand what is going on.

Without multiple and, preferably, conflicting interpretations of information, the CEO has no opportunity to make her own judgment as to what is right or wrong. Even if she wants to know what is going on, how many CEOs have the depth of training to really understand what is legal and what is not? It is not black and white at all; and if it ever was it is becoming increasingly gray.

Take Kenneth Lay: The whistle-blower told him that something inappropriate was going on in accounting. But could Lay make the call as to whether it was kosher or not? The world has become so complex and the laws so elaborate that it takes a professional to interpret what is right or wrong—and often even *they* do not agree. Did Lay have enough expertise and confidence to disagree with his highly paid CFO? Should he have?

DOUBLE ADVOCACY

In my consulting practice, I strongly recommend double advocacy.

Never, *ever*, should a CEO be in a situation where he has only one source of information on strategic issues and thus is subject to a single-sourced recommendation. This is the same principle typically applied to lawyers or surgeons: When in doubt, always get a second opinion. And since the need for strategic decisions is continual in companies that are subject to an accelerated rate of change, they should be structured to provide continual double advocacy.

With double advocacy, the CEO is warned by each side about the repercussions of the other's plan of action, and he is in a position to decide what to do, proactively, rather than wait until an audit tells him that what was done was the wrong thing to do—or go to jail and know for sure.

This principle should apply to the President of the United States, as well. For example, he has to rely on reports the CIA gives him. If they are the only channel through which he receives "intelligence" (information)—in other words, if he has no dissenting opinions to consider—then his space to maneuver and to use his own intelligence (judgment) is severely limited.

Realistically, in a single-advocacy system, the emperor has no clothes, to use a children's tale as an analogy. The CIA may have spent ten manpower years studying an issue, analyzing it with the expertise derived from one hundred combined years of education and experience. Then they present a position paper for the President's analysis. How much time and knowledge does the President have? Can he dedicate an equivalent number of years? Obviously not. He can act like he is in command, but whoever made the recommendation is the power behind the throne.

What he needs is an equally qualified organization, highly professional and knowledgeable, that takes the same case as an assignment and comes up with a separate, preferably dissenting, analysis. Now the President can listen to both positions and the supporting evidence or assumptions that led to each. He is given a choice of recommendations, and thus has a better chance of making the correct judgment.

True, the double-advocacy system and structure is less efficient because there is double effort spent on the case—but it is an effective system. The cost of a mistake made in a single-advocacy system far outweighs the cost of double advocacy.

In democratic societies, public policy decisions are made in a double-advocacy system: We have liberal and conservative views, whose proponents debate each other openly with freedom of expression and freedom of dissent.

Democratic systems are not efficient. They are effective. Dictatorships with single advocacy, on the other hand, are efficient, but we all know the disasters they bring to their societies.

AVOIDING BUREAUCRATIZATION

One more point: The Sarbanes-Oxley Act, as a solution to the problem of lack of accountability, is scaring the daylights out of boards of directors. Out of fear, they are starting to micro-manage. But board members are only part-timers, and often they do not know the business in detail. So authority is moving further upstream, away from where the action is, and that can cause even more bureaucratization than is usually mandated by size and the increasing complexity of operations. And it can lead to more bad decisions.

As change accelerates, we understand less and less what is going on. In a situation of uncertainty, an institutionalized rather than happenstance double advocacy is necessary to interpret data, so that the decision-maker will not be dependent in her judgment upon a single interpretation of that data. The more change and uncertainty there is, the more important the rule of double advocacy becomes.

Furthermore, the more change, the more training we need, and that includes training our boards of directors and CEOs.

STRATEGY FOR THE NEW MILLENNIUM[1]

ISSUES of strategy and planning depend not only on the latest forecast or trend in the marketplace, but also on where a company is on its lifecycle.

Every organization grows, develops, and, sometimes, dies on its own intrinsic and organic lifecycle, from its founding vision and Infancy through the challenges of a young company in Go-Go and Adolescence, to Prime, and beyond that to the aging stages.[2]

As organizations change on the lifecycle, they suffer the dangers of internal disintegration. What will characterize the 21st century is that the speed of change will accelerate even more. Organizations that change the fastest can also disintegrate the fastest.

Emerging strategies must focus as much on the internal processes as on the external opportunities. The new strategy should cause change without disintegrating the company. "Lead change while keeping us united" could be its slogan.

The strategy for keeping a company united differs depending on the stage of the lifecycle. Strategy should be derived from an analysis of two factors: the need for internal integration of the different sub-systems of the organization; and the need for external integration with the changing market. External integration connotes the energy a company requires to identify its clients and satisfy their needs. Internal integration is what it takes to coordinate efforts to meet this goal.

For example: A young company must plan for rapid sales growth, reached by external integration with its market. But then, having achieved booming sales, it must direct its attention to building structure, controlling

---

[1] Originally published in *Executive Excellence* (now *Leadership Excellence*) magazine, December 1998; reprinted with permission.

[2] Ichak Adizes, *Managing Corporate Lifecycles* (Santa Barbara, CA: Adizes Institute Publications, 2004).

costs, and insuring profits, or the orders will overwhelm the systems. That is done by internal integration. The strategic goal of a company should be to reach and maintain a state of Prime, a condition where flexibility (needed for external integration) and control (needed for efficient implementation of strategy and reached through internal integration efforts) are in balance. Having a strategy that does not fit the organization's stage on the lifecycle is like giving a child medicine that's appropriate only for adults.

Strategies for Lifecycle Positions

Courtship

The company begins as a vision in its founder's eye. The strategy in this stage of the lifecycle calls for vision tempered by reality. There are questions to be answered: What exactly is my company going to do? What is the value-add of the product or service, and how valuable is it really? Who is the customer? And finally: Am I willing to make the commitment? The strategy must incorporate commitment expressed in sacrifices that the founder is willing to make that reflect future risks and realities.

Infancy

In Infancy, the stage where the commitment is made and the risks of opening a company are taken, a company's strategy should be to produce a stellar product or service that satisfies its clients and competes effectively. Sales are vital, but cash flow should top every list of concerns. The goal of Infancy is survival.

Go-Go

This is a rapid growth stage, when founders, having achieved success, often believe they can do no wrong. But many companies run aground because the founder doesn't recognize the need for discipline and structure. Having created products or services that actually sell, the company now should be seeking increasing market share and long-term prospects, rather than the short-term deals once needed to survive. The strategy is to focus on core capabilities, to decide what not to do, to set priorities, to make hard decisions about what to put on the back burner. But at the same time as it seeks market share (even at the expense of profits), the Go-Go company has to keep a tight grip on costs. Discipline and control of growth are needed, and the implementation of a complementary team in decision-making is called for to provide the founder with reality, analysis, and controls. Without such a complementary team, the company runs into the danger of "founder's trap," with the result that when the founder dies, the company dies, too.

Adolescence

In Adolescence, companies often suffer from a temporary loss of vision due to extensive internal fighting among its top managers, generated by the differences of styles that a complementary team will have. The founder's strategy should be to provide forces of integration: vision and values. It is a period of convergence, a time to prune the tree so its energies grow upward. It must dispose of ventures that are not within the company's core competence. Adolescence calls for redefining the business the company should be in. Re-engineering is needed.

Prime

> *Transformation is difficult, because normally people want a new strategy without yielding the old one. Everyone wants "more" rather than "instead."*

Prime is a condition and not a destination. To avoid sliding into aging, the organization needs to stimulate the entrepreneurial spirit. Strategically, a Prime company should be spinning off new businesses or new markets and looking for opportunities to diversify, whether by internal growth, acquisition, or merger. Diversification is more than just adding more revenues and people.

Earlier, everyone's focus was on sales. In Prime, marketing dominates. The company's market plans have to be in line with the market's demands, or opportunities will be missed. In Prime, a constant equilibrium between flexibility and control must be maintained; otherwise, control will overwhelm flexibility and the company will slide into the aging stages.

THE AGING STAGES

A company in Prime can slip fairly easily through the aging stages of Aristocracy, Witch-hunt, Bureaucracy, and finally, Death.[3] (The last stage will be covered at another time.)

What characterizes aging? A company beyond Prime has lost focus and drive. It's time to redefine the business, spin off what doesn't fit, and crank up the company's rusty skills and neglected strengths. Over-control, typified by bureaucratization of the organization, destroys the energies the company needs to recapture the entrepreneurship of its early days.

An aging company needs to diversify, but it is wasting its time unless cultural diversification accompanies business diversification. Transformation is difficult, because normally people want a new strategy without yielding the old one. Everyone wants "more" rather than "instead."

How do you determine your company's strategy in this new millennium? Look at your company's position on the lifecycle and what its needs are for each stage. To choose a strategy that ignores the organization's location on its lifecycle can mean disaster.

---

[3] For more information on the aging stages, see the chapter on "Prime and the Preventable Stages of Aging," starting on page 88.

PART 3

TEAM BUILDING
(MUTUAL TRUST
AND RESPECT)

THE SECRET OF SUCCESS[1]

I have discovered the secret of success of any system. It allows me to predict whether a marriage, a country, or a manager is going to succeed.

I do not care whether you define success as becoming a billionaire or being able to lie on the beach and do nothing. The success of any system—whether it is micro- or macro-, whether it is a single human being, a family, an organization, or a society—can be predicted by one, and only one, factor: the ratio between external integration and internal *dis*integration.

External integration is defined as the amount of resources an organization invests in identifying and satisfying clients' needs. Internal disintegration is how much managerial energy must be wasted in miscommunication, internal fighting, internal politics, and mistrust, while attempting to make something happen within the organization.

External integration is a function of matching opportunities and capabilities. In the business world, another name for external integration is marketing—and if you take all the books on marketing and summarize them, and then you summarize the summary, and so on, you will get to the essence: how to match changing opportunities in the marketplace to your organization's changing capabilities. In other words, how the organization can become integrated with the market. In personal life, it is called career planning; on a macro level it is the industrial policy of a country.

Internal disintegration is a function of whether or not mutual trust and respect (MT&R) exist in the organizational culture. If there is little or no MT&R, the energy spent on internal disintegration will be very high. Another name for it is "internal politics."

How does the formula below predict success? Because we know from physics that every system, at any point in time, has a fixed amount of energy. What I discovered is that in an organization, this fixed energy is allo-

[1] Compiled from various Insights and other essays, 1993–2009.

cated in a predictable way. First it goes to deal with internal disintegration; only the surplus goes to external integration.

This applies to the individual as well. Example: Your friend is very sick. You go to visit him in the hospital. But the hospital allows only five minutes for a visit. Why? Because the patient has no energy. Where is his energy? The energy is being used to heal the sick organism.

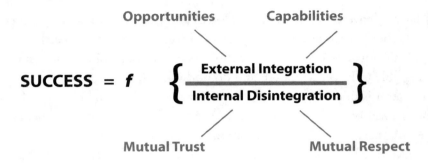

$$\text{SUCCESS} = f \left\{ \frac{\text{External Integration}}{\text{Internal Disintegration}} \right\}$$

Opportunities   Capabilities

Mutual Trust   Mutual Respect

In the same way, if a person suffers from low self-esteem, which is a combination of low self-respect and low self-trust, he will be riddled with inner conflicts. Such people may be good-looking, smart, and rich, yet they will be unlikely to have a successful relationship or career. Most of their psychological energy will be spent "between their ears," dealing with personal problems that stem from their low self-respect and self-trust.

Let's look at the next level. Let's assume we have people who are "centered" and do have self-respect and self-trust. They personally have energy to deal with the outside world—but they have a disastrous family situation, devoid of trust and respect. Let's say they have problems with their parents or spouse or children.

Where is their energy spent now? Research shows that executives who go through a divorce are virtually useless to the corporation for about three years. They can't succeed during that time, not because they are objectively bad, but because their energy is necessarily being diverted somewhere else.

One reason—but it might be a major one—for the relatively slow rise in productivity in the United States is the breakdown of the American family. Certainly, low American productivity can't be blamed on a lack of technology or financial resources.

AT THE ORGANIZATIONAL LEVEL

At the next level is the organization. You have people who know who they are and who they are not, and who have a supportive, respectful, and trusting family. All their energy is available to deal with their careers—*but* the organization, as a whole, lacks MT&R. Co-workers walk with their backs against the wall for fear of being stabbed. Marketing is fighting sales; production is fighting engineering; accounting is fighting everyone. When a client arrives, what is he told? "Come back tomorrow. I am exhausted today."

This is a critical stage for an organization, during which miscommunication and/or misunderstanding of co-workers' different styles, needs, and expectations come into play. What is needed is a system of MT&R within the organization.

"Trust and respect" are words that have been thrown around a lot by politicians and the media in these times of acute political and social change. But they are more than just political phrases, slogans, or media sound bites. They have a hard functional edge; and they are a real part of the dialogue and concrete interactions that any organization—business or government— must learn to use if it is to effectively and efficiently control conflict and change. Good managers—successful managers—command MT&R.

The key to managerial success is building a complementary team. Successful companies are the product of a complementary team, whose members, by definition, are constantly disagreeing with each other. How this internal marketing—the resolution of conflict—is handled depends on the special character of each organization. Creating a culture in which internal conflicts can be handled *constructively* minimizes internal disintegration, thus allowing the business to focus its energies on the franchise of customers and clients.

WHAT MAKES A SUCCESSFUL ECONOMY?

But now, let's assume we have an organization with common vision and values, and the right structure, process, and people. It has developed and nurtured MT&R, but it operates in a society riddled with corruption and hatred among religions, nationalities, and races. Now what? Can it compete well internationally? Where is the energy of the country going? How much energy can be left if the union is fighting management, the military is fighting the government, and the government is fighting the people? A country can be rich in gold and mines and land, all the natural resources, but it cannot succeed if its relationships are bankrupt.

Compare the successful economies of Japan and Switzerland, nations with few physical resources, to some of the developing nations rich in oil, gas, diamonds, and other resources. These developing nations can't use their resources constructively, because of their traditions of tribalism and internal conflicts. Colonial powers exploited them, and native governments often behave the same way after independence.

During the Imperialist period, the occupying powers brought to their colonies the missing elements of administrative order and entrepreneurship. But in order to dominate, these colonial powers, particularly England, would often turn one religious or ethnic group against another, fostering disintegration. The English excelled at this Roman strategy of "divide and conquer." Later, when the colonists left, as in the case of India, they took with them the entrepreneurial function, leaving behind a huge administrative structure and a broken sense of integration—all of which lowered productivity. This is the 20th-century inheritance of many Third World countries.

THE EFFECT OF A SOLID FOUNDATION

On the other hand, look at Switzerland and Japan. Switzerland overcame the deep regional, language, religious, and ethnic barriers that marked its early history to become a smooth, efficiently run country. Japan has been an even more striking example of the consequences of integrated relationships. Although in recent years there have been cracks in the system, "Japan, Inc." has built its achievements on the complementarity of its culture and society—or "teaming," as it is often called. There are very few Lone Rangers there. Both decision-making and implementation rest on the solid foundation of an integrated society and business culture.

Europe today has the potential to be a giant. It is rich with cultural diversity, a market economy, and open borders. It can become a serious contender for world leadership—*if* it can overcome its history of disrespect and mistrust. By building and using MT&R as a tool for integration, it can transform its fifty-year failure to work together into unprecedented success. If it does, and if it is able to internally integrate itself, both the United States and Japan will have a serious competitor in the 21st century.

THE COMMON DENOMINATOR

Looking at the personal, social, and national spheres, we can see one basic and common denominator: Success comes from within.

Too many companies worry exclusively about strategic planning and about how to beat their competitors. But success comes from the inside. If we are strong inside, we can deal with any outside problem by handling it as an opportunity. If we are weak inside, then every outside opportunity will be perceived as a problem.

Japan's success is not the *cause* of America's problem; it is the *manifestation*. The problem with America is America, not Japan. The American system has less MT&R than the Japanese.

As the United States attempts to meet the conflicts and changes of the 21st century, these are critical factors. We are not going to stop change. Conflict will never go away—because conflict is what change creates. What we have to learn is how to manage change in a constructive way. That means building a socially effective nation, by developing and supporting MT&R— learning how to "be" and directing our internal energies outward.

STEPS TO SUCCESS

Being aware of your own vulnerability, trusting that you can find a solution, and respecting the complementarity of the team are the secrets of success.

And remember that success is not the destination but condition of the journey.

The way to improve a person's or a company's or a country's performance is not by changing strategy first, but by changing the internal environment first. Once you change the internal environment, the right strategy and direction will emerge more easily. Without an organizational culture of MT&R, even the best strategy is unlikely to be implemented successfully.

How to Convert a
Committee into a Team[1]

I traveled to Canada some time ago to give a lecture to a large Canadian company. The night before the lecture, the chief executive picked me up at the airport and invited me to the hotel hospitality suite. The executives who would be attending the meeting the next day were all there playing poker, three tables, four to a table. I watched the game. The energy was high. They were joking and laughing, even though hundreds of dollars were changing hands. After midnight the adrenaline was still flowing. "Great game," they all said. "Let's get together and do it again soon."

I got to thinking. If the same executives were seated around a committee table trying to come to a decision on how to allocate the company budgets, they would probably be exhausted and drained of energy after only a couple of hours. It would be a chore, not a pleasure. Odds are, no one would say, "Let's get together and do it again soon."

What's the difference between a poker game and getting something done at a committee meeting? Why do so many people hate management by committee?

The difference is in the rules of conduct.

Societal Rule Structures

The Dutch historian Johann Huizinga saw history as a game of rules. When you break the rules, society falls apart. A revolution happens.

Without rules, a meeting tends toward anarchy. People keep interrupting each other. People get angry, disrupt the flow of the meeting, and conclusions are not well understood. Little or nothing gets accomplished.

In meetings, as in good marriages, we need both unity and differences.

---

[1] Originally published in *Successful Methods* magazine, February 1994; reprinted with permission.

The danger is that if we don't follow the rules, we achieve only organized chaos or a false unity. What distinguishes good team management is the presence of mutual trust and respect (MT&R), based on rules of conduct. When you break the rules, you are violating MT&R.

The joker in the deck is that not everyone communicates in the same way and with the same verbal and visual cues. Good teams are made up of (P)roducers, who must produce results; (A)dministrators, who organize so that things get done right, in the right sequence, with the right timing and intensity; (E)ntrepreneurs, who are risk takers and who focus proactively on changes in the external market; and (I)ntegrators, who are necessary to build a team effort. To make a good decision, all four (PAEI) types must participate.

People with certain styles tend to gravitate toward certain organizational rules. This makes for a real communications bramble patch in trying to get direction and sense out of a meeting.

For example, the producing people and the entrepreneurial types in an organization make decisions quickly and are ready to jump into actions or ideas. To reach either of them in an argument, you have to get to the point.

Administrators, on the other hand, are more interested in the *how* than the *what*. They move slowly and need time to digest the material.

An entrepreneurial-type manager may argue a point to an administrator and notice that the administrator is not arguing back. The entrepreneur will probably take that to mean agreement. In fact, it probably doesn't mean that at all.

> What's the difference between a poker game and getting something done at a committee meeting? Rules of conduct.

Communicating with highly entrepreneurial types requires thinking like an (E) type. You can't simply provide the solution and explain how to do it. The entrepreneur would probably say, "Wrong problem, wrong solution." (E)s tend to resist any idea unless it is their own. So you have to take their creativity into account and use it. Ask them, "What do you think?" "What do you suggest?" "How would it fly better?"

All hell breaks loose when two entrepreneurs bring clashing visions to a meeting. As Tom Monaghan of Domino's Pizza recounts in his autobiography, *Pizza Tiger*,[2] in its early years his company experienced a crisis

---

[2] New York: Random House, 1986.

caused by the lack of teamwork among its managers. Part of the problem, he admitted, was that he and his operations man, Dick Mueller, were both creative (E)s. "When we disagreed on how to do things," he wrote, "we were like two rams on a frosty morning."

CHANGING MEETING BEHAVIOR

You know you are in trouble at a meeting when what I call "back-up behavior" begins to appear around the table: When people are tired or upset, they often revert to their default style of communicating, ignoring the needs of those to whom they're speaking. Producers, feeling they are losing control, become little dictators: "Enough! I've have it. Here's what we're going to do, and I do not want to hear any more discussion ..." Administrators usually freeze and become very, very quiet ... and obstinate. Integrators, those who work across departments, just sway with the wind. "Oh, is that what you want to do? Fine. No-o-o problem." Entrepreneurs are the most dangerous in meetings: If they feel they are losing control, they attack.

But people *can* change their meeting behavior. If the meeting structure of an organization is changed, and people learn the rules that nourish MT&R, then eventually they start acting with MT&R. And business gets done.

Here are my rules for changing the structure of committee meetings and converting a chore into effective teamwork:

Rule 1: Start the meeting on time. You can often tell the entire organizational structure from the order in which people show up for a meeting: The more important they are, the later they come. That sets the wrong tone for mutual respect. Setting a penalty for every minute of tardiness reinforces the rule of respect.

Rule 2: Take breaks. Take a ten-minute break every eighty minutes. Ring a bell at the beginning and end of the break even if you have to stop a speaker in mid-sentence. Respect for the meeting's form will eventually increase respect for its content.

Rule 3: Learn to listen. One of the problems at meetings is that we are so busy rehearsing what we are going to say that we don't listen to what *other* people are saying. This is particularly a problem with

(E) types, who always have a pocketful of ideas to drop on the table. They are so busy listening to what they are thinking that they do not hear what others are saying in the meantime.

Rule 4: Learn not to compete for "airtime." When there is no rule for who should speak next, either the most powerful person dominates, or else everyone rushes to make a point before anyone else does. Here is what I call "the rule of right": When a speaker finishes, she looks to the right. The next person to talk will be the first person to her right who signals with a raised hand. Entrepreneurial managers always have to say something; administrators take their time to mull things over. These contrary styles are often misunderstood. Establishing a speaking order takes the pressure off everyone, and it reinforces respect for all ideas and response styles.

Rule 5: The rule of language. Words can set off wars: "I disagree!" "You're wrong!" "That's ridiculous!" Even phrases like "What do you mean by that?" have an inherently confrontational judgment behind them. Substitute phrasing such as: "I have a different opinion," or, "Here's another alternative."

> In meetings, as in good marriages, we need both unity and differences.

Rule 6: First names only. It's hard to address someone by her first name with aggression or anger, or even formality. First-name communication tends to keep the climate friendly.

Rule 7: Hard rules and soft rules. Certain meetings require control and discipline, whereas others need a maximum flow of discussion. If less control is necessary, impose soft rules (rules 5 and 6 only) to set the tone for your meeting.

Rule 8: Pay the penalty! Set a small monetary fine for speaking out of turn or breaking any other rules. Will it work? Yes. Jim Hennessy of Advanta Mortgage noted that fines are "fast and furious at first"—some (E)-types will gladly pay money to keep talking—but they begin to decline as the rules sink in. In the meantime, Hennessy reported, the penalties add up to a nice annual contribution to the local children's hospital.

Rule 9: The rule of democratship. Rules 1 through 8 help foster a spirit of democracy at meetings—all parties are heard, and the whole group is involved in decision-making. But once the decision is made, no dissension is allowed, just as in a dictatorship.

MUTUAL TRUST AND RESPECT

Communicating with business teams—or in any other business environment—requires that managers control and harness the energies of the team's complementary members. Some companies build a set of rules into their organizational policies. Others will call on the rules when they get into particularly tight meeting situations. The point of these rules is not to suppress conflicting opinions, but to discipline them.

WHY MUTUAL TRUST AND RESPECT?[1]

I have been teaching, preaching, prescribing, and inducing mutual trust and respect (MT&R) in organizations for forty years now, and studying what causes it to grow or diminish. At the last Adizes Convention, in Las Vegas in 2009, I tried to further articulate: Why do companies succeed when there is MT&R, and why, when there is no MT&R, do organizations eventually crumble? Why is the same true for families and for societies?

What is it that MT&R provides, does, contributes?

Here is my latest insight on the subject: It all has to do with energy.

Every system has energy. Where does it come from? From the people who comprise the organization. That is why managers seek people for their organizations who are energetic, passionate, and dedicated.

Every organization is a system that needs energy to operate.

When the energy does not flow freely—when it gets stuck somewhere, somehow—there is less energy available for the system to operate with. When there is no mutual trust and respect, it is as if there are barriers in the energy flow; the organization is less energy-sufficient, which renders it competitively disadvantaged.

MT&R makes the system transparent. When there is mutual trust, energy flows. The same with mutual respect.

Let us analyze this last point in more depth, starting with mutual trust.

Mutual trust exists when the parties share common interests—at least in the long run, if not at present. They perceive that their mutual interests will be fulfilled over time, and they have faith that if one party gives now, that giving will be reciprocated eventually.

The opposite of trust is a suspicion that the other party will take advantage of your good will and not reciprocate. Obviously, when you feel that

---
[1] Adizes Insights, September 2009.

kind of suspicion, you filter what the other party is trying to tell you. The energy transmitted in the communication will be blocked.

How about mutual respect? In Hebrew, there are two meanings for the word "respect": "to honor" and "to value." To honor is ritualistic. It is (A)-based. To value is (P)-based: I value those who contribute to my interests, those who add value.

When I talk about respect, I mean "to value." Thus, to respect means to give the other party a chance to express their questions, doubts, and disagreements, because you have faith that they will add value to you, faith that their disagreement stems from understanding something you have either not paid attention to or have ignored.

With such faith, it is easy to see how energy will flow. Without such *a priori* belief—i.e., if you believe that the other party is just wasting your time, and there is no chance their disagreement will teach you anything—energy will not flow. It will be deflected.

THE INEVITABILITY OF PAIN

To trust and respect someone who argues with you is painful. It takes energy. It can be exhausting. So why does MT&R give energy? Just the opposite would seem to be true, no?

> When there is mutual trust, energy flows. The same with mutual respect.

Debate takes energy from those who have no trust and/or respect for each other. By contrast, those who have MT&R are energized by debate.

Now note, you cannot start out with distrust and disrespect and expect anything good to happen. It does not work that way; you cannot say, "First show me that I can trust and learn from you, and if I am convinced that you are trustworthy and adding value with your disagreements, *then* I will trust and respect you."

Why not?

Disrespectful and distrusting debates exhaust those involved. Because it is painful, it decreases rather than increases MT&R.

But the other way around does work. *Start* by assuming that other people are trustworthy and can add value with their disagreements. Listen! Give them a chance to interact. Test them. If they are not adding value, *then* stop the interaction with them. (Some people have something to say; others have to say something. Avoid the second group.)

But always *start* with mutual trust and respect.

It is like believing in God. If you start by not believing and require proof of God's existence to become a believer, you will remain a skeptic forever. "For believers there are no questions. For heretics there are no answers," says the Jewish Talmud.

But if you start with the belief that God exists, you will find endless proofs of God's existence. In every tree. In the sunrise and moonlight. In the smile of a baby. It is everywhere. Even in prison ...

How you start is crucial. It affects how you will continue.

The more mutual trust and respect there is, the more energy is available to be managed.

THE BUSINESS OF
MUTUAL TRUST AND RESPECT[1]

LET us discuss how to implement mutual trust and respect (MT&R) at different levels of analysis.

We already know how to apply it to organizations. At Adizes, we have taught it and practiced it now for forty years worldwide. What have we learned from our experience applying MT&R in organizations that can also be applied on a personal, family, social, and international level—and eventually to our "mother ship," Earth? (We should be looking at space, too: We are already polluting space. But let's stop today with Earth; that is enough of a challenge.)

Let's be careful, though. What applies to one level of analysis does not necessarily apply to a higher or lower level of analysis.[2]

ON THE PERSONAL LEVEL

What does MT&R mean on a personal level? The rule appears to be: If the choice you make increases your self-respect, do it; if it decreases your self-respect, don't do it. If it increases your self-trust, do it; if it decreases your self-trust, don't do it.

How should we define self-respect?

First, let us discuss the difference between respect and *mutual* respect.

According to Immanuel Kant, respect means that you recognize the undeniable right (i.e., sovereignty) of the other person to think differently. We are not promoting fusion, sameness. We are seeking integration of differences. I do not want to be you and you are not expected to be me;

---

[1] Adizes Insights, September 2007. Originally given as part of a Founders' Session speech at the 29th Annual Adizes Convention, Palic, Serbia, July 2007.

[2] I thank Principal Associate Carlos Valdesuso for making this point to me.

nevertheless, we should be able to work together—not despite, but because of our differences.

How? When there is mutual respect, our differences are constructive, because we differ in an environment in which we can learn from each other's differences. That's why the Adizes symbol is a hand: Every finger is different but together they work like a hand. We do not have a hand if all the fingers are the same, or if they are different but cannot work together.

Integration, not fusion; harmony, not cacophony. Harmony isn't everyone singing the same note, but different voices singing in complementary tones.

In organizations, to promote mutual respect we create an environment in which it is safe to think differently and express one's differences of opinion without fear.

What does self-respect mean now that we understand *mutual* respect? How do we create a safe environment in personal life, and what does "safe" mean? Safe from whom?

It appears to me that we must recognize, legitimize, accept, and even rejoice that we have different, opposing thoughts even within ourselves: that we have a "Parliament" between our ears. We have lots of political parties there. The Liberal party tells us, "Do it," while the Conservative party warns us, "Don't you dare do it." In making decisions, there is a lot of in-fighting—self-doubt and disagreement—in our own heads.

To me, self-respect means to respect my own internal differences of opinion, which means to recognize that all my thoughts are legitimate, even when they contradict each other.

I know some people who get very upset because they can't get a simple, clear answer from their own brains—and the clarity they expect from their brains they expect from others' brains, too. Calm down. Listen to the voices of dissension inside your head, and understand that it is OK to be in doubt, to have noise in your head. Listen to the noise, calmly, without judging which arguments are right or wrong. Listen to the discussion and make the different "parties" talk to each other—without denial, without anger, without rejection—and listen to them *all*.

I disagree with Descartes, who said: "I think; therefore I am." I am above my thoughts. If you doubt it, try meditation. Watch your thoughts. Be above them. Some thoughts are dangerous to your health and well-being. So watch your thoughts and don't get ruled by or attached to them.

You need to accept yourself—which means that you should accept all of your thoughts as they occur, even if they are inconsistent with each other. You should even acknowledge that some sinful ideas pop into your head from time to time. You're human. Welcome to the club.

Self-respect means that you appreciate—not just tolerate—your own voices of dissension, that you understand that it's more than OK to be in doubt. You recognize that self-doubts and conflicts are good, because if we listen to the conflicting opinions, we learn a lot. It is beneficial and constructive to have such conflict.

Self-respect is necessary for mutual respect, because if you cannot cope with your own differences of opinion, how are you going to accept and tolerate someone else's differences of opinion? If you can accept your own differences of opinion, it is much easier to learn from other people who disagree with you.

WHY DISAGREEMENT IS GOOD

Here is an analogy that I hope will help you understand why you need people to disagree with you:

What happens if you try to solve a problem that is beyond your computer's capability to process? You'll find that you have to go to a bigger computer. But let's assume there is no bigger computer. The solution is to develop a computer network: many computers that talk to each other. Jointly, they have as much if not more processing power than a large computer. But this power can be achieved only if the computers can talk to each other; and that might be difficult to achieve because different computers might have different operating systems.

Your brain is like a computer. When you are in doubt and cannot solve a problem, what does that tell you? That you have limited processing capability, using your own limited brainpower, to process this problem. When that happens to me, what do I do? I start putting together a network of "computers." I go to Paula, to Carlos, and to Sunil, and I ask them for advice. I look for people whom I respect who have a different style, like a different operating system.

And what happens? First of all, I have added processing capacity: More brainpower is involved in solving the problem, but the processing capability is different because the people's styles are different.

Why do I need different styles?

Assume Carlos is a better administrator[3] than I am. By asking for his help, I free my brain from (A) processing, giving me extra brainpower to practice entrepreneurship, which is my strength. The (PAEI) complementary styles network is more powerful in processing a complex problem than any individual person can be, because there is no person who can process complex (PAEI) problems all by himself and be right on every problem, every time, forever.[4]

But what happens now that there is a network of different styles of management working together? Instead of disagreeing with myself, I now disagree with you and any others who think differently from me. When you express a different viewpoint from mine, you are representing that part of my brain that was disagreeing with me earlier. We already know how upset I was when my own brain was conflicted between my (E) and my (A). Now, when you represent the (A), the more you say things that the (A) part of my brain agrees with, the more upset with you I become. It looks as if I am fighting with you, but in reality I am fighting with myself.

At Adizes, we've solved this problem. The Adizes method offers the language and tools to enable different managerial styles to communicate with and complement each other—so that together they can manage complex problems caused by change better than any individual can.

I am suggesting that we need to do the same, not just with others, but within ourselves. We need to create a safe, constructive learning environment within ourselves.

How? Understand and acknowledge that it is normal and acceptable to have differences of opinion—even within yourself. Don't waste energy being upset about it. Legitimize dissension. Disagreement is an opportunity to learn. Listen to your own voices of dissension. Calmly. Respectfully. Without being too hard on yourself. And if you cannot solve a problem by

---

[3] For more information on the (PAEI) elements and styles of management, see the chapter "(PAEI): The Organizational DNA Code for Managing Change" in Part 1 of this book, "The Roles of Managers/Leaders," starting on page 37.

[4] For further details, see Ichak Adizes, *The Ideal Executive: Why You Cannot Be One and What to Do About It* (Santa Barbara, CA: Adizes Institute Publications, 2004).

yourself, find someone who disagrees with you (without being disagreeable), someone from whose differences of opinion you can learn.

The Necessity of Trust

Now let us proceed to the subject of trust.

We know from the Adizes methodology that trust is based on faith that there is, or will be, a common interest. Why faith? The reality is that a true common interest, a win-win situation, is rare. In fact, we are constantly involved in a conflict of interests—a win-lose situation. Every minute of the day we are in conflict about our choices; for example: "I want to eat this cake, but I know it is not good for me." Or let's say I take you to dinner, and I pay for it. I am losing and you are gaining, since you don't pay. So where is the common interest?

To feel that there is a common interest, there must be faith that my own interests will be represented eventually, even though they are not being addressed right now. In other words, I believe that next time, you will invite me to dinner. In the long run, our interests will balance out.

When you have faith, you believe that there is give and take—or, better said, give and receive. In a trusting relationship, I will wash the dishes this time. I will give up my time, but it's no big deal because I have faith: I trust that next time, you will give up your time to wash the dishes.

> Harmony isn't everyone singing the same note, but different voices singing in complementary tones.

What about self-trust; what does self-trust mean? Self-trust is what should guide you in conflicts about, for example, that cake you wanted to eat, or maybe did eat, even though it was not good for you.

Self-trust is not about making the right decision every time. It is about learning from your mistakes and being willing to try again. Success is not measured by how infrequently you fall down, but by how fast you get up. Or, as Mary Kay eloquently put it when asked the secret of her success: "Do you want to see the scars on my knees?"

When you fall, when you make a mistake—and we all do—have faith that you can get up again. Do not lose your spirit. Trust yourself; know that a failure is not forever; try to see what you can learn from it, and trust that next time you will do better.

Years ago I was invited by Alan Bond, of Australia, to watch the America's

Cup, which he won that year. (He told me that he used my methodologies in order to win it.) During dinner, the phone rang and he got up to take the call. When he came back, his face was a bit drawn. "What happened?" I asked him.

"I just lost $20 million," he said.

"How does it feel to lose $20 million?" I wondered.

"Well, I look at it this way, Ichak," he said. "Very few people can take a course in life where the tuition is $20 million, and I am one of those fortunate few. Now the question is: Did I pass the exam or not? Did I learn something worth $20 million? If not, then I failed this life course; I paid $20 million in tuition and did not learn the $20 million lesson."

Whenever something bad happens to you, do not ask, "Why did this happen to me?" Ask instead, "*What for* did it happen to me?"—meaning, "What is there for me to learn? What lesson was I supposed to learn from the experience?" When we ask, "Why did it happen?" we frequently look for the cause but not for the lesson.

For example: You got fired from a job. The "why" answer would be, "Because they do not like me," or "Because my boss prefers someone else." In other words, all kinds of excuses.

To answer the "what for" question, you will have to ask yourself: "What should I learn from this experience? What did God want me to know?"[5]

MANAGEMENT BY PRIDE

There are all kinds of management theories: management by results, management by process, management by values. I would like to propose a new one: management by pride.

The word "pride" has very clear significance for me. Are you proud of what you do? If you are not proud of what you do, you are doing the wrong thing. That doesn't mean you aren't producing results. But have you done the best you could? Are you proud of your work? Are you proud of your actions?

Sometimes we notice a person who is comfortable in his own skin. He is not in conflict with himself. Does this come from faith, self-respect, self-trust? I don't know what it is, but I do know that if someone is proud of his actions, that means he is not fighting with himself. He accepts his own differences of

---

[5] I thank Principal Associate Carlos Valdesuso for making this point to me.

opinion and has faith in his ability to learn from whatever happens. He can take the heat. He is proud of who he is or what he does or did.

As a formula, I suggest this:

$$\text{self-trust} + \text{self-respect} = \text{pride}$$

Do not lose pride because you are internally in conflict and cannot decide and need someone else's opinion, or because you failed at something. Ask yourself each time: What can I learn from this experience?

Is being proud all you need to be successful? No. The Nazis were very proud people. In order to know whether you are on the right road, you must first be conscious of what you are doing. Then, ask your conscience: Does what you are proud of promote mutual trust and respect? Are your deeds nurturing constructive diversity, or subverting it? If we follow this kind of reasoning, we see that the Nazis' pride was destructive, regardless of how proud they were of themselves.

On the Family Level

Now, let's analyze what to do at the family level. Is what we do as parents or partners promoting the existence and strength of the family or destroying it? Are we raising our children to follow God or the Devil? To follow construction or destruction? To learn trust and respect or to learn *lack* of trust and *lack* of respect? Do we promote love or hate? Are we teaching our children to know what pride is all about and what to be proud of?

It appears to me that some of the principles we teach organizations in order to help them achieve mutual trust and respect can also apply to families. It makes sense to schedule periodic family meetings to discuss the family mission; to discuss who does what, and what is not getting done and why; to discuss whether we as individuals are being equitably rewarded in this family; to discuss how we handle our disagreements—do we disagree by being disagreeable—etc.

On the Global Level

Let us now move to the next level of application: the world we live in. Today, while we progress technologically and our standard of living gets higher, our quality of life is getting lower. We are witnessing global warming and pollution—not only water and air pollution, but social pollution. (To me, homelessness is a manifestation of social disintegration, of social pollution.)

Unless we choose the constructive direction, we are going to destroy the place we live in. So, what does it mean to trust and respect the environment? What does it mean to respect trees; what does it mean to respect the earth; what does it mean to respect the air? I don't know. We know that respect means "acknowledging the sovereignty to be different"—but how does that apply to the environment?

I am now working with the government of Montenegro, a new country. They are excited and impatient about development: They want highways, hotels, high-rises. But I see how the highways are leaving scars on the mountains, and how the high-rises on the mountaintops look out of place and detract from the beauty of the scenery.

In comparison, look at so-called "primitive" villages: Do you realize how they "hug the environment," how their houses fit their surroundings? Nothing is strange or unnatural. How organic it looks. The so-called "primitive" man respects the environment better than we do. Development is destroying the world we inhabit. We respect the bottom line, while disrespecting the environment we live in.

What about trust? What does it mean to trust trees and rocks and nature? I am lost here and invite others to figure out how mutual trust and respect applies to macro systems such as the environment. But if common interest is the guiding light, then perhaps trees have their own interests, which we violate. How about rocks?

On every level, MT&R seems to be the driving force, the vehicle through which we make choices that can help us live either longer or shorter. It is our compass toward constructive rather than destructive change.

We know how to promote MT&R in organizations. But when we go to a macro system, we still have a job to do.

I invite you to think, challenge, and disagree with me. I look forward to learning from your criticism.

THE FUTILITY OF EXPECTING[1]

LET'S say you interview someone for a job. She absolutely vibrates with the expectation that you're going to hire her. She even shows a bit of displeasure if the interview goes in the wrong direction. You might cut the interview short, and for sure you wouldn't hire her.

You probably know people who go to a restaurant and are annoyed if everything does not go "as expected." They become too aggressive, unpleasant to be around.

What is going on?

It is OK to want, but not to expect.

What is the difference?

Wanting means that you are alive and would like to see something happen, but you do not *assume* that it *must* happen. You do not assume that you are, or should be, able to make it happen.

When you expect, when you wish, and even subconsciously when you pray, you are assuming somewhere deep inside that if you try hard enough, what you wish or pray for will actually happen. So it is up to you to control the situation. If it does not happen, you become annoyed at whomever or whatever you perceive as having stood in the way of getting what you expected: You get annoyed at God for not responding to your prayer; at your children for not fulfilling your wishes; and at your spouse for not living up to your expectations.

But in reality, you are annoyed at yourself, for failing to deliver what you believed you should have been able to deliver.

When wishes are not granted and prayers are not answered, people are miserable and feel as if they have failed to control the results they wished for. And this misery can be continual, because there is no end to wishful thinking; thus there is no end to expectations that may never be fulfilled.

---

[1] Adizes Insights, January 2009.

Do your best to reach your goal, but if it does not happen—surrender. Assume it was not supposed to happen. Recognize the fact that you are not omnipotent. Realize that you can't control everything.

ACCEPT AND SURRENDER ...

You must stop wishing, expecting, and praying as a way of "making a deal with God." Prayer should be an expression of accepting the wish of God and surrendering, not of begging God to fulfill your prayer.

This feels disempowering, right?

But take the time to read about the Flood in the Old Testament. Even God realizes that He or She cannot make us righteous. It is up to us. Thus, when it rains, God brings the rainbow to remind Him/Herself to stop expecting that S/He can make us righteous, and to stop the Flood. S/He did His/Her best and gave us the rules, but now it is up to us. S/He does not expect to control us. So who are we to be bigger than God and get upset when our wishes and desires do not get realized?

Put a picture of a rainbow in your office to remind you that even when you do your best, what you want might not happen. Accept that there are limits to what you can control and do.

Want everything, but expect nothing.

Is that all?

Yes—but it's not so simple.

... OR, CHANGE YOURSELF

What if you have a spouse who repetitively, consistently does not give you what you want from your marriage? Telling yourself not to expect, not to wish, not to pray, to accept the reality although you don't like it, is depressing and fatalistic. Right?

What to do, then?

You have to reformulate the problem. Focus not on what you expect or don't expect, want or do not want from your spouse. Your spouse is not the problem. Focus on what *you* can control: What do you want from *yourself*? In other words, if you cannot get what you want from your spouse, decide what *you* can do about it.

Acceptance is one solution. Another solution is to get yourself a spouse who does what you like without your having to expect it; who does what needs to be done naturally, without your having to pray for it. In business, hire people to work for and with you who naturally do what you want done without your having to motivate them and expect from them and beg and control them.

Management books tell you that one of your tasks as a manager is to motivate people.

The textbooks are wrong.

> Do your best to reach your goal, but if it does not happen— surrender.

Don't hire people you need to motivate, people whose attitudes you need to change. The management profession is not for social workers. The people you hire should be a motivated bunch to start with. Your job is to not *de*-motivate them.

Get out of the prison called "I Expect." It only leads to misery.

Tell people what you want. Listen to the problems they have making it happen. Deal with them. And then, what you want should happen—*without* your having to motivate, beg, or pray. If it does not happen, either you made the wrong decision or you have the wrong people.

On Expectations
and Job Interviews[1]

I received a question from an associate, Nebojsa Caric, that gave me a new understanding. The question was how to handle the fact that people have one set of expectations when they seek a job, but that over time their expectations change.

My insight is this: During the interview, you should ask the candidate what he *wants* the job to be. Take notes.

Then ask what he expects from the job. Take notes.

Wanting and expecting are not the same thing; as an example, I might want to win a lottery, but I do not *expect* it to happen.

Motivation and frustrations are both functions of expectations, so those expectations should be identified during the interview and differentiated from what a person wants. The problem is that people don't always clearly differentiate between what they want and what they expect.

So, after you've written down, separately, your candidate's wants and expectations, read the list of wants back to him, and ask which of those wants, if not fulfilled, would make him feel frustrated, and which ones he would be able to let go of.

The ones that would make him frustrated are expectations in disguise.

Then, go over the list of expectations and ask the same question. The expectations he could let go of are only wants in disguise. Take them out.

Finally, you should have a complete list of expectations. Ask yourself: Can you fulfill this candidate's expectations? If you cannot, this is the wrong person to hire, even if he is qualified. If you *can* meet those expectations, put it in writing and have the candidate sign it.

When, a year later, he has a new set of expectations—for example, a raise

---

[1] Adizes Insights, January 2010.

in salary—pull out that list and let him read it. Discuss the differences, and realign expectations for the new year.

Notice that the (E) style is going to have mostly, or all, expectations. That is what makes him entrepreneurial. As George Bernard Shaw said, "Reasonable people adapt themselves to the world. Unreasonable people attempt to adapt the world to themselves. All progress, therefore, depends on unreasonable people."

> Ask yourself:
> Can you fulfill
> this candidate's
> expectations?

(E)s *expect* that what they want *will be*. That is what makes them unreasonable, demanding, and narcissistic. That is the price we pay for progress.

The (P) style is the reverse. They will have only "wants" And no expectations. They are here to serve, to do what needs to be done, and they want to do the job. (P)s expect to fulfill *other* people's wishes—*other* people's wants. Since what others want is a bottomless pit, (P)s work endless hours with no time to train or delegate, and end up becoming Lone Rangers in their managerial style.

The (A) style will have mostly expectations and a few wants, while the (I) style will have mostly wants and some expectations.

Try it.

THE IMPORTANCE OF
BEING GENUINE; AND WHAT
IS WRONG WITH TRYING[1]

WHAT does it mean to be genuine, and why is it important?

When someone is genuine, that person is at peace with herself. People at peace with themselves seem to have fun. They seem to enjoy themselves at whatever they are doing; or else they would not do it. They exhibit a high level of energy, clear eyes, and an ever-ready smile. They are not trying to impress you or anyone else. They are present both physically and emotionally. They seem to be behaving naturally; you do not sense tension when you are with them. They do not seem to be trying to make you do something or trying to convince you to agree to anything. They do communicate, but without tension.

What is going on?

I believe that people who are at peace with themselves can behave that way because they spend little or no energy on what I used to call "internal marketing" and now call "internal disintegration." Internal disintegration occurs when there is a lack of self-respect and self-trust.

People who lack self-respect do not have the ability to listen to and honor their own voices of dissension. They do not honor their own experiences. They do not learn from their past. They seem to be in conflict with themselves.

And those who lack self-trust do not listen to their intuition. They do not listen to their bodies. As the expression goes, they are not "together." They are insecure about their decisions and wonder whether their behavior is appropriate or not. They are not sure how sure they should be, so they try to cover their inadequacies. They are not at peace with themselves.

---

[1] Adizes Insights, June 2006.

When people are at peace with themselves, they accept their inadequacies. Such people know they are not perfect, and they accept that. They see no need to hide, to wear a mask; no need to pretend to be what they are not. They are sure that they are not sure. They know when they do not know. They do not try to be right or avoid being wrong. What is, is. They do not try to impress. What you see is what you get.

WHAT IS WRONG WITH TRYING ...

And this brings me to a big illumination:

I suggest that you might not want to hire someone who tells you that she is trying very hard to succeed.

People who are "trying" are, by definition, not at peace with themselves. They are *trying* to be someone they are not, instead of accepting who they are and what they do.

> You might not want to hire someone who tells you that she is trying very hard to succeed.

Have you ever seen someone *trying* to act, or *trying* to sing? You wish they would stop. An actor should not *try* to act; she should *act:* she should *be* the person she portrays. Someone who *tries* to sing is self-conscious about her singing, which always makes the attempt look embarrassing.

I used to think that a person who works hard at whatever she does and tries hard to succeed is someone to be appreciated and even emulated.

Now it occurs to me that the opposite is true. If someone has to try, she is not where she should be or doing what she should do.

Take me, for instance: When I lecture, I do not *try* to succeed at all. I get up on the stage; all I know is the two sentences with which I am going to start the lecture, and how much time I have been allotted. I know I have enough material to lecture for a full ten days without repeating myself. I know what I know and I am prepared without trying. I have no notes, no PowerPoint presentations. After the first two sentences, I am watching the audience and lecturing what I feel they should know. I am having fun. My lecture flows naturally. I have been told more than once that I am an excellent lecturer.

But if you assigned me to do bookkeeping, I can tell you that I would have to *try* very hard to complete my assignment, and even so, it probably wouldn't be very good. Not because I do not know accounting—I do; I have a degree in it—but simply because I hate it. I hate sitting and dealing with numbers. It is not natural for me.

Here is another example from my professional life: I have been *trying* very hard to manage my Institute. For years. It just occurred to me that if I am trying so hard, it must not be a natural thing for me to do. If I am trying so hard, I am not having fun. I am suffering and becoming easily exhausted.

How strange. If I lecture to a thousand people, even for several days, at the end of the experience I feel energized. Managing my Institute, on the other hand—even for one day—requires a vacation.

This conclusion is not easy for me to accept. I teach management. I write about management. So how can it be that I have to *try* to manage well? Should it not be something that I excel in? Am I a con man parading as an expert in management, when in essence I can talk the talk but I cannot walk the walk?

The answer is that I am a philosopher of management, an observer of the dynamics of management. I understand it. I can analyze it; but do not ask me to do it. I am like an art critic: Even the best of them do not necessarily know how to paint.

So stop trying, Ichak. It is time to say it is not for you. Get someone to manage who does not have to try, who actually has fun doing it.

How many inventors and founders of companies *try* to manage, *try* to succeed? And that is why they fail. Being an entrepreneur does not guarantee that you can manage, no matter how hard you try. The rest of your management code will determine whether you can manage.

HIRE SOMEONE WHO DOESN'T TRY

In job interviews, the candidate is often asked how hard she tried in her previous job, or how hard she intends to work on the new assignment. Usually people are proud to say that they will try very hard.

To me, now, this seems like a bad sign. The answer you really want to hear is: They enjoyed what they were doing without any trying. They were having fun, and they intend to have fun in the next job; and if it does not work that way, then it is not for them.

But my experience is that people fear admitting that they're having fun. It seems so frivolous. Some religious sects, such as the Puritans, consider having fun almost sinful.

This applies to your marriage as well. How many of us spend years trying to make our marriages work? What a waste of our lives. It should work without our having to try too hard.

Who hasn't tried to go on a diet? And we know that diets do not work well. Why? Because trying means we are not at peace with what we are doing. We hate the diet. And hate takes energy. To lose weight, you should love being skinny rather than hate being fat.

Skinny people do not try to be skinny. They simply are, because they love what they eat, and they eat right. Without trying. They are at peace with what they eat and how they eat it.

> My experience is that people fear admitting that they're having fun. It seems so frivolous.

When you do what you are at peace doing, you get *more* energy in doing it. When you try, the harder you try, the more energy you spend. At the end of the day you are totally exhausted from trying, and still, you have not produced the ecstatic results you expected.

Scary conclusion, is it not?

It is scary to me because it means admitting that your failure or deficiency will not be ameliorated or eliminated by trying—even by trying *hard*. On the contrary, it will only mask the deficiency. It will only postpone your finding out what you *can* succeed at without trying.

If I have an executive who is telling me how hard she is trying to do her job, I believe that means I need to change either the job or the person. She is in the wrong position.

If you think about it, this illumination is a call to freedom. There are natural fits, where you can succeed without trying. Give yourself a chance to find what that might be, and stop wasting your time trying to succeed at something that is not for you.

You do not have to try to succeed. You just have to find what is natural for you.

Or, instead of trying, how about *trying out*, meaning making the first attempts to see if you like something or are good at it. That is fine. But if those attempts are taking too long—and for some people they are lifelong—and you aren't having fun, then that it is a sign that what you are trying out is not working out. You are banging your head against a wall, and it might be time to realize that this is not for you. You were not designed to swim underwater like a fish. You just are not a fish. So stop—and find what you can be successful in, naturally.

When you accept yourself as you are, acknowledging your deficiencies and loving yourself in spite of them; when you are comfortable in your own skin, comfortable with what you do and with whom you do it, you will feel genuine, full of energy—and guess what? You will even be more attractive, because people love to be with people who give energy instead of taking energy.

STONE AGE MONEY[1]

I recently heard a great lecture by Dr. Douglas Lisle, an evolutionary psychologist. It was about "Stone Age money" and how it affects our behavior today.

The lecture gave me some insights I want to share with you.

During the Stone Age, and for a long time thereafter, there was no money as a means of exchange.

So if I did something for you, how would you pay me back? Sometimes with goods you could offer me, but mostly with gratitude, a sense of "I owe you." You would be expected to reciprocate the favor.

Those who did the most for the village—who were the best hunters, for example, who thus fed the village—got the most recognition and became chiefs, or something similar.

This went on for thousands of years. The result is that we have developed a sort of "chip" in our heads—a storage mechanism like a bank account—to receive, store, and pay gratitude.

We need gratitude. Period. That need is deep in our subconscious.

Now, what does this need for gratitude mean for management?

> Merely getting paid for work is not enough.

It means that merely getting paid for work is not enough. If you just were paid, but your employer did not show any gratitude, you would feel as if you had not been paid at all.

Whoa! This was news to me. How often have you heard people say: "You got paid, so what are you complaining about?"

Think about it: The highest rate of suicide among medical professionals is among dentists. They get paid in money only; no gratitude for drilling into your teeth.

---

[1] Adizes Insights, October 2009.

The highest rate of turnover in the human services industry is among consultants. They just get paid money. No gratitude. Like prostitutes.

Hello, managers: Wake up! If you only pay your workers in money and fringe benefits, then you are not paying them in "Stone Age money," and they feel gratitude-deficient. It is hardly strange that they are not cooperative. Their deepest need—something that developed and was nurtured for thousands of years—is not being met. This can sometimes produce dysfunctional repercussions for the companies we manage, manifested in lower morale and productivity.

"Always say, 'Thank you,'" your mother told you. Listen to your mother. She was right.

PART 4

PROBLEM-SOLVING

WHAT IS A PROBLEM?[1]

WHENEVER we do not like something, or something is bothering us, we call it a problem. If it is raining and we get wet, it's a problem. If a spouse is an alcoholic, it's a problem. And the crisis in the Middle East is also a problem.

But calling anything we dislike a problem does not help us solve it. In fact, it actually hampers our ability to solve it, because it does not guide us correctly to mobilize the energies that are necessary for solving it.

IT MUST BE CONTROLLABLE

Let me suggest that a problem should be defined not only as something we do not like, something undesirable and/or unexpected, but also as something we can *control*—i.e., solve. If it is out of our control, if there is nothing we can do about it, then it is not our problem. That is an unfortunate fact.

For instance, I wish I were taller. I used to consider my height a problem. It took years for me to realize that I cannot control my height. But I can control my weight.

Please note that I am not saying you need to be able to solve the entire problem by yourself. As an individual, you can control only so much. With the cooperation of others, however, you can solve many more problems than you can individually.

So the word "control" should not be understood as what you can accomplish by yourself; rather, it should be defined as what could be accomplished, assuming you can get the cooperation of the people you need. If you can mobilize all of the people whose authority, power, and influence (CAPI) will be necessary to solve the problem, and direct them toward solving it, that is also control.

Being controllable is necessary but not sufficient to define a "problem."

---

[1] Adizes Insights, August 2006.

People often mistakenly define a problem by its cause, asking, "Why?" "*Why* is this person an alcoholic?" "*Why* are interest rates unpredictable?" The assumption is that the root cause of the undesirable fact *is* the problem that needs to be solved.

But I suggest that there is no end to the question "Why?" A child can defeat a Nobel Prize-winner by simply repeating "Why?" to every answer she gets. Eventually—usually after three to six "whys"—the answer will be, "I do not know." Try it yourself.

WHO, WHAT, HOW, WHY

> Without that anchor of knowing <u>who</u> can do something about the problem, looking for a cause is just an academic exercise.

So instead of starting with *why*, focus on *who*: Who can solve the problem—at least as we understand it at that moment? Figuring out *who* is best equipped to solve the problem helps establish *what* the problem is and *how* it should be framed. Once that decision is made, the designated person or people should be assigned to find out *why* the problem exists and what to do about it.

It is very possible that once the cause has been determined, the problem might need to be *re*defined, and again the starting point is to figure out the best person to handle it. At that point it can be reassigned to a new person or team to solve the newly defined problem.

If, in the process of analyzing a problem, we conclude that we cannot solve it and that other people are needed, then we know it's time to reconstitute the team.

But without that anchor of knowing *who* can do something about a problem, looking for a cause is just an academic exercise. We understand the problem better, but what then?

ANECDOTAL EVIDENCE

Here are some examples, from both personal and business life, of how to define a problem.

Personal: As long as you continue to believe you can make a difference and cure your spouse of being an alcoholic, it is *your* problem. If it takes the extended family to make her change or get help to change, it is an *extended family* problem. But let's say your spouse refuses all help and refuses to change. The alcoholism is not your problem *or* the family's problem anymore. It is her problem alone.

But now, what is *your* problem? *Your* problem is: What are you going to do with your life? Do you want to continue living with an alcoholic?

Business: A banking client of mine once claimed that one of the bank's problems was that interest rates were unpredictable. In my view, that was not their problem, because the bank had no control over the Federal Reserve's rate decisions. In fact, I told him, the bank's problem should be redefined as: "We do not have a strategy for dealing with unpredictable interest rates"; or, "We do not have access to a system that would enable us to better predict interest rates."

As you can see, the definition of the problem changes depending on who can control it.

MAKE CONFLICT CONSTRUCTIVE: STRESS AND THE ORGANIZATIONAL CLIMATE[1]

LET'S face it: We're all stressed out. The tendency is to work longer and harder, and then collapse. We want to slow down, to fit in a vacation or some golf, but there's too much work to do. It seems impossible to deal with clients' needs today and, at the same time, anticipate change in the future. And the more we do, the more the work piles up, and the greater the stress.

What's going on, and what—short of yoga—can we do about it?

It's no secret that the root of the problem is the high velocity of change in our postmodern society. Change demands effective decisions and action. That creates conflict, because we rarely make decisions in a vacuum—and conflict is the source of stress. The reality facing all of us in today's business climate is that the higher the rate of change, the more conflict there will be—along with its dysfunctional byproduct, stress.

In fact, change creates problems that are both opportunities and threats—what I call (in a literal translation from Mandarin Chinese) "opporthreats." What we are seeking, then, is quality management—to resolve problems by making quality decisions and implementing them efficiently.

But quality decisions and efficient implementation often seem incompatible. How often do we see outstanding decisions not implemented and bad decisions somehow becoming operational reality?

The source of this apparent incompatibility in management stems from the diversity of styles needed for decision-making and from the diversity of interests needed for organizational implementation. In addition, in the fast-paced markets of today, the speed of change inflames the conflicts inherent in this diversity of styles and interests.

---

[1] Originally published in *Manage* magazine, February 1996; reprinted with permission.

One solution to reducing stress is to reduce change. Stop the train and get off, move to a slow track, give up, take it easy. But change (and conflict) is life; you can't walk away from it. To slow down in today's competitive markets is to commit organizational suicide. Remember that the quietest place in town is the cemetery.

The other way to deal with stress is to refocus the internal energy of your organization. You can convert conflict into functional action, harnessing the destructive energies of conflict into growth. Conflict can then become a constructive force in your company, instead of a destructive and disintegrative force with its pervasive byproduct: stress.

Take a lesson from the Japanese. One of the reasons the Japanese have been so successful and so quickly responsive to change is because they make decisions together slowly, which enables them to implement decisions quickly. A German manager once asked me, "How come the Japanese are so fast with innovations? We have the same R&D budget." I responded, "They are faster because they are slow." He thought I was kidding.

The Japanese organizational management systems have been based on mutual trust and respect (MT&R) that is coded deep in their culture and society, and this has been instrumental in their ability to both effectively and efficiently deal with change and conflict. It is a dynamic use of the principle of "slowing down." (Although it should be noted that more and more, the Japanese are failing to put their own principles into practice, which has resulted in increasing stress and even suicide.)

As a leader, you need to create an organizational climate that harnesses the energy of conflict and stress.

There are three dimensions to this new environment:

DECISION-MAKING

There is a tendency for executives to rush in and make decisions "decisively" and independently, left and right, like the Queen of Hearts in Alice's Wonderland: "Off with their heads!" The idea is to get a solution as quickly as possible. But there is no use running fast if you're running down the wrong road.

The trick is to integrate all of the organizational roles in the decision-making process. Effective and efficient management over both the long and short term require that four roles be performed.

These roles are functional, but individuals will have management styles in which one or more of these attributes dominate: The (P)roducer—the (P) role—produces the results for which the organization exists. The organization must be (A)dministered in the right sequence with the right timing and intensity. The (E)ntrepreneurial role focuses on proactive changes in the external market (environment) and leads in creativity and risk-taking. The (I)ntegrator is necessary to build a team effort.

It is unlikely that any one manager can perform all four of the (PAEI) roles needed for effective and efficient decision-making, although we might like to think so. That means an organization needs to bring into play a complementary team and a decision-making process that integrates the different styles, attitudes, and opinions of these four basic organizational roles. This process ensures that conflict is brought into the open and into the dialogue. Making a decision together takes time, but subsequently, decisions are implemented quickly. People trust each other to do the required tasks. In a badly managed organization, people make decisions fast because they are acting individually; but implementation will take a very long time because there is no support or understanding of the decision.

MUTUAL TRUST AND RESPECT

Conflict is not abstract. It has a face: the face of whomever you have to deal with in dealing with issues of change. Conflict without understanding is an emotionally exhausting process. And technology sometimes gets in the way of really hearing and understanding the people around us. Miscommunications and misperceptions of the other point of view only tend to ratchet up the conflict and the stress. There are different techniques, about which I have written elsewhere, for handling meetings, communicating with the four functional types in an organization, and developing systems of mutual trust and respect. The starting point is to recognize that your most important role as a leader is to create a climate and culture where mutual trust and respect are nurtured and supported.

The role of the leader, then, is to create the right organizational structure to handle change and conflict. There are many levels of change, just as there are different levels of the perception of change, and executives today need to integrate their companies to handle change, not only for today, but for the future. The strong foundation of a complementary team within your company will integrate decision-making and implementation.

This foundation must be constantly maintained, even as you deal with current change. It's like digging a mine: You dig to move ahead, then shore up your infrastructure, then dig more, then shore it up again. You need to shore up internally as you deal with the external market. By building a system of MT&R, you are answering the need to create a mechanism for dealing with the rate of change, and taking the edge off stress within your company and within yourself.

STRESS IN OUR PERSONAL LIVES

We often say that stress "spills over" into our personal lives. But it is not so much a case of it "spilling over" as of being at the core of the problem. I have already said that the common denominator of success in any organization—a family, a business, or a government—is the ratio between internal marketing (how much managerial energy is needed to make something happen within the organization) and external marketing (the amount of resources, for production, sales, marketing, etc., required to satisfy customer needs).[2] Your personal stress level may be an indicator of the imbalances caused by a company that lacks integration through MT&R. Stress in business feeds conflict in your personal life, and the imbalances and stress in your personal life feed the business experience.

The more you resolve the conflicts of change, the more change is created, and the more you will be facing conflict and stress. The solution to handling stress and the fast rate of change today is to create a structure in which people can relate to each other as a complementary team. Then, the energies of destructive and dysfunctional stress become harnessed into growth and positive, enjoyable, business experiences.

---

[2] For more detail, read "The Secret of Success" beginning on page 125, in Part 3 of this book, "Team-Building (Mutual Trust and Respect)."

THE DUALITY OF EVERYTHING; OR, HOW TO DELEGATE[1]

IT is nothing new when I say that there is duality in everything. We would not know what being skinny was if we did not define what being fat is. There would be nothing to exhale unless we inhale.

This duality also applies to decision-making, in both business and personal life.

In my lectures, I often say that you do not know what you know until you know what you *don't* know. If someone tells you what she knows about a subject, ask her what she does *not* know about that subject. That will tell you how much she *really* knows. If she claims to know it all, she is full of hot air and you should carefully examine what she claims to know.

HOW DECISIONS SHOULD BE MADE

To finalize any decision that involves change, you must answer the four imperatives of decision-making: *What* to do, *how* to do it, *when* it has to be done, and *who* should do it.

Deciding what to do without deciding how and when it should be done or who specifically should do it, can produce a disaster. In military affairs, for example, when a commander orders a unit to clear a village of an enemy contingent (the *what*), but does not spell out the *how*, in this case the values that should govern such activity, he risks allowing hundreds of civilians to be killed.

In the same way, if you do not spell out *when* something needs to be done, by the time the task is actually completed it may be too late to be effective.

Finally, not spelling out exactly *who* is responsible for getting some-

---

[1] Adizes Insights, October 2008.

thing done might mean that your decision never gets implemented, because everyone expects someone else to do it.

But deciding what to do (and when and how and by whom) is not enough. Deciding how to do something needs its accompanying duality: how *not* to do something. Deciding when requires also deciding when *not* to accomplish something; and deciding who is the right person to carry out the decision also requires deciding who is *not* the right person.

THE ROLE OF EXPERIENCE

Ironically, it is easier to decide what, how, when, and who, than to decide what not, how not, when not, and who is not the person to do something. That is because what we know is by definition limited, while what we don't know is limitless.

Determining the "not's" should be done either by someone who has experience with poor decisions, and thus has learned what, how, and when not to do things; or someone whose wisdom has accumulated over time by watching others fail. (Intelligent people know how to solve a problem. Wise people know how not to get into the problem in the first place.)

Thus, even if you know what to do, or how to do it, etc., if the decision is a strategic one, look for someone, or even several people, to evaluate your decision—to tell you what not to do; how not to do it; what is the right timing of the implementation; and whether you have chosen the right person for the task.

> Deciding who is the right person … also requires deciding who is not the right person.

And any time you delegate, even when you are careful to specify all four imperatives, you still need to supervise and monitor the execution of the task, because no one can imagine how the person you delegated to might overdo the *what*, or violate the *how*, or not meet the time limits, or further delegate to someone you consider to be inappropriate.

PROACTIVE MANAGEMENT

It is not necessary to find the negatives—what not to, how not to, etc.— by monitoring execution and pointing out mistakes as they are made. You can, and should, determine the negatives through "simulation": Tell a person what to do, and ask her how she intends to do it. You might discover in the simulation that she is heading toward making a mistake. Correct it in time. And ask her when she believes she can complete the task for sure. You might find out that she cannot carry out the task in the appropriate time frame.

Delegation is not a linear process or a one-way street. It is interactive. As you correct the person you have delegated to, you are teaching her, and she is gaining experience. In addition, the decision you made will be carried out the way you intended.

By asking questions intelligently, you might be developing the wisdom of your subordinate.

PERSONAL LIFE

The duality of this process has repercussions in personal life, too. Some people brag about the self-control they demonstrated in deciding *not* to eat something fattening. But what makes you sick or overweight is what you *do* eat. You might pass on the pound cake but become overweight anyway because you eat too much cheese or eat food with too much oil.

You have to watch what you eat and what you do *not* eat.

Everything comes in pairs. Not only the sexes.

BARRIERS TO DECISION-MAKING[1]

I was on my honeymoon flying with my bride to Israel on El Al Airlines. Long flight. I checked the pouch in front of my seat for something to read and found a bag with a puzzle containing four different geometric pieces that together constituted a flying airplane.

The instructions were to put the puzzle together in the shape of a rectangle.

Easy. Right?

Not at all. I tried and tried and could not do it. I started feeling embarrassed; my bride was following my efforts, and I imagined her wondering what kind of a moron she had married.

Pitying me, she offered to help. Guess what? She could not do it, either.

Across the aisle was a professor from Stanford Law School, who was also watching. He started making some cynical comments about the intelligence of the academic staff of UCLA (I was a professor there at the time). Then, he tried it too and could not do it.

Now I felt I had the right to be upset, and I called the stewardess over to complain: "What kind of sadists are the people at El Al Airlines, to want to humiliate passengers and give them puzzles that have no solutions?"

She was puzzled, and said, "I do not know what your problem is. Kids do it in less than a minute!"

Got it. The key word was: "kids."

I turned the pieces of the puzzle upside down so that I could not see the picture of the plane, and, lo and behold, I put the puzzle together in seconds.

I turned the puzzle back around and guess what?

You *could* make a rectangle—*if* you allow the plane to fly *upside down*, with the cockpit facing earth!

The reason all of us intelligent professors could not solve the puzzle was

---

[1] Adizes Insights, December 2009.

because we decided *a priori* how the plane should fly. We decided what the solution should be first, and then tried to force that solution on the problem.

This was a great lesson for me.

Never Assume

When approaching a problem, begin with a totally empty head. Do not assume anything. Let the problem "talk to you." Be blind, as I was when I turned the puzzle upside down.

The solution, if you approach it from an unbiased perspective, will actually present itself to you. It becomes clear by itself. Just be *open-minded.*

If a couple is having marital problems, ask the kids what is going on. Surprisingly, they will hit the nail on the head. With one sentence, they will usually make it clear and to the point.

Why can kids see it so much better than we adults—*especially* educated adults? Because we have a solution in search of a problem. We know what the problem *should* be; we have patterns and names for problems, and formulaic solutions, and we try to force the evidence to fit the pattern we have in our heads already.

In research methodology, this is called formulating a hypothesis.

Don't do it.

The famous philosopher and sociologist Ivan Illich argued that our contemporary education system, instead of teaching people to learn and think for themselves, actually programs them to live up to the expectations of the establishment. He was probably right. Certainly it is true that our schools spend more time teaching people the "right" answers than teaching them to ask the "right" questions.

Go fresh. Empty. Virginal. Intentionally ignorant. With no fear of admitting, "I do not know."

Is, Want, and Should

Years ago, I was consulting for a large bank in Mexico whose president was a highly respected man, although he had no college education. His vice president told me: "Unhindered by education, he can think."

What I have learned from this experience for my consulting practice is to shut up—both my mouth *and* my mind. I just listen and look at the problem as if it is the first time I have ever heard of anything like it.

Let the problem talk to you; let the points on the map start connecting to give you the picture. Don't force the connections.

I know this sounds confusing, so let me use another analogy: I was just in Israel for President Shimon Peres's annual get-together, where there was an exhibit of some new technologies that Israel is developing.

One company had software that analyzed patterns. Let us assume you have a trucking company, and you have to do lots of repairs. The software will eventually tell you the problem.

> Let the points on the map start connecting to give you the picture. Don't force the connections.

"Aha! It is data mining software," I said.

"No," the company president told me. "In data mining, you have an algorithm and you use it to mine the data. You develop the algorithm based on what you believe the issue is.

"Our software develops the algorithm by analyzing the data. The data gives us the algorithm."

Exactly: Let the data talk to you. Be sure you do not start with a hypothesis. Starting with a hypothesis is what I did with that puzzle: I assumed that the plane has to fly correctly. And guess what? This plane was different. My assumption of what *should* be and what I *wanted* it to be was blocking my ability to see what *was*.

In order to solve problems, you must know first what the problem *is*, and in order to find what *is*, you have to relax what you think it *should* be and what you *want* it to be.

President Obama's Health Care Plan: What Went Wrong?[1]

I F you want to know if a meal is a good one, one way to find out is to taste it. That will tell you if the food is edible or not, all right. The problem is, you might get sick from the test.

How about smelling the dish? That is what dogs do; no matter how hungry they are, they smell the food first before they eat it.

But smell can be manipulated.

I suggest to you that there is a better way to evaluate what is submitted to you for consumption: Watch how the meal was prepared.

Imagine watching someone cook a very complicated dish while totally ignoring the recipe. You do not have to be a chef to conclude that what she is cooking won't necessarily be edible, and you might feel ill just smelling it.

I have watched how both Hillary Clinton and President Barack Obama developed their health care plans. Neither one was "cooked" properly, and that is why both plans had difficulty obtaining the necessary votes to be implemented. Even if President Obama's plan ultimately passes in Congress, there is a danger that so many political compromises will have to be made in order to force it through that, although it was designed as a racing horse, it might end up a three-legged camel.

PROBLEMS VS. PRE-PROBLEMS

What went wrong? Both President Obama and Hillary Clinton made the same mistake: They used problem-solving technology when, because we live in a democratic society, what they actually had was a pre-problem. (The

---

[1] Adizes Insights, September 2009.

following insight uses Adizes tools, and I'm afraid only those who have read my books or been through training will be able to fully understand it.)[2]

Both assumed that since they had a plan they liked and believed was a good one, that it would be implemented.

Both approached the problem as if they had CAPI (coalesced authority, power, and influence), when they did not. What they needed to do was to get the CAPI group together; establish that there was, in fact, a problem; and then lead them to take ownership to design the solution.

Instead, Obama, and Clinton before him, finalized a plan without consulting the people needed to accommodate that plan. They skipped a necessary step in decision-making: They went from illumination to finalization, and only then submitted their plan for accommodation.

At that point, when efforts were made to accommodate the plan by suggesting some compromises, those efforts were resented.

The missing step had come back to haunt them.

In plain English, they developed a plan and *then* tried selling it. A common mistake. That is how most people approach problems: They decide on a solution and then try to convince others that the solution is good.

> Obama, and Clinton before him, finalized a plan without consulting the people needed to accommodate that plan

What often happens, however, is that the "buyers" might have their own finalized solutions, too. What we have then is two trains on the same track but going in the opposite direction, pushing, huffing, and puffing ... but hardly moving. Or perhaps a better metaphor is two male moose locking horns for the favors of the female (the electorate).

Both Clinton and President Obama solved the problem first and tried to get CAPI later. Shoot first, ask questions later ....

No CAPI

President Obama consulted the American Medical Association, which represents no more than 17 percent of doctors. The independent doctors were not heard. In developing his plan he consulted the insur-

---

[2] For more information on problems and pre-problems, see my book *Mastering Change: The Power of Mutual Trust and Respect* (Santa Barbara, CA: Adizes Institute Publications, 1992), pp. 133-148.

ance companies, but not the Republican leadership who had the votes he needed.

Hillary did worse. She consulted no interested parties whatsoever. Her plan was developed in secrecy, by "consultants" and "experts"—first-class chefs who, in their infinite wisdom, decided what their patrons should eat and then tried to force-feed pork to vegetarians.

What they should have done is gotten the CAPI group to "cook" the solution together.

They did not do this. They saved the conflicts for the end rather than handling them in the beginning—another classic mistake that I frequently encounter in my consulting work.

Problems must be solved by, among others, those who are going to implement the solution; otherwise, we end up with what doctors call "non-compliance": The medicine is good but the patient ain't taking it.

WRONG ROAD MAP

The plan's development did not follow an effective road map of decision-making.

First of all, I believe even the diagnosis was incorrect, because public outrage about the health care crisis was not loud enough to create the CAPI necessary to solve the problem.

> The plan's development did not follow an effective road map of decision-making.

I suspect the task was not well defined, either—because *who* should have the right to be insured is still under debate. (Should illegal immigrants be included or not?)

But even had the diagnosis and the task definition been done properly, the design characteristics of a desirable solution were handled badly, if they were handled at all. Why? Because the CAPI group, even had it been assembled (which it was not), would not have been able to agree on the criteria of the desired solution until the diagnosis and the task were settled first.

Without agreement on the diagnosis and the task, there is no chance of being able to develop the criteria of a desired solution or to support the solution later on.

We have compounded mistakes here. It is obvious that the decision road map was not followed, the dish was not prepared correctly, and those who needed to "eat it" felt they were being served frozen steaks with burned potatoes.

It's true that sometimes people will eat anything, because being hungry is worse. But it did not have to be a badly prepared plan, did it?

As you can see, I am not debating the content of the plan. I refuse to taste the dish. I know how badly it was cooked.

WHAT CAN BE LEARNED FROM RICARDO SALINAS'S MANAGEMENT STYLE?[1]

RICARDO Salinas has been a client of Adizes for the last twelve years. During this period, the company he leads, Grupo Salinas of Mexico, has grown from $250 million in capitalization to $3.5 billion in capitalization. Today, the group contains a very large retail chain, Elektra, which is all over Latin America; two cell phone companies, Unefon and Iusacel; two television networks, Television Azteca (Channels 13 and 7), and a network in the United States, Azteca America; plus a bank—Banco Azteca—and pension and insurance companies, among others. It employs more than 60,000 people.

I have watched Ricardo, the CEO and the majority owner of the company, manage. He implements brilliantly some of the basic tenets of the Adizes methodology.

THE CONCEPT OF 'DEMOCRATSHIP'

I have never met an executive who commands such vast, deep knowledge of the subjects of retailing, media, banking, and telecom. Most people command one field of knowledge. Ricardo always surprises me by proving again and again that he does know what he is talking about.

How does he do it?

This is where the velvet glove comes in. To learn, he is all charm and openness and vulnerability. He listens well and is not afraid to ask, and ask again and again, until he truly understands the subject down to the smallest detail.

---

[1] Adizes Insights, May 2006.

He is truly open-minded and democratic in making decisions. But once that decision is made, he becomes a tyrant, a steel hand. No deviation from the decision is accepted or goes unpunished. People truly fear him. He can become very unpleasant if one challenges his decision once he makes it.

So he knows when to be open and when to be completely closed.

He perfectly exemplifies my argument that a person can be open-minded in making a decision, admit ignorance, and learn, and then make a decision and be an absolute dictator in implementing it.

Most people who are dictatorial are afraid to show their weakness or ignorance on any subject. And those who admit their ignorance are afraid to make a decision—because they've admitted ignorance.

> He knows when to be open and when to be completely closed.

Ricardo is different; he is a study in contrasts that work very well together. He knows when to smile and be charming and open and vulnerable, and when to be an absolute pain and closed-minded in the extreme.

He genuinely practices democracy in decision-making and dictatorship in implementation—what I called democratship.

A truly rare species. And a very successful one.

PART 5

MANAGING CHANGE

HUMAN RESOURCES: WHY IT DOES NOT LEAD CHANGE[1]

IN forty years of consulting to companies worldwide, I have never succeeded in leading a company through change via its human resources department. In fact, I have learned over time that being assigned to work with HR is the kiss of death to any major initiatives for change. Nothing will happen. The most that will happen is a training workshop, and that is it.

As a rule, when I discuss needed changes with a CEO, I discourage him from bringing the human resources VP into the discussion, because I already know from experience that the participation of this VP will cause the mountain to give birth to a little mouse, as in the famous fable, and we will end up with a new workshop on communication skills or some team-building, feel-good program.

If the purpose of our work is to engineer a paradigm shift in what the company does or how it goes about it, a disruptive change that will require structural changes or significant new resource allocation, the HR people will block it in a very polite way by dragging their feet until the initiative dies.

WHAT IS GOING ON?

Why is the human resources role detrimental to change, while CEOs, marketing officers, chief technology officers, and chief strategists in the company embrace the need for change? Should not HR have a key role in managing change? And if so, why does the HR department, by and large, have the least clout and power base in a company? Why is it hardly ever consulted on major strategic initiatives?

Let us try to illuminate this observation: A well-managed organization is effective and efficient in the short and long run.

---

[1] Adizes Insights, March 2006.

To be effective in the long run, it needs to be proactive to change. It needs to adapt to what the foreseeable future dictates.

To lead change, when there is no full certainty what the future is going to be, involves creativity and the ability to take risks. That is not what human resources departments do, nor is it the dominant style of the people who staff HR departments.

The tasks of the HR department largely involve administrative roles: salary and benefits administration, hiring and firing, training that is geared to making people more effective and more efficient in what they are already doing. It is linear change. Better, or more, but not different. Not disruptive change. Not development, even though the department is usually called "human resources development."

Disruptive change is too scary for HR, because it introduces stress into labor relations. The role of the HR department is not focused on proactive change. It deals mostly with efficiency and administration.

As a result of the mainly administrative role that HR is expected to play, those who end up in HR tend to manage in an administrative, often bureaucratic style. They are not aggressive, change-oriented types, like marketing and strategic-planning people ought to be. They are friendly and see that everything works according to the rules and procedures. Consequently, they are not allies for change. The HR department finds major change counterproductive to its purpose of maintaining order, and disturbing to its need for harmony and industrial peace.

WHAT CAN BE DONE?

My recommendation to all the companies I have consulted to is to create two different departments for the human resources function. One deals with administration and is called HRA: human resources administration. It is involved with salary administration, performance evaluations, hiring, firing, and training employees to perform better within the present structure and roles.

The second department is HRD—human resources development— which deals with changing organizational structures and the necessary role changes that accompany such changes: organizational development, team-building, improving communication, coaching middle management, serving as the ombudsmen for people employed in the company, etc. This department worries about the future and how to prepare the organization for that future, while HRA worries about the present and how to make it most efficient.

Will the two departments be in conflict?

You bet.

That is precisely why each time a company is structured in such a way that HRD is expected to perform *both* roles, virtually no human resources development will occur in that company. The efficient bureaucrats of HRA will stifle any efforts to lead change by the development people. Those who measure success by current efficiencies and results will consider HRD people inefficient and insufficiently effective. In that organization, HRD will die or become so co-opted that its role of co-leading change will decay to zero.

> Disruptive change is too scary for HR, because it introduces stress in labor relations.

In their structure, organizations should not mix roles that are supposed to produce efficiency in the short run with roles that are supposed to produce effectiveness in the long run. My experience shows that it simply does not work.

DEFINING LEADERSHIP; OR, WHERE DID I, OR 'THEY,' GO WRONG?[1]

WAITING for a plane in Kiev, Ukraine, I picked up the January 2009 issue of the *Harvard Business Review*. Although I do not typically read this magazine, because it is so alien to my way of thinking, I did so because I was bored.

As I should have predicted, I became quite disturbed by some of the articles. They made me wonder: Am I on the wrong track, or is it the establishment, as represented by Harvard, that's on an old, outdated path?

For example, on page 21, in an article by James M. Kouzes and Barry Z. Posner, in their discussion of what it means to be a leader, they say:

"Leaders on the front line must anticipate merely what comes after current projects wrap up. People at the next level of leadership should be looking several years into the future. And those at the C suite must focus on a horizon some ten years distant."

But Michael Kami, who was the chief strategic planner for Xerox forty years ago, has said—and I agree with him—that planning is not good enough. In today's increasingly turbulent environment, it is almost impossible to anticipate what will happen ten years hence.

How many companies predicted the oil crisis of the last century, or the credit crisis of this century, in spite of all the prediction models and the millions of dollars spent on them?

We live in what Peter Drucker has called an "era of discontinuity,"[2] and

---

[1] Adizes Insights, May 2009.

[2] Peter Drucker, *The Age of Discontinuity: Guidelines to Our Changing Society* (New York: Harper & Row, 1969), see "Preface to the Original Edition."

who can predict discontinuities? If the future is more or less like the past, we can predict it relatively easily—but discontinuities are very difficult to predict with any accuracy or workable benefit.

So what to do? Kami already said it: Predict less, and work more on making your company more flexible, so that it can easily change direction as conditions change.

Now, what does it mean to be flexible?

Eliminate hierarchies, as some current gurus recommend? I say no, because then you destroy accountability.

Have no fixed strategy or budgets? Obviously not. Thank God, at least the well-meaning gurus have not got *there* yet.

So, what then?

Create, nurture, feed, and reinforce a culture of mutual trust and respect, so that change is not threatening.

> *Creating and nurturing the right culture is what leaders do.*

It is easier to turn on a dime when there are no suspicions of hidden interests and agendas. It is better to learn from each other's differences in opinion, and thus make better decisions, than to have disrespect for each other's contributions and suffer from the common maladies of think tanks, where people cannot stand each other.

Creating and nurturing the right culture is what leaders do, especially in our current turbulent environment, in which flexibility is essential for success.

In my book *The Ideal Executive: Why You Cannot Be One and What to Do About It*,[3] I stated that the difference between a manager and a mismanager is whether he has a zero anywhere in his (PAEI) code. If so, he is a mismanager. If not, he is a manager, although not necessarily a leader.

A leader must excel in at least two of the four (PAEI) roles (denoted in the code by capital letters), and it is imperative that one of them be (I). What the other role should be depends on his task. For marketing, it is (E): (paEI). For accounting, (A): (pAeI). For a CEO, it will depend on where the organization is in its lifecycle.

We are all leaders as long as we are sensitive to those we lead and the environment in which we operate; as long as our style is functional to the

---

[3] Santa Barbara, CA: Adizes Institute Publications, 2004.

task at hand at the time it is needed. So I strongly disagree with Kouzes and Posner: Predicting the future is not sufficient to make a person a leader.

A LEADER'S PRIORITIES

And here is more:

In the same article, on page 23, the authors write: "From Day One, the new leader must put shareholders' interests first ... and promote value creation."

Sounds right. This is the cornerstone of microeconomic theory, and Milton Friedman, the Noble Prize-winner in economics, made it practically a religion: The main responsibility of management is to the stockholders.

It's wrong.

> When you focus on stockholders' value creation, you blur your attention to the market, to your customers.

That is managing *by* earnings per share rather than managing *for* earnings per share. There is a big difference represented by that one word, and that difference is what management focuses on.

Your mind is like a camera. Do you focus on the mountains and see the person close to you as somewhat blurred, or do you focus on the person in front of you and find that the mountains become indistinct?

When you focus on stockholders' value creation, you blur your attention to the market, to your customers.

That is why CFOs who become CEOs despite a lack of marketing or sales experience predictably, and repeatedly, lead their companies over the cliff. They are not watching the road. They are watching the dials.

FOCUS ON REVENUE

Management should focus on clients—on increasing repeat sales, which are an indication of client satisfaction. They should focus on post-purchase service. On pre-purchase market-needs creation.

It is the market that produces revenue. Without revenue, no matter how much you cut costs, you are heading south.

It is so easy to miss this point. When you focus on increasing stockholders' value, you might focus exclusively on the cost reduction side of the P&L and ignore the fact that the market is slipping away—which is exactly what happened to the car industry in the United States. It had been led for far too long by financial geniuses who focused on stockholders too much and on clients not enough.

Your first and most important stakeholder is the client. Your organization exists first and above all to satisfy the changing needs of the market.

Focus on that, and if you do well there, at a cost you can afford, stockholder value will follow.

Management *for* the stockholders, not *by* the stockholders.

IS STRUCTURAL CHANGE
NECESSARY?[1]

IN the March 2006 issue of the *Harvard Business Review*, an article by Robert S. Kaplan and David P. Norton titled "How to Implement a New Strategy Without Disrupting Your Organization" claims that, "Given the costs and difficulties involved in finding structural ways to unlock value, it's fair to raise the question: Is structural change the right tool for the job? We believe the answer is usually no." The authors then proceed to recommend the Balanced Scorecard approach.

I beg to differ.

Let me give you an analogy I use in my lectures to explain my methodology for changing organizations.

Assume that you are in a powerboat that is about to hit a rock if it continues going forward in the same direction. To avoid the rock, it must change direction—toward, let's say, the right.

How useful do you think it would be to stand on the deck and scream: "Right! Right! Come on, guys, we need to go *right!* You are a team. A *good* team. And I trust you! ..." etc.

This is all good motivational talk, right? But all by itself, it won't work. And that is the mistake that some executive coaches trained in psychology or sociology continually make. These executive coaches are all oriented toward interpersonal human behavior. Their efforts to change direction by using motivational talk and cultural change may eventually cause the change to happen—but usually it will be after the boat hits the rock, or perhaps a split second before.

Why?

Because changing a culture to create teamwork to, in turn, generate strategic change, takes time. The reason is that each interest that will be affected

_____

[1] Adizes Insights, July 2010.

by the planned change must agree to the change. But no one is going to agree until she sees that the status quo is more threatening to her than the proposed change might be. At that point, she will cooperate to make the change. However, by the time it has become clear that the status quo poses a threat; the situation is more than likely a desperate one.

Now, assume you have a first-class navigator with a very well-balanced scorecard also standing on the deck, and that this navigator has explained to you that you need to make a change, and has shown you where you have to go. Will *that* by itself work?

Obviously not. And that is another mistake many consultants make: They recommend strategies for change and then simply expect their expensive recommendations to be implemented.

What really makes a change happen?

Let's continue to use the analogy of powerboats for organizations. What determines the direction of a powerboat is the power structure—how the engines are aligned. If we want to change direction, we must change the power structure. For example, if we need to go right, we must increase the power of the engine on the left and decrease the power on the right. Once we do this, we will see the boat turning about.

Knowing where you want to go, no matter how detailed and balanced your plan may be, does not alone make change happen. You need to realign your power structure—i.e., your chart of responsibilities and authority—in the new direction you need to go. And if that is difficult and expensive, well, consider the alternative: the costs of *not* making the change.

THE MOTORBOAT CALLED BRAZIL

In Brazil, the inauguration of left-wing President Luiz Inácio "Lula" da Silva in January 2003 seemed to herald a huge political change from the policies of its outgoing president, Enrique Cardozo. But during my visit there, I could discern no significant changes in the country.

Why not? Because the engines of the motorboat called Brazil are frozen; thus, no matter what you pledge or promise, or how much you stand on the deck shouting and pleading, the boat continues on its set course.

In the case of Brazil, what is "frozen" is government expenditures. In order to cut the cost of government, a constitutional amendment would be necessary—which would require a majority vote. The problem is that unless the situation there becomes desperate, there is little chance of achieving a consensus among so many government representatives.

My forecast for Brazil: There will be no economic reform in Brazil until the economy destabilizes to the point of obvious crisis. This crisis is being postponed for as long as Brazil is a major exporter, mostly to China. But if the world economy stagnates, the crisis will eventually come to Brazil, which cannot easily cut its government expenditures.

> Knowing where you want to go, no matter how detailed and balanced your plan may be, does not alone make change happen. You need to realign your power structure.

Kaplan and Norton are simply wrong. To say that structural changes are difficult and costly and thus to be avoided is like saying that medicine is costly and tastes bad and that therefore we should try to cure ourselves by visualizing good health instead.

To know where you want to go is necessary. But not sufficient.

You must also organize yourself to get there; otherwise your attempt to create change will end in the realm of daydreaming. We know this from consumer strategy: How you position your forces depends on whether you want to attack or defend. You won't do well attacking if you position yourself to defend, and the reverse is also true.

GETTING THE RIGHT RESULT

Let me give you an example from my consulting experience of how changing the power structure is indispensable to changing direction.

It was at least twenty years ago that I was asked to consult with a defense electronics company. They told me that because the Cold War was ending, the national defense budget was being cut, and they wanted to move into consumer electronics. They had already tried many times but with no success.

How had they tried to do it?

They had hired a bright young MBA, who spent days, if not months, studying the subject. This MBA wrote up a detailed and well-documented report analyzing all the reasons why the company should go into the consumer electronics market. The report was outstanding, with lots of tables, statistics, and whathaveyou. After he'd submitted his report, the company appointed him project manager in charge of consumer electronics.

And nothing happened.

And the company became very frustrated.

So I looked at the organizational chart. Herein lay the problem: The head of military electronics had the engineering department reporting to him—all 1,500 engineers. He had assembly reporting to him. He had quality assurance and control reporting to him. In fact, most of the company was reporting to him.

Meanwhile, the newly appointed project manager in charge of consumer electronics had barely a secretary reporting to him.

What about the remaining departments?

Finance made and monitored the budgets, and naturally it tried to avoid threats to the quarterly results that were reported to the stock market.

Do you think finance would support military electronics or not?

As you might expect, finance would talk about the need to change, but when the tires hit the road and the time came to allocate resources, it sided with the short-term outlook: with consumer electronics.

And what about the CEO? He wanted the change, but he also needed the support of his executive committee, which talked the talk but did not walk the walk.

And the poor MBA—young, new, and inexperienced in company politics—what about him? He would make his presentations, everyone would agree to his findings and "hmmm hmmmm …" a lot, but everyone in the company continued to hold her own department's interests above all others and protect them fiercely.

So I recommended to the CEO, and also led the group to realize, that if they wanted to make a strategic change of direction, it had to be accompanied by a strategic change of the power structure.

> We try to avoid the pain that structural changes produce. But that does not work in the long run.

At the end of the process we initiated, that structure looked quite different. There were *two* market managers: defense and consumer. Each had product marketing and marketing research and a sales organization. But the engineering department, where most of the power was, reported to the president. Each market manager had a separate budget with which to buy services from the engineering department. And consumer electronics had a bigger budget than military electronics. We were "milking the cow to feed the calf." Finally, the VP formerly in charge of military electronics was assigned the responsibility for consumer electronics.

Now how long do you think it took to make the change in direction?

If I want to know where a company is going, rather than where it *should* be going, all I have to do is study the organizational chart and understand the power structure. It tells me where the "boat" is going. Not where it *should* be going, but where in reality it *is* going.

We live in a world of instant gratification; we want everything faster, simpler. We try to avoid the pain that structural changes produce. But that does not work in the long run. It only creates more frustrations and more pain.

To change the direction of a river, you must change the structure of that river's contours.

WHAT COMES FIRST?[1]

MANY executives are confused about the correct sequence of changing structure, strategy, leadership, and vision: What to do first?

Alfred Chandler led us astray when he claimed, more than thirty-three years ago, that "structure follows strategy."[2] My colleagues now claim that structure follows leadership, values, and vision. I claim that Chandler was incorrect then and that my colleagues are missing the point now. They are confusing the *is* with the *should*.

Structure *should* follow strategy. In reality, however, strategy follows structure, because organizations are political entities. If you know what the power structure is, you can predict what the strategy will be, because people follow their self-interests. Strategy is the manifestation of those self-interests, because it reflects the power structure. It *should* not be that way, but that is irrelevant. Focusing on what *should* happen rather than on what *is* happening leads to misdiagnoses and inadequate treatment.

Years ago I was facilitating the rejuvenation process at Bank of America and restructuring the company first, rather than doing the strategy first. A partner of the Boston Consulting Group who attended my meetings challenged me. He said: "You might be rearranging the chairs on the Titanic; shouldn't you be worrying about where this organization is going first? While you are reorganizing how people sit, they might be traveling in the wrong direction."

His criticism kept me awake for several nights. But then I remembered an experience from my teenage years. When I was a senior in high school, my city sent twenty teenagers, including me, to France as a youth delegation.

---

[1] Originally published in *Executive Excellence* (now *Leadership Excellence*) magazine, September 1995; reprinted with permission.

[2] Alfred D. Chandler, Jr., *Strategy and Structure: Chapters in the History of the Industrial Enterprise* (Cambridge, MA: MIT Press, 1962). Chandler (1918-2007) was the virtual founder of the academic study of the history of business and the rise of the modern corporation.

We took an overnight train ride from Biarritz, the site of our youth camp, to a meeting in Paris. Being teenagers, we all tried to fit into one compartment. Some of us were sitting on each other's laps, reclining across several people. But as soon as we all finally fell asleep, one of us wanted to go to the bathroom. Commotion galore! "Move your hand!" "Watch where you step!" There was no support for "change" in those circumstances. The entire compartment had to be disturbed simply because one person had to go to the bathroom!

In poorly structured organizations, sometimes it is easier to "wet your pants" than to make a commotion and invoke the wrath of your peers.

Where is the typical consultant standing as he is making his analysis and recommendations? Outside the train, right? Standing above, Godlike, observing the train as if it were a toy and shouting, "Change the direction; go toward Rome!" He might even toss a 200-page report into the train compartment proving that a change in direction is necessary—but would people actually implement that change? I suggest that that report would be round-filed, as are most consulting reports. Someone might read it and cynically think to himself, "This *should* be done. He is right. But I can't even go to the bathroom without getting everyone upset, and he wants me to *change trains?*"

And where is the CEO—a CEO with correct vision, attitude, and values—sitting? Is he even on the train, or is he also outside the train? I suggest that he is as much a prisoner of the political situation as the others. The CEO might make some waves, might provide a vision, but will there be true support for change or will people resist it? Are leadership, vision, values, and wishes sufficient?

> To change vision, we have to change people's perceptions of self-interest—a structural issue. To change structure, however, we need a vision.

As they are caught in the traps of their own self-interest and self preservation, how easy is it, really, for people to develop a new vision of what the company *should* do?

To have a new vision that people share, a vision that leads to action, there must first be a change in the present structure of self-interest, to allow and encourage people to freely visualize their new self-interests.

I realize that there is a chicken-and-egg problem here: To change vision, we have to change people's perceptions of self-interest—a structural issue.

To change structure, however, we need a vision.

My own approach is not to start with vision, values, *or* leadership styles. What I do first is make decision-makers aware of their interdependency, of how "tied up" they are.

Secondly, people in the organization need to become aware that if they do not cooperate and enable each other's movement, they will be riding toward a disaster. They need to change direction. At this point, I do not get into detail about *which* direction. I simply try to create awareness of three realities:

1) Yes, we are in trouble;
2) Yes, we need to change; and,
3) Yes, we need each other to change.

Once that consciousness is created, the organization needs to be coached to make some changes—usually some tactical changes first, which will reinforce the notion that cooperation can work. Once that sense of trust is created, strategic changes can be made more easily in the future, because people will trust others to cooperate.

ESTABLISH THE MISSION

Next, a general vision of the new direction (though not of any specific destination) is made. I call it "the mission." No specific goals, just a general mission statement establishing why the organization exists.

That leads us to rearrange "how we sit"; in other words, to generate the first draft of that mission, some structural changes must be made so that the organization is at least facing in the right direction.

For instance, let us say that a bank comes to the realization that making money as a savings-and-loan business is no longer profitable, and that it needs to convert itself into a fee-based financial-services organization. Once that realization is reached, we can discuss what organizational changes are needed. Once we rearrange "the seating" by creating a new structure that enables flexibility, we can start planning strategy.

"Mission" is why we need to change. "Strategy" is how we are going to reach that mission.

Strategy discussions will lead to more changes in the structure.

In designing a structure, we might ultimately do more than a hundred drafts—going back and forth, from function to form, from form to function: structure to strategy, and back again.

As we do that, a positive sense of interdependency is constantly nourished. Mutual trust that change can be made qualitatively is established, and everyone understands that we need to change direction as well.

My approach is to define the mission and vision as generally as possible. Mission and vision are only the means to get the organization to change its structure as soon as possible. Then, with the new generic structure that enables flexibility, a strategy can be developed, which will lead to further adaptations and refinements of structure. This means that in the process of facilitating structural design, the top management, with my help, designs many structures until the final one emerges to be implemented.

The sequence is as follows:

1) Agree that there is a problem and that we need each other in order to solve it;
2) realize that cooperation is needed to produce change;
3) envision the mission of the organization;
4) produce the first draft of a new structure of responsibilities;
5) formulate strategy;
6) redefine structure;
7) deal with questions, doubts, and disagreements about the structure by continuously improving the structure.

GETTING TO 'MANAGEMENT BY RESULTS'

Next is to deal with the staffing problem: who will take which position in the company. We can either staff the positions with the people the company already has, or hire new people from the outside. Issues of resource limitations emerge. The chart changes again to fit this new organizational limitation.

This process produces an organizational chart of responsibilities—which is necessary, but not sufficient, to have a working organizational structure.

When responsibilities are well defined and understood, we proceed to define the goals of each unit in the organization. That is where "management by results" comes in.

Once that is accomplished, we next discuss and define the levels of authority needed to accomplish goals within each area of responsibility. That might lead to further improvements to the organization chart.

When the levels of authority are agreed on, we proceed to discuss what rewards people will receive if they reach their goals within their areas of responsibility and authority. Changing the rewards system might lead to more adaptations to the chart.

Reorganizing a company is not a linear process. It has to be participative, systemic, and systematized.

> *Agree that there is a problem and that we need each other in order to solve it.*

Leadership and vision, without a holistic structural change that encompasses responsibilities, authority, and rewards, are as empty as daydreaming. Many organizations have vision and values statements all over the place, but they have no positive effect; on the contrary, they can create cynicism, because the employees know the organization isn't "walking its talk."

To change organizational behavior, we must first rearrange the political and reward structures. That will give rise to a new vision and attitude and even create a place for a new leadership.

AWARENESS, CONSCIOUSNESS, AND CONSCIENCE[1]

IT takes time for ideas to develop and mature. For instance, I started writing the book *Leading the Leaders*[2] about twenty or thirty years ago. I took notes on top of notes, reading them and rewriting them until I was finally ready to share them with others in a book.

What I am going to present today is not clear in my mind. It is not well articulated. Maybe twenty years from now (may we live so long), it will have become clear enough to be presented without embarrassment. Nevertheless, I want to share these inarticulate thoughts with you. You are my colleagues; it is through sharing, questioning, and challenging one another's ideas that we begin to think more clearly, rationally, and analytically; we learn; and thus jointly advance our ability to manage change without destructive conflict. I thank you in advance for being willing to bear with me as I present these random thoughts.

> *A ship is safe in harbor, but that's not what ships are for.*
> – John A. Shedd[3]

As you all know, I start my lecture on change by arguing that change, by definition, creates both problems and opportunities. It creates problems because everything is a system, and all systems are composed of sub-systems. When there is change, the sub-systems do not change in synchronicity. This lack of synchronicity creates gaps. Those gaps are manifested in what we call problems.

---

[1] Adizes Insights, August 2007. Excerpted from a speech given at the Founder Session Presentation, the 29th Annual Adizes Convention, in Palic, Serbia, July 6, 2007.

[2] Santa Barbara, CA: Adizes Institute Publications, 2004.

[3] John A. Shedd, *Salt from My Attic* (Portland, ME: Mosher Press, 1928).

I suggest in that lecture that all problems—be they medical, emotional, organizational, physical, social, or political—are manifestations of disintegration caused by change. The faster the change, the faster things fall apart, and the graver and more numerous are the problems facing us.

Problems caused by change, however, can be addressed proactively because they can be predicted. They can be predicted because their cause, change, is predictable too. Change has a lifecycle, and every stage in the lifecycle has its predictable problems.

Since everything is subject to change, everything has a lifecycle: stars, rocks (those of you who were at the convention in Greenland probably remember that we touched the oldest rock on Earth), trees, and people. Organizations have a lifecycle, too.

Now, while everything has a lifecycle, not all entities have the same lifecycle. They have different time spans. Some butterflies have a lifecycle of one day, while a star can live for millions of years. The challenge is to manage organizations to become stars instead of butterflies.

One day, as I was delivering this lecture and, as usual, repeating over and over that everything has a lifecycle, I suddenly had doubts about what I was saying.

I remembered a rafting trip I had taken with my 13-year-old son, Sasa, a year or two earlier, down the Colorado River in the Grand Canyon. We were rafting down the river as the guide was telling us about the age of the colorful rocks we were looking at. Then it occurred to me: Wait. Granted, not all entities have the same life span. But the biggest difference is between those entities that can choose to prolong their life span and those that have no choice.

THE ROLE OF CONSCIOUSNESS

Rocks and stars cannot choose how old they will be. They age with time, and scientists can tell you the age of a rock or a tree because their life span is predetermined. Even animals don't have a choice. A horse or a dog will have a certain life span, a predictable number of years. They do not have the choice to prolong that life.

We humans have a choice. We can have longer or shorter life spans than our ancestors had. It depends on the choices we make. Furthermore, we can affect how long our organization, or even our global environment, will "live."

But in order to do that, we have to be conscious. What differentiates us from animals or anything else is how conscious we are. The more conscious, the more human we are.

Now, what is consciousness, and how is it different from awareness?

If we are shivering, we are aware that we are cold. We are *conscious* when we understand the repercussions of being cold, when we really understand what will happen if we do not take cover.

Consciousness is an understanding of the meaning and consequences of our actions. Conscious people do not just react to drives and feelings—like hunger or fatigue—as animals do, or spread their roots in search of water, like trees do. What makes people different from animals or trees is this search for meaning,[4] and the need to understand.[5]

But being conscious is not the same as living consciously.

What does conscious living mean? Is it enough to know what is going on and be aware of its repercussions?

My insight is that *living* consciously means taking a certain level of responsibility: *acting* on what we are aware of and understand. It means to walk our talk.

Some organizations claim to be "conscious" of pollution: In other words, they are aware of the pollution and understand the repercussions if the pollution continues. But they do nothing about it. I suggest that they are *aware* and *conscious* of the pollution problem; but they do not *live* consciously.

How many of us are aware of overeating? We are conscious of the possible repercussions, such as diabetes and high blood pressure. Still, we do not act.

WHAT IS MISSING?

In order to act, we need more than consciousness. We need a conscience.

Note that in the English language the words "consciousness" and "conscience" are similar. The same is true in Serbian: "consciousness" is *svest* and "conscience" is *savest*; I wonder whether this is true for other languages, too. "Awareness" in Hebrew is *mudaut*, which comes from the root "to

---

[4] For more information, see the writings of Victor Frankl.

[5] For more information, see the writings of Carlos Slutsky and Sara Cobb.

know." To act, one needs more than knowledge. In Hebrew, "conscience" is *matzpun*, which has the same root as *matzpen*, "compass," and *tzofan*, which means "code."

I suggest the following interpretation: Conscience is one's compass in life, pointing toward the right road to take. If we listen to it, it will bother us until we take action. However, conscience must be decoded. One needs not only to listen to it but also to try to interpret what it is telling us. To do that we need to be conscious, to understand the repercussions of what we are aware of.

It is not easy to live consciously in modern times, when one's conscience is under constant siege. Our values are constantly being challenged by technological changes, and we, as a civilization, are increasingly confused in determining what is right and what is wrong. (When does life start or end? Is cloning of people acceptable? Is stem cell research right or wrong?)

We live in a new jungle. The old jungle of primitive man was very scary; but I suggest that the new jungle is much more dangerous than the primitive one. In today's jungle it is more difficult to know what is what and who is who. In the primitive jungle, if you saw a lion, you recognized an enemy. Today, we look at a sheep and don't know if it is truly a sheep, or a wolf in sheep's clothing.

For example, the food advertised for us to eat, and the quantities we are served: Is this food our friend or our foe? Is it going to nourish us or slowly kill us?

As I drive down the highway, confronted by thousands of billboards, I am conscious of the new jungle. I wonder which of those smiling models is a modern version of the Biblical snake, trying to seduce me to eat, drink, smoke, and in doing so get me kicked out of the "heaven" of the healthy.

What should we be conscious of in this new jungle? What rules should we follow to decode the code and be able to follow the compass of life?

I believe that the code is mutual trust and respect (MT&R). If our actions undermine MT&R, our compass is not pointing to true north. That will lead to disintegration and destructive conflict.

My conclusion is that living consciously is following religiously the principles of MT&R: being conscious of what happens when we do not follow MT&R, and being aware when we violate MT&R.

Managing External Change: The 'Information Superhighway'[1]

W E may be overloading human potential at current levels of technology, as seen in our relationships with others.

What's ahead for us on the "information superhighway"? Experts talk of the technological possibilities but seldom speak of the long-term impact on culture and business. Nor do they ask, "Will it give us the freedom to better use our time?" or, "Will it improve the quality of our lives?"

A geometric progression in computer technology is smothering us with information. Half of business equipment spending now goes toward technology.

To many, the possibilities in information technology suggest a revolution in knowledge, a quantum leap for humankind. One envisions the weaving together of a new learning environment and a new information society. In business, the "virtual corporation" is said to be the wave of the future, with a new mastery of information and ways of managing people.

But does that necessarily mean more productivity?

MORE INFORMATION = GREATER EXPECTATIONS

I believe that the impact of the information superhighway will be to make us more productive—but, ironically, will also make us feel *less* productive and more disempowered. We will lose more and more mastery of our environment, as citizens, workers, decision-makers, and do-ers.

Why? The answer has to do, first of all, with information overload. The new information systems ensure that there is always more that can be done.

---

[1] Originally published in *Executive Excellence* (now *Leadership Excellence*) magazine, April 1995; reprinted with permission.

That exponentially increases expectations—and happiness, we know, is a function of expectations.

As expectations rise, commensurate real-time performance can't follow. We are finding a "highway syndrome" along the information highway: Suppose there is a surge in heavy automobile traffic. We increase the number of lanes to reduce the congestion. Now we can travel faster. But the lower congestion and wider highways attract more people to the suburbs, and soon the highway is more congested than before. Ultimately, instead of improving transportation, the additional lanes have helped create deserted downtowns and long commutes.

Similarly, rather than saving time, more information and capability may actually increase our workload and frustrate us, because we're not using all the tools we believe we should or could use. The information highway will change the quantity of information, but not necessarily the quality of communication.

Having increased options does not increase productivity, happiness, or health. In fact, it could work the other way. For example, take the United States: It is a rich nation with endless opportunities to feed itself. And what happens? I have never seen a nation with as many obese people as the United States. The more developed the country, the more its citizens must worry about weight control. Having more food choices does not make us healthier. In fact, if we overindulge, it could potentially kill us.

To be sure, technology is attempting to resolve the problems it creates: blue lasers and molecular disk drives, parallel processing for desktop environments, and artificial intelligence technology are only a partial list. But is there a point where human control and interactivity end? Is the next step a world in which technology drives the culture, as Jacques Ellul predicted in 1964 in his book *The Technological Society*?[2] Technology, he argued, would soon become both the strategy and the mission: an end in itself.

Already, the product of this information-driven world is more and more the creation of a manqué world for workers and citizens—the opposite of the new learning environment often described as the goal of the information superhighway.

The image we are being fed, of a "campfire of technology" around

---

[2] New York, NY: Knopf, 1964.

which we tell our stories and interact as humans, sounds rosy but may be misleading. We can rewrite the music of the masters, re-cut films, rewrite history, and solve as individuals the problems of humankind. But having lost a sense of what is real, we might become increasingly inauthentic in our behavior. In 1993, Howard Rheingold wrote in *The Virtual Community*[3] that virtual reality allows people mastery in a world otherwise controlled by teachers, bosses, parents, and professionals. But what is "real" reality in these circumstances? Aren't we getting increasingly confused between what is real and what is a simulation of reality?

Even at today's level of technology, we tend to tune out and switch off in our relationships with others; we treat each other as if the other were not a person but a program on radio or television. What will the information highway and virtual reality bring to our social mores and behavior? Lonely people interacting via video and computer screens, without direct sensory and human feedback? That is quite a distance from the ideal of the educated citizen that John Dewey described at the beginning of the 20th century[4] —productive, decisive, social beings who can creatively think and act in a democratic setting.

We should not put all our faith in technology to solve the problems of the future. The solution lies in learning first how to "be," as human beings, and how to relate to each other—in politics, in ethnic relations, as families, and as creative beings. Then we will be ready to use the technology, rather than letting the technology use us.

Long before Karl Marx began to analyze the economics of alienation in *Capital*,[5] he described the alienation of the worker[6] as a loss of control over both the process and the products of his labor; a gradual estrangement from his fellow laborers, whom he perceives as threats to his earning power; and eventually, estrangement from human nature in general.

Today, the information superhighway seems to be calling up the same bleak, ironic vision.

---

[3] Howard Rheingold, *The Virtual Community: Homesteading on the Electronic Frontier* (Reading, MA: Addison Wesley, 1993).

[4] John Dewey, *Democracy and Education* (New York: Macmillan, 1916).

[5] Karl Marx, *Capital: A Critique of Political Economy* (London: Dent & Sons, 1930).

[6] *Economic and Philosophical Manuscripts of 1844* were Marx's unpublished notes, discovered by scholars in the early 20th century, in which he worked out his Theory of Alienation.

Twelve Tips for Keeping Your Business at Prime[1]

LOTS of elements, from personal lifestyles to bottom-line business savvy, go into bringing a corporation into what I call Prime—the golden point where flexibility and control are in perfect balance. Every company has its own unique lifecycle; but nothing remains permanent in the lifecycle of a company, whatever its size. Change is the order of the day.

Here are twelve tips for bringing a company to Prime and keeping it there in the changing winds and turbulent economies of the 21ˢᵗ century:

1) *If you delegate too early, you abdicate.* Decentralization becomes a goal later in the lifecycle, but delegating authority too early in the company's history, before there is structure and procedures and policies—before there is "law and order"—is tantamount to abdication. It is both desirable and necessary to have a strong, centralized, even autocratic management in the early stages of an organization's lifecycle.

2) *Conflict is change is growth.* Conflict is indispensable to growth. Period. There is no conflict only when there is no change—i.e., when you are dead—and there is no growth without change.

3) *Stop conflict from being destructive.* The way to make conflict constructive is to establish a climate of mutual trust and respect (MT&R).

4) *Agree to disagree.* The critical variable in determining success or failure is how well you maintain mutual trust and respect within

[1] Originally published in *Manage* magazine 44, 3 (1993), pp. 14-17; reprinted with permission.

the company as it grows by leaps and bounds, spreads out in many directions, and its success starts to show. Successful companies are the product of a complementary team—whose members, by definition, continually, but respectfully, disagree with one another.

5) *MT&R is not just a question of good attitude.* Good attitudes are necessary but not sufficient for mutual trust and respect.

What else is necessary?
- a rewards system that rewards cooperation;
- the right amount of discipline in communication;
- common vision and values;
- a functional structure, because "good fences make good neighbors."[2]

When these factors exist and are nurtured over time, attitudes of mutual trust and respect will grow and become effective.

6) *You don't know what you don't know until you know it.* Often we assume we have a solution when we start. But problems change rapidly, so solutions must also change rapidly. The right solution is a continuous search for the right solution.

7) *Know when less is actually more.* There are stages in the lifecycle (Go-Go, for example) when you should be looking for less to do rather than what else to do. Confusing the two can make you bankrupt.

8) *Getting there.* Measuring success exclusively by profit is as erroneous as measuring a season by one ball game. You can win and still be losing because of *how* you won. If you are just winning without looking at the how, complacency can set in and eventually defeat you. You can't win by watching the scoreboard.

9) *Sales and profits aren't always a match.* More profits and more sales can be achieved only when an organization is in Prime—that is,

---

[2] A 17th-century proverb, cited by Robert Frost in his famous poem "Mending Wall."

when an organization has established controlled flexibility. Prior to that, a young organization is flexible but not controllable, and sales may go up while profits suffer. After Prime, when an organization is less flexible and exerts more control, profits may be increased by cutting costs at the expense of client satisfaction, and sales may go down.

10) *Deciding and doing may involve different people.* To manage anything—whether it's in business or personal life—means making good decisions, implemented with minimum energy and resources. But not all decision-makers are good implementers. Thus, a complementary team built on mutual trust and respect is needed.

11) *When a "yes" is a "no."* Creating a win-win environment is no easy thing, because not everyone means the same things when they use the same words. An administrator may listen to an entrepreneur without saying a word. The entrepreneur might think this silence is a golden "yes," when in fact it is a shrieking "NO!" The trick is learning to work with everyone else's style of communicating.

12) *Risk failure.* Those who can't afford to lose will never win. If you can't take risk, you'll never explore the possibilities of winning.

PART 6

COMMUNICATION

THE NEW TOWER OF BABEL[1]

I N my consulting work, whenever I notice conflict I stop the discussion and work on defining the words we are using. I have found from experience that many of the problems that cause miscommunication, and thus conflict, stem from the fact that people use the same word to mean different things.

It reminds me of a story from the Old Testament: When the people started to build the Tower of Babel, God mixed up their language and they had difficulty communicating.

My interpretation of this story is that up until that time, people were nomadic. When they became urban and settled, they started building towers, which was a significant strategic change. There were new, previously unknown phenomena and new experiences that needed new words. Take the word "scaffold": The word, which describes a structure used to build towers, was unknown to nomadic culture because nomads didn't build towers.

I believe that because of all the modern world's technological advances, we are experiencing a second Tower of Babel phenomenon. There is enormous confusion because new phenomena are being created for which there is not yet a vocabulary. People use old words to point to new phenomena, or create new words no one has ever heard, and confusion reigns.

DIVIDED BY A COMMON LANGUAGE

I spent a whole day in one company just defining the words "module" and "sub-system." There was tremendous mobility in the company because it was growing fast. People brought vocabulary from their previous jobs to the new one, and since they had come from many different companies, the result was a new Tower of Babel. People weren't able to communicate. It

---

[1] Adizes Insights, May 2009.

went so far that what one person understood the word "budget" to mean was different from what another person believed it to mean.

In another company, I spent almost two days in very heated debate over what was meant by the word "engineering." I was helping them to restructure the company, and in order to restructure engineering, we had to first define what it means.

I was amazed: We filled two full walls with flip pages on which we wrote down all the existing types of engineering. There was the easy-to-understand electrical engineering, separate from mechanical and civil engineering. But then we hit a real block: systems engineering. What was that? A debate ensued, with some people claiming that it did not exist, while others, whose degrees were in systems engineering, threatened to resign from the company because they felt disrespected.

There was also product development engineering and sustaining engineering. But where did product development engineering end and sustaining engineering start? And what was the difference between maintenance engineering and sustaining engineering?

> For some reason that I do not yet understand, discussions about word definitions generate a lot of emotion.

Complicating the discussion was that people sometimes "upgraded" a position—giving it higher status by assigning it a new label. Like calling what used to be maintenance engineering "sustaining engineering." (I've found this phenomenon in sales, too. Some people don't want to be mere salesmen, so they call themselves "marketing engineers." How silly!)

There was something called value engineering and something called human resources engineering, not to mention re-engineering, which referred to organizational restructuring; and quality control engineering, as different from quality assurance engineering; and financial engineering, as different from accounting. It was impossible to restructure the company until all the different meanings were cleared up.

People usually dislike this exercise. For some reason that I do not yet understand, discussions about word definitions generate a lot of emotion. People get really upset defending their definition or understanding of a word, as if the Lord gave it to them personally on Mount Sinai. I have to use all my skills of integration to keep the group from falling apart or stopping the session altogether.

To release stress, I tell a joke to show them why defining words is important:

A young man goes to the doctor and says, "I want a castration." The doctor is surprised and tries to convince the man not to do so, because he is still young, etc. The young man insists that it is his religious conviction, and he wants to do it, and that is that.

The surgeon makes him sign a release, wheels him to the operating room, cuts his testicles off, and wheels him to the recovery room.

When the young man wakes up, he sees another young man in the room's other bed.

"What are you here for?" he asks.

"For a circumcision," the other man answers.

"Ah, that is what I meant!"

To be an effective tool of communication, words must have an agreed-upon meaning.

> *I believe that because of all the modern world's technological advances, we are experiencing a second Tower of Babel phenomenon.*

COMMUNICATION STRATEGIES FOR LEADING TEAMS[1]

T HE late Robert Hutchins, the longtime president of the University of Chicago and one of the great social thinkers, often spoke of Western society's goal as moving toward a "Civilization of the Dialogue." And it is true that civilized dialogue is essential if people with different styles and interests are to come together. But without attention to other people's styles and assumptions, you cannot have a productive conversation. The diverse perspectives that should be a source of strength and wisdom become debilitating.

Say you want to get a colleague's point of view on an important business issue. (E) types toss off solutions, some only tangentially related to the problem at hand. Ask them to outline a solution to a problem and they will probably lose interest. They are focused on the future, not on the present. As Ted Turner, a classic entrepreneur, once remarked, "All I remember is tomorrow."

(A) types, on the other hand, want more data. Administrators can find the holes and pitfalls in any proposal, but they can also get lost in minutiae.

(P)s often rush to judgment, just to be out of the meeting and back to producing. And integrators consider any decision reached without full consensus to be an unacceptable risk.

Conversations between any of these types can escalate into shouting matches or collapse in cold silence, in which not even the silence means the same thing to both parties: For (E)s, silence means agreement; for (A)s, disagreement—just the opposite!

To communicate effectively, first recognize your colleague's management and communications style. Then prepare for every important conversation

---

[1] Adizes Insights, February 2004; also published in *Leader to Leader* magazine, Winter 2004.

by tailoring your approach to your colleague. If you want to take advantage of the diverse perspectives of a team, it does no good to conduct a conversation entirely on your own terms. Rather, you must find ways to encourage your colleagues' contributions.

If you're proposing an idea to an entrepreneurial type (for instance, a VP of product development), focus on opportunities, not problems. If you'd like the support of an administrator (often an HR or finance chief), stress efficiencies that the proposal will bring. Also, gauge the optimal time for a conversation, allow plenty of time to hash out the details, keep the session within the time allotted, and bring a written agenda.

By contrast, for a producer (typically a sales or production VP), more than a 20-minute conversation is likely to be counterproductive; keep things short and to the point.

And to get the best response from an integrator, speak first to other stakeholders and then mention early in the meeting that you have talked it over and already have agreement on all the key issues. Just bear in mind that this is the *worst* approach to take with an entrepreneur.

Remember, to come to the best decision, you need an intellectually honest and open discussion with the person you are talking to. You will not get that unless you create an environment in which that person can be heard.

> Bad decisions <u>can</u> be made by consensus.

MANAGING GROUP DECISION-MAKING

In one-on-one conversations, you can tailor your communication style to your colleague's. In a group, however, many different styles and interests come into play.

That may not matter if the team is simply reviewing the status of a project or sitting through a PowerPoint presentation. But if you're setting a new course of action and want the shared wisdom and eventual buy-in of a diverse team—in short, if you need to come to a decision that will require change—it's another story. You must recognize the individual differences that lead one manager to push for quick answers and another to demand more data. Such differences, if ignored, are what make so many meetings so frustrating.

The answer, however, is not to run a meeting according to your own style, or that of any single type. Inevitably, someone will be misunderstood, and resentment, resistance, or confusion will result. Often, teams trying to avoid displays of anger or unpleasantness will descend into management by committee, an unfortunate situation in which people are more concerned with compromising with each other than with reaching the best result. Bad decisions *can* be made by consensus.

What's needed is a set of rules, a methodology that disciplines people to advance through the decision-making steps together—not in their own way, at their own pace. Those rules ensure that when a decision is reached, everyone involved is confident that his voice has been heard.

Leaders can improve the group decision-making process by recognizing the eight cognitive steps that everyone goes through in making a decision:

1) *Defreeze:* Step back and disengage from other concerns.
2) *Accumulate:* Gather your thoughts and reflect.
3) *Deliberate:* Recognize patterns and make sense of information.
4) *Incubate:* Sleep on what you have learned (or, as the Spanish say, "Consult your pillow").
5) *Illuminate:* Synthesize the big picture and see a solution—the "Aha!" moment.
6) *Accommodate:* Reconsider your second thoughts and doubts.
7) *Finalize:* Bite the bullet and decide, so that you can take action.
8) *Reinforce:* Seek reassurance that you've decided wisely.

Most of us can recognize these elements of the decision-making process from our own experience. In team decision-making, the trouble stems from the fact that no group moves through this process in lockstep. Some managers, typically (A) types, cannot easily move from accumulation to deliberation; they never have enough data. Meetings led by (A)s usually end just about where they started; nothing gets resolved easily. (There is, however, a request for more information.)

Other managers, for instance (E)s, get caught between the illumination and accommodation cycles; for every doubt that is raised about an idea, the (E) will offer a new idea and thus a different solution. You end up with many ideas but no decisions. And so on.

The lack of discipline in working and advancing together in making a decision has other manifestations in the conduct of the meeting, exemplified by people who arrive late, or interrupt others, or intimidate others for a quick solution.

Leaders can use several techniques to enhance team communication and effectiveness. For instance, to defreeze the group—that is, to help people leave other worries behind and openly engage in a question—ask them how they feel about the subject at hand. Acknowledge your own excitement or concern from the beginning.

When accumulating information, put aside discussions of how or why something occurred; just get the facts on the table.

During group deliberation, make sure everyone's observations have been aired; then ask people to look for patterns or relationships among the facts presented.

Likewise, to illuminate the best solutions, start by identifying every idea people have. Put aside, for the moment, concerns about expense or logistics. Address these in the accommodation stage.

PUTTING THE PIECES TOGETHER

Team decisions are unlikely to occur in a single meeting; the process may unfold over several weeks. The team leader may want a facilitator to help keep the conversation on track, and, in any case, will need to understand the highs and lows that people on the team are likely to encounter along the way. (A) types, for instance, often revert to the high of accumulating data to avoid the pain of deliberation. Likewise, (E)s seek quick illumination but dread the painful compromises of accommodation. (P)s hate the whole roller-coaster ride and want to finalize immediately.

> *Bringing together the interests of people across an enterprise is the essence of leadership.*

The key is to be sure that the team advances together, rather than allowing each team member to advance at his own speed, disregarding others and getting annoyed that others are not following. With these principles in mind, the leader should bring order and efficiency to meetings. Even more important, he must ensure that the management group arrives at decisions together, in a spirit of mutual trust and respect.

Even though everyone needs to participate in the decision-making, consensus is not mandatory. The final word belongs to the person in the room who has the authority to commit resources and is accountable for the decision. The purpose of the team decision-making process is to help that decision-maker to become as informed and knowledgeable as possible.

Senior executives can act with greater confidence and credibility by providing an open and transparent forum that allows and even encourages divergent points of view. When the participants walk through each step of each decision together, I have found that their ultimate decisions are more broadly supported and better implemented.

Bringing together the interests of people across an enterprise is the essence of leadership. Rather than seeking instant alignment after a decision is made, leaders should bring to the meeting those whose cooperation will be needed to implement the decision. When self-interests get unearthed up front, common interests can ultimately emerge. Resistance to change is dealt with before the change is announced.

For example, a $5 billion high-tech company used this approach in a successful turnaround. Seeing a steady erosion in its market share, the company convened several management teams to diagnose its problems and develop solutions. The changes involved a reorganization of the company and caused pain to many managers and staff. But ultimately it was supported by the key stakeholders, all of whom had a chance to join in a structured decision-making process with clear rules of conduct.

Decisions get implemented more easily when true alignment exists. That alignment comes from the interaction of people, values, structures, and processes *before* decisions are made, and those interactions are fruitful only when leaders seek out divergent views and complementary strengths.

Successful leaders know that they cannot be right on every decision all the time and forever. They need to seek out the wisdom and expertise of those around them whose styles complement their own. Such diverse teams hold the answers to gridlock and dysfunction. How leaders manage the team's interactions and communications can make the difference.

Insights from Linguistics, Part 1[1]

ON my recent trip to Russia to receive an honorary doctorate from the Academy of National Economy of the Russian Federation (following Stanley Fisher, who received it last year), I made a discovery that confirmed an illumination I had thirty years ago.

I have reported about that illumination in my tapes and in one of my books. Let me summarize it quickly, explain what experience generated it, and present to you what I recently learned about it in Russia.

Around 1972, I was lecturing in Monterrey, the economic powerhouse of Mexico, to their top industrial management. At that time, since I did not yet speak modern Spanish, I lectured in English via simultaneous translation.

I dislike using simultaneous translations. One reason is that I use jokes in my lectures, and occasionally, by the time the audience laughs (if they do at all), I am already on a different subject.

On that particular day, frustrated, I asked the audience if they would mind if I lectured in classical (or medieval) Spanish. How do I know classical Spanish? I am a descendent of the Spanish Jews who were expelled from Spain in 1492, during the Inquisition, because they refused to convert to Christianity. Those Jews, called Sephardim, spoke a form of medieval Spanish, called Ladino, at home and among themselves for hundreds of years. My grandmother did not know any other language but Ladino. So I learned to speak it from her. If you listen to it, it sounds like a mixture of Spanish, French, Portuguese, and Italian.

So there I was in Mexico with some of the most respected and powerful Mexican oligarchs, trying to deliver 20th-century material in 15th-century language. And guess what? Something very interesting happened.

---

[1] Adizes Insights, May 2007.

At a certain point in my lecture I noticed that the audience was not following what I was saying. So I asked them in 15th-century Spanish, in Ladino: "Did you hear me?" They replied that in modern Spanish, "to hear" is a completely different word. In modern Spanish, the word I had just used, *sentir*, means "to feel." I had asked them if they'd "felt" me when I'd meant to ask them if they'd heard me.

The word *sentir* also exists in other languages, with other meanings: in French it means "to smell"; in Italian, "to listen." Five hundred years ago, one word was used to signify all of them: "to hear," "to listen," "to feel," even "to smell." In effect, the word meant "to sense." In modern Spanish there are still remnants of various older meanings of the word *sentir*. When one is hard of hearing, Mexicans describe that as "*mal de sentido*," which is like saying "hard of *feeling*." And they call a one-way street "*un sentido*," as if to say "one-way feeling."

My illumination was that if one word had once had all these meanings, it must mean that back then, when one heard, one also listened and felt. In other words, one actually sensed what was going on.

MORE EVIDENCE OF DISINTEGRATION

Then, about ten years later, when I was consulting for the Greek government, someone told me that the same linguistic phenomenon exists in the Greek language. In Corfu, an island a bit isolated from the rest of Greece where people speak a somewhat more classical Greek, they, too, use one and the same word to mean "to hear," "to listen," and "to feel."

Now, in Russia, I have found that in Ukrainian, which is a Slavic language, the word *chut* means "to listen"; while in Russian and in Serbian (another Slavic language), it means "to hear."

Thus, it seems that my illumination of thirty years ago has been confirmed: Regardless of culture, land, or language, five hundred years ago people were apparently more "together": When they *heard*, they also *listened* and *felt* what was going on.

Modern man has different words for these different phenomena—which means that today it is possible to hear without listening, to listen without feeling, and even to hear *and* listen and *still* not feel what is going on. We are disconnecting.

How sad this is. We need psychotherapists to be our intermediaries, to help us feel what another person who is in pain is trying to tell us. We need to take courses on how to become more aware, and we have to pay to be trained to feel. We use words that indicate an increasing insensitivity, increasing distance from each other: "tune out," "turn off," "fade out."

An animal is more integrated than we are. For example, my dog: When I get home, he comes to smell me, and from the smell he knows how I feel; he senses whether to go to a corner and leave me alone or that I am ready to play and scratch his tummy.

Compare that to people, even those I am very close to: By the time they've listened to what they've heard—and then actually *felt* what I've said—I might have become too desperate to communicate anymore.

Are we falling apart? While we are technologically advancing, are we "losing it" as humans? Does development on one hand lead to disintegration on the other hand? Do centripetal forces necessarily give birth to centrifugal forces? Ironically, while the globe is becoming a big village, countries are breaking apart, and blind nationalism is pushing us further away from each other. Are centripetal and centrifugal forces operating at the same time? Is there a balanced, zero-sum game going on somewhere?

Does anyone else have examples of this phenomenon in their language? Whether yes or no, what is your reaction to this illumination?

> *Does development on one hand lead to disintegration on the other hand?*

WHY CERTAIN AUDIENCES ARE PASSIVE

Here is something else I learned from the Russian trip:

I lectured three times in Russia, and each time I had quite a distinguished audience: some leading business people, some academics, and some MBA students. There was, however, a common denominator at the three lectures, which were delivered in Moscow and St. Petersburg: The audiences were very quiet. I felt no energy from these audiences.

I usually get an audience excited. This time it was worse than it usually is in Sweden, or even Germany, where the audiences are also very passive. (The liveliest audiences are in Israel and China. For me, lecturing in Israel is always the most exhilarating but also the most exhausting experience. Nothing goes unchallenged.)

I was very surprised by the passivity of the Russian audiences. As people,

they are quite gregarious. What was going on? But when I shared my observations with the president of the Russian Management Association, he was
not at all surprised. He told me the following: In the Russian language, the
word for "I" (me) is *ya*, which is also the last letter of the Russian alphabet.
Russians discourage individualism, which they perceive as somebody
jumping ahead of others. So they sit quietly and listen to the "authority."

One of the goals of the Russian Management Association, its president
said, is to encourage individuals to step up, to challenge. In order for a
market economy to work, you need entrepreneurs who dare to challenge the
status quo and, in doing so, compete.

Was this collectivist behavior a remnant of the Communist era, when
people did not dare to challenge authority, or is it a much older attribute
of Russian culture? If it is the latter, that could explain why Communism
first took root in Russia, rather than England or Germany, where Karl Marx
developed the theory.

Hmmm. ...

SPEECHLESS

Here is another observation:

In some languages, certain words have no translation, which tells you
something: If the word does not exist in a particular language, perhaps the
speakers of that language do not recognize or appreciate the phenomenon
that the word signifies.

I have previously reported that the word "management" has no translation in any of the more than fifty countries I have lectured in so far. Except
for Hebrew, all the languages use the English word "management" because
their own languages have no literal translation.

Why is this happening? Is it because the managerial process as we know
it is a Western/American invention rather than an indigenous process that
the rest of the world recognizes as its own?

What do you think?

Here is another case: When one of my books was being translated into
Swedish, I got a call from an editor who told me that there is no Swedish
word for "entrepreneur." The editor wanted to use the word "creative"
instead. He added, however, that during the Middle Ages, a Swedish word
meaning "entrepreneur" actually did exist. How interesting this is. Since the

word died out over the years, could it mean that maybe the phenomenon also died?

In France, the word "entrepreneur" (which is a French word) is now used to describe a real estate developer. It is not a generic word signifying anyone who builds any business, as we use the word in English. It is possible that the French narrowed down the meaning of "entrepreneur" because the phenomenon of entrepreneurship is also dying in France—while the word "administration" is flourishing: There are dozens of schools for administration, but not one for entrepreneurship.

Can we further say that the decline in the use of the word *and* the practice of entrepreneurship might partially explain the economic woes of the French economy? I know this argument is a bit of a stretch, but what do you think?

> Today it is possible to hear without listening, to listen without feeling.

Another interesting finding from the trip: In modern Russian, there is no word for the concepts of either "accountability" or "privacy." How might this affect the development of market forces, competition, and managed entrepreneurship?

I also mentioned previously that not all languages have a translation for the English words "effectiveness" and "efficiency." Hebrew, for instance, has a word for "efficiency," but not for "effectiveness." They translate "effectiveness" as "purposeful," which might be acceptable to describe long-term effectiveness (to have a purpose *is* long-term effectiveness), but does not describe short-term effectiveness.

The fact of that missing word for short-term effectiveness explains a phenomenon that I've observed both in business and political meetings in Israel. The participants in these meetings can get very Talmudic: lots of arguments and vocal disagreements. But after a while you wonder: What are they disagreeing about? What is the agenda? They debate a lot and waste a lot of time, making their meetings not very effective. This would not happen in the United States, where the short-term focus is maintained and the meetings are effective and end with decisions.

In Sweden, too, the language is missing one of these words. I cannot remember whether it was "effectiveness" or "efficiency," but knowing their culture, I would bet that the absent word is probably "effectiveness." The Swedes are very organized and thus efficient—but effectiveness is not a strength.

Does anyone have other examples of words that exist in English but not in other languages; or words in a different language that do not exist in English?

Not Exactly 'Yes'

Take the Japanese word *hai*: It does not exist in English. It is often loosely translated as "yes." But many Americans doing business in Japan have gotten into trouble because of this translation: They believe that their Japanese counterpart, in saying "*hai*," has become fully committed to a plan or idea, when in reality that is far from being so.

Hai is translated as "yes" because that is as close as the translator can get in English, while in Japanese it means: "Yes, I hear you. Tell me more." It is not the real confirmative, binding commitment that "yes" means in English. In Japanese, *hai* is better translated as "I am not saying 'No.' Let us continue talking." The word *hai* reflects the Japanese cultural preference for non-confrontational negotiations, while for us in English, "yes" is yes and "no" is no. It's much more black and white.

There is so much to learn from traveling.

Insights from Linguistics, Part 2[1]

I N a lecture to the Young Presidents' Organization (YPO) in St. Moritz, Switzerland, I was lecturing about the indispensability of conflict created by change: Whenever there is change, necessarily there will be conflict— because we think differently about how to handle the opportunities and threats created by change; and also because our interests are impacted differently by those changes. That all means: conflict.

The way to make this inevitable conflict constructive rather than destructive is by creating a climate of mutual trust—to have faith in the long-term common interests of others—and also a climate of mutual respect—being willing to learn from others whose opinion is different from yours.

To create mutual respect, we need to surround ourselves with people from whom we can learn—not *in spite of* the fact that they think differently, but *because* they think differently. These people are called "colleagues." The word "colleague" comes from Latin: *co-,* which means "together" and *legare,* which means "to bequeath" or "to send as an emissary." Colleagues do not necessarily *start* together, but through listening to and learning from each other's opposing arguments, their opinions may ultimately find common ground.

In the audience at this particular lecture was the chief rabbi of the Swiss Jewish community, and as I looked at the rabbi I realized that in Hebrew, the word "colleague" (*amit*) comes from the same source as the word *imut*— "confrontation." To me, that means that there are no collegial relationships without confrontation, or conflict. Then, I realized that the word "truth" (*emet*) also comes from the same source.[2]

---

[1] Adizes Insights, June 2007.

[2] This point, however, has been challenged by a Hebrew linguist.

My interpretation is that, in Hebrew, since the source of the words is the same, a colleague is someone you are in conflict with, someone you do not agree with—*but*, through respectful discussions and disagreements (i.e., confrontation), you can arrive at the truth. Truth comes through confrontation, conflict: We can learn from our disagreements—*if* the conflict is handled with respect.

There is more to it, I think. Since the three words have the same root, I suggest that, at least in the Hebrew language, no one has a monopoly on *the Truth*. We have to confront each other and discuss in order to reach truth.

LINGUISTIC COMMON SENSE

That brings me to another insight, this time from Middle English.

What is the meaning of *"common* ground," *"common* wife," *"common* law," *"common* man," and *"common* sense"?

"Common" means "everyone." "Common grounds" are grounds everyone can walk on. "Common wife" means that everyone acknowledges she is your wife. By the same token, "common sense" means that everyone shares an attitude or opinion.

If someone is not allowed to walk in a certain area, then it is not common ground; if someone disagrees with an opinion or argument, then by definition it is not common sense.

I am always bothered by people who try to intimidate others during a discussion, yelling: "That's absurd; it defies common sense!" They are claiming a monopoly over what makes sense. In order to find out what constitutes common sense, you cannot close yourself up in your study and contemplate your navel; you have to go out to the street and look for people who disagree with your thoughts. That forces you to keep perfecting your argument until you arrive at common sense. This is called learning.

> We have to confront each other and discuss in order to reach truth.

That is how I have developed my management methodologies. I present my theories to everyone—top executives, workers on the line, even analphabets—and let them challenge my points. Then, based on their comments, I revise my arguments and let a new group challenge them—on and on, continually. After fifty-two countries and forty years of changing my mind and modifying my theories, I often get to a point where people listen and say (sometimes with a dismissive shrug), "Oh, but that's just common sense."

Here is another insight from analyzing the roots of Hebrew words:

Over the years I have tried hard to understand what mutual respect really means. In the Hebrew language, I found an answer.

In Hebrew, the words for "tolerance," "patience," and "pain" have exactly the same root: *SVL*. The only differences are the vowels: "Tolerance" is *SoVLanut*, "patience" is *SaVLanut*, and "pain" is *SeVeL*.

My interpretation: There is no respect without tolerance. How can you learn from someone who disagrees with you unless you can tolerate hearing, listening, and understanding her conflicting opinions? And how can you tolerate without patience? But to be patient and tolerant—to hear, listen, and feel something you do not agree with—is very painful.

So in the Adizes methodology, in order to change the organizational culture and develop mutual trust and respect, I have developed tools that help people handle the pain that comes with working and debating with people who do not agree with you. These tools teach you how to learn, and how to be patient and tolerant, which are all essential in changing a culture.

> How can you tolerate without patience?

And here is yet another insight from Hebrew:

HVH, as a root, means "present tense," or "now." But in Hebrew, when you put a *Y* in front of a verb, it means "in the future."

Now look at the consonants in the name of God: *YHVH*.

HVH means "present" and *Y* means "future." Put them together and you get "Make your future today."

When you add the vowels, you have *YeHoVaH*. The word *hova* means "it is an order," or "obligation." My insight is that if you were permitted to pronounce the name of God (which Jews are forbidden to do), you would be saying something along the lines of: "Stop living in the future. Make that future be today. That is an order."

KNOWING WHEN
NOT TO SPEAK[1]

RECENTLY I was asked to say a few words at the retirement party for Dan Maydan, president of Applied Materials in Silicon Valley, California. Applied Materials has been a client for more than ten years. Here is what I said:

What comes to my mind, as I think about my long acquaintance with Dan, is his unique wisdom as a leader.

It has been my privilege to coach and consult to companies throughout the world for more than forty years. In doing so, I have met and worked with many top executives and even prime ministers and presidents of nations. Once in a while, I come across an executive we all can learn from. Dan Maydan stands out in that crowd.

When Dan started leading the company, it had only $40 million in sales; when I came to consult to Dan and the company almost twelve years ago, it had $400 million in sales. By 2000, at its peak, the company had grown to over $10 billion in sales.

What was the leadership style that led to such growth?

LISTENING INSTEAD OF TALKING

Let me tell you why Dan stands out and what we can learn from him.

I have met many outstanding executives who know how to speak well. But there are very few who know how *not* to speak.

Sitting in meetings with him, I have noticed that although Dan is chairing the meeting, he almost never leads the discussion. He simply lets the meeting take place, allowing anyone to speak as they will. He sits quietly and seems to be dozing.

---

[1] Adizes Insights, September 2005.

If you did not know him well, you might believe the guy had retired on the job. But if the discussion takes a wrong turn, he perks up—and suddenly you've got the distinct feeling you've just touched a hot stove. He informs everyone in the most assertive and articulate terms why it is the wrong direction and what the direction should be—and then he retreats back into silence and lets the discussion proceed.

Working with him, I learned how to interpret his silence: As long as he is quiet, the meeting is going well.

Why this style is functional becomes clear when you understand the other characteristic of Dan's managerial style: Dan's calendar is almost always empty. Whenever anyone asks to see him, the answer is, "Come in now!"—not in two months' time. And he has all the time in the world for you. He is never hurried.

Again: He listens carefully and does not give you a solution. "What do you think we should do?" is his usual question, and if the answer is a good one he says, "Great! A wonderful idea! Why don't you go ahead and do that?" If it is a bad idea or a bad analysis of the problem, he will tell you why, but again without giving you a solution. He'll send you back to think some more until you have the right solution.

VISION AND DIRECTION

The common denominator in both aspects of Dan's managerial style is this: He never tells people what, specifically, to do, or how to do it.

He provides the vision and the direction, and from there he lets people figure out for themselves what to do. As people articulate their decisions, he listens intently, only getting involved when he feels that what they want to do is inappropriate or misdirected.

Thus, his focus is on constantly articulating the company's vision—by setting direction and then monitoring people to ensure they do not deviate from it in their decisions. When they do, he explains the problem clearly so they can learn.

This has several advantages. One: It stimulates creativity. Executives have to think, not just carry out orders. And when they are corrected, they learn why their plan or idea had inherent problems they hadn't considered or did not even know existed.

That is true coaching. People learn nothing from just following orders.

People learn when *they* decide what to do, having done their best in making that decision, and when someone else who knows better shows them, if necessary, where the faults are.

The second advantage is that it is obvious that Dan is respectful of those reporting to him. He values what people think, and if what they want to do makes sense to him, he enthusiastically supports them. A leader who always tells his subordinates what to do is insinuating that those subordinates cannot think, and that he alone can make the right decisions. Since Dan supports the decisions his people arrive at, they leave his office filled with energy and ready to implement the plan. They own the decision fully. They feel respected and accountable—and they have learned a lot already.

The third advantage to Dan's style is that it takes far less time to correct wrong ideas, which happens only periodically, than to solve every problem in detail and then supervise its execution.

That is why he always has time. Why his calendar is empty. Why he has time to listen. And in listening, he learns a lot—both about the company's problems and about the quality of the people reporting to him.

What does it take to have such a style?

There is no question that Dan has an ego. How could he have become a president and built a $10 billion company from scratch without an ego? But unlike others, he knows how to control his ego and how to nourish the egos of others: how to build people up. And he has succeeded. Many of his former employees in attendance at this retirement party are now CEOs or presidents of their own companies. You might say that Applied Materials, under Dan's leadership, was the best experiential school for CEOs.

One more characteristic of Dan's style is worth mentioning.

For most people who are busy building a global company, time is at a premium; a complaint I hear almost universally is that there is no time for personal life, for family.

Watching Dan work, I was impressed by how well he balanced work with family: his absolute dedication to his late wife, Dalia, may her memory be blessed; his children and grandchildren; his community; and to his own good health and exercise.

It takes just this kind of balance in life, together with a controlled ego, to build a successful family and successful executives—which are the true assets of any company and any conscious person.

IS THERE A PROBLEM WITH OBAMA'S MANAGERIAL STYLE?[1]

YES, as a matter of fact: He talks too much!

Words don't always have the same "weight." How seriously they are taken depends on who speaks them.

Let me give you an example from my consulting experience—and this was not even a word, just a gesture! It was in Mexico. The company was owned by an old, very aristocratic and autocratic "don." During my work with a group of the company's leaders, I noticed that the discussion suddenly died, and I could not figure out what had caused it to end so abruptly. During a break, I asked the vice presidents who were at the meeting, "What happened?"

"No use discussing it," they said. "He [the don] has already decided against it. Did you not see how he moved his head left and right, even a bit annoyed? It is no use talking anymore."

I went to the don and asked him why he was so adamantly against the proposal we were discussing.

"I am not at all against it," he said, surprised.

"So why did you shake your head left to right, annoyed?" I asked.

"There was a fly trying to land on my nose." he replied.

THE DANGER OF OVER-ANALYSIS

If this had happened to a third-level administrator, she could have shaken her head as much as she wanted. No one would have paid any attention. No matter how strenuously she objected to what was being proposed, she would have been, if not utterly ignored, at least disregarded.

The higher up you are in the hierarchy, the more seriously your words and

---

[1] Adizes Insights, August 2009.

body language are taken. Many executives whom I coach do not understand this. They talk too much. What worked for them as junior executives
becomes a major problem when they ascend to the top of the organization.

My prescription is this: The higher up the organizational ladder you
climb, the bigger your ears should be and the smaller your mouth should be.

President Obama has big ears all right, literally and figuratively. He
listens, but he also talks too much. Says too much. So far, his eloquence and
charisma have saved him, but the day is coming when he will make a blunder
he can't fix. He will later try to explain that what he said was not what he
meant, but it will be one explanation too many: His charisma will evaporate,
and his eloquence will be rechristened as "just big-mouth, hot-air Obama."

He says too much, too often, too freely, and on too many subjects. An
example of this tendency was his comment on the arrest of Harvard Professor
Henry Louis Gates. Gates was arrested for disorderly conduct in front of
his Cambridge, Massachusetts, home when he refused to identify himself
to police who were investigating a possible break-in. Obama, who initially
remarked that the police had "acted stupidly," later backed off, saying he
"could have calibrated those words differently"—although he stopped short
of an official apology.

"No-drama Obama" was the wonderful expression used to describe his
style while he was running for President. The style he needs to practice now
is "Shut up, Obama": Because he is the President, every word he speaks is a
potential black hole that can swallow up his credibility in no time.

WHY POLITICIANS LIE
OR TELL HALF-TRUTHS[1]

DURING my career, I have worked with eight prime ministers and many, many CEOs of very large corporations all across the world. I have observed an interesting similarity in their styles, in the sense that they all keep their cards very close to the vest. They make you feel as if they agree with you, only for you to find out later that the opposite is true. You discover that the impression you had of reaching an agreement was not reflected in their actions in the field.

Some CEOs of large corporations act like politicians, akin to top leaders of the executive branch of government.

Why do they keep their agendas close to the vest? Why do we find that both groups use half-truths? Why do they appear to agree when, in fact, they disagree?

Here is my insight: As you climb higher up in the corporate hierarchy, the importance of your role as an integrator becomes greater. You are not in charge of sales, or product development, or finance, etc.; you have others doing those jobs for you. You do not have to do strategic planning, because even that is delegated, sometimes. So what is your role as CEO of a large company? Your role is to integrate.

What does that mean?

Your stakeholders, your top management, and other groups all have competing points of view and interests. So as an integrator, you must maneuver and try to listen in order to find the most appealing solutions to all the different political power bases. Then you must focus on implementation.

This is politics—exactly what prime ministers of democratic countries must do.

---

[1] Adizes Insights, July 2009.

In both cases, political maneuvering requires employing "big ears and a small mouth." You have to be able to listen, not only to what is being said, but also to what is *not* being said. And you have to be very careful what *you* say, because what will appease one constituency might alienate another.

Thus, speaking in half-truths is part of the job if you are going to be a successful leader of a large, complex system. To be politically astute, or to know how to maneuver, sometimes means keeping your thoughts to yourself. You have to make everyone feel that his voice is being heard, without seeming to commit yourself to one voice at the expense of another.

It reminds me of how parents behave with children. You do not explain too much to them. You do not get into arguments with your kids. Your agenda is your business, and it is up to you how to "sell" them on your decisions.

So, are people like children and our leaders like parents?

There is a similarity. Like children, who want parents they can trust, we want leaders we can trust, and that means that we want them to be open and transparent to us.

But I suggest to you that in the complex world we live in, this is a utopian expectation. It cannot and will not happen.

Judge Actions, Not Words

It is time to stop being childish and realize the complexity of the situations our leaders have to deal with, and accept their close-to-the-vest behavior as normal and expected. We should not judge them by what they say or have said, but by what they do.

In my coaching of top executives, I tell them: "If you are not politically competent, or if you do not know how to please people and still maintain your course, then you cannot climb up the hierarchy of large corporations." That is the reality.

> You have to be very careful what you say, because what will appease one constituency might alienate another.

An executive vice president who was a candidate to become the CEO once told me, "I hate politics. I told the board point-blank that if I become the CEO, I will fire the VPs for marketing, sales, and new product development."

There was no chance the board would let him do that, but he wanted to be totally honest and disclose his agenda.

Guess what? He did not get the job and, to my mind, the board was right. He would have created havoc in the company. He would have been, politically speaking, a bull in a china shop.

The higher you climb in an organization's hierarchy, the smarter you have to be politically, and that means, yes, not disclosing everything you intend to do. You must learn to keep your cards hidden and accept the fact that you will be criticized for lying, because what you *say* you will do is not always what you *will* do.

That is the nature of the beast, and we'd better grow up and realize that it won't change, no matter whom we elect.

PART 7

MANAGEMENT EDUCATION

WHAT IS WRONG WITH MANAGEMENT THEORY?[1]

WHAT would you think if you read about an animal—say a tiger or a wolf—that kills and devours its prey, but then goes on hunting and killing even after its appetite is sated?

You would say such a creature was not normal, that its behavior was unnatural. You would worry that this animal might kill everything alive in the prairie, leaving nothing for the future. You would try to find it and kill it. Right?

Many managers of companies behave just like that animal does: No matter how much they produce and how many resources they use, they want more. And more. They roam dangerously, without restraint, over the economic prairie.

When I read the advice of current management gurus, I notice that they think the same way: Regardless of where you have arrived or what you have already achieved, you must always be looking toward the next goal. Keep running. Keep going. If you are at the very peak of the mountain, then you must pick another mountain with an even higher peak to climb next. There is always another goal, and it is always bigger or higher.

And there we go, building and creating far beyond our actual needs. In order to sell more and more, we try to create "needs" that our clients do not even know they have. "More, more," is the motto of business. That means using more and more resources and, in the process, destroying the prairie.

It was not always like this. If you look at so-called "primitive" societies, they behave in a more natural way: They kill to eat, and no more. They cultivate the land to grow as much as they need, and no more. The rest of the time, they celebrate and associate. We "modern" men work more and more

---

[1] Adizes Insights, February 2008.

and accumulate more and more, as if the more we have the better we are. We fail to realize that, accumulatively, more is less: Today, for example, there are fewer animal species alive than even last year. Many are disappearing. And so it goes for flowers and trees, too. We *seem* to have more, but in essence we have less.

What Does It Mean?

That we need to rethink our goals.

There are two types of goals: deterministic goals, which usually are quantitative—the more (or less), the better—and constraint goals, which are conditions we do not want to violate—and not to violate them is a goal in itself.

A constraint goal does not regard "more" as better, or "less" as better. You might define a constraint goal as: "Reach this number [a certain blood pressure, for example]—and stick to it."

Profit should be a constraint goal, not a deterministic goal: In other words, as long as we keep within our self-imposed boundaries, we are satisfied.

Then what should our deterministic goal be? To serve humanity without doing harm. In some professions, that already *is* the goal: Think of the medical profession's Hippocratic Oath, which says, in essence, "First, do no harm."

Would you go to a doctor whose goal was to maximize her income? She might kill you by over-prescribing and under-serving. A physician's job is to provide the best medical care she can provide. *Adequate* profit, not *maximum* profit, should be the secondary goal. That is being professional.

In contrast, management schools and their high priests are teaching people to become not professionals but wild animals with one goal in mind: to kill more prey than anybody else.

It is time to change management theory and its measurement of success—before we completely destroy the prairie we live in.

HOW TO DEVELOP
ENTREPRENEURSHIP[1]

In 2007, I attended the Central and East European Management Development Association (CEEMAN) annual convention. One of the topics discussed was how to develop entrepreneurship. Here is what I had to say:

S CHOOLS of management are preoccupied with the subject of entrepreneurship, because the entrepreneurial spirit acts as the foundation for effective leadership. Without entrepreneurship, management schools can only train staff people or bureaucrats; they are training employees instead of employers.

I suggest to you that entrepreneurship is not a problem of developing nations. They have plenty of entrepreneurs. When people in developing regions are provided with opportunity, they will likely start a business. For example, the streets are full of peddlers, who exhibit entrepreneurial spirit; and some people, when denied the opportunity to express it in the open market, will turn their focus to the black market instead.

This entrepreneurial spirit is prominent among developing nations because there is no work, and it becomes essential to come up with something to do in order to survive. In order to get out of the slums, creativity and the willingness to take risks are encouraged from a young age.

I believe that the development of entrepreneurial people is a problem for *developed* countries.

Why?

I suggest to you that a certain part of the entrepreneurial spirit is a genetic characteristic, like a talent for music or sports. To me, to develop an entrepreneur is not to create him from scratch. It is, rather, to take his innate

---

[1] Adizes Insights, December 2008.

talent and help him learn how to use his talent effectively, without killing that talent in the process.

Take, for example, the training of artists. Sending highly talented painters to art school can actually be detrimental to their innovative artistic output. They might lose their courage to be different. Something similar can happen to young entrepreneurs who attend business schools in developed countries. There, they learn many rules, theories, and case studies of failed companies, any or all of which can promote risk-aversion. After graduation, they prefer to look for a well-paying job rather than start a business.

Consider the Internet and digital technology as illustrations. The leading companies, like Google, Dell, and Apple, were not established by MBAs, but by some geeks working out of their garages without the "benefit" of any business education.

If a business school student is creative, which is a component of being entrepreneurial, he will go into consulting or investment banking. But very few business school graduates start their own companies. Starting a business requires a certain level of romanticism and naïveté; it requires not knowing too much about how difficult the process will be.

WHY DO ENTREPRENEURS IMMIGRATE TO DEVELOPED NATIONS?

So, in developed countries, where do the entrepreneurs come from? Many come from the developing countries where this talent, as I said, is ample.

But why do they come?

Entrepreneurs from developing countries do their best to immigrate to a developed country, like the United States, because they are looking for the infrastructure and business environment necessary for success: The capital markets work, the judiciary system works, telecommunications and transportation work, and there are large pools of qualified people from which to hire employees. Conversely, the environment of an immigrant's country of origin—typically an emerging economy—commonly lacks an advanced infrastructure.

Additionally, the business environment in developing countries is not supportive. For example, in market economies, everything is permitted unless specifically prohibited. It is the opposite in countries in transition, where the dictatorial climate of the past still lingers. There, everything is prohibited unless specifically permitted, and getting those permits takes time, connections, and often bribery. Furthermore, in capitalist societies, government traditionally stays out of business endeavors and does not compete with private enterprise. In the mixed economies of emerging countries, where the role of government is not as well defined, if there is economic opportunity in the marketplace, the government *will* compete with private enterprise.

Thus, I suggest to you that schools of business in emerging economies need not worry about how to develop entrepreneurial people. They should worry more about how not to undermine the existing entrepreneurial spirit, with ineffective or stifling education, programs they copy from developed countries. What emerging economies need is a supportive infrastructure: a banking system that works, a judicial system that is not corrupt, an educated labor force, and a supportive government that encourages rather than competes.

> Starting a business requires a certain level of romanticism and naïveté; it requires not knowing too much about how difficult the process will be.

Developed countries, on the other hand, have a great infrastructure but dying entrepreneurial spirit and often import it from abroad. (I wonder if there are statistics on what percentages of today's American entrepreneurs are immigrants. I suggest it is high.) If developed countries want to stimulate the entrepreneurial spirit, their management education system should be less structured and more experiential.

Developed and developing countries have different needs and thus should have different solutions for advancing and nurturing entrepreneurship. But in both developing and developed countries, entrepreneurship is essential for leadership and economic success.

BUSINESS SCHOOL LEADERSHIP IN TIMES OF CRISIS: WHAT CEEMAN CAN DO[1]

I have been asked to talk about how business schools, and specifically those in CEEMAN (the Central and East European Management Development Association), should react to the current crisis.

Let me start with a story.

When I was a kid, my mother would tell me not to go outside in the wind after a hot shower, because I would catch a cold. I wondered why I would catch a cold after a shower, when people in Finland—and I hear the same is true in Latvia—like to sit in a sauna and sweat, and then jump into cold water. They do not catch pneumonia. They do not die. Rather, they feel invigorated.

Why do *I* get a cold just by sticking my nose out the window, whereas another person can roll in the snow and feel invigorated?

What is the difference between them and me? What is going on?

It is not the cold, or the wind, or the air-conditioning, that makes me sick. It is my body, which is not capable of dealing with change; if it was, I could jump from a sauna into cold water and even enjoy it.

We usually try to see a problem as something *out there* that is giving us trouble and causing a crisis. But the truth is that the problem is in *here*, within us. When you are healthy and used to change, change is invigorating. But if your immune system is weak, a change will get you into trouble.

Not every person, company, or country necessarily has problems in times of change. It depends on how healthy the system is. Now, what does "healthy" mean? What does it mean to be a healthy organization or a healthy country?

---

[1] Keynote presentation before the Central and East European Management Development Association (CEEMAN) annual conference, in Riga, Latvia, on September 23, 2009.

The system is healthy when it can deal with change without falling apart. And what makes a system healthy or unhealthy?

With Change, Systems Fall Apart

Change causes disintegration because all systems are composed of sub-systems, and sub-systems do not change at the same speed. Inconsistent change causes disintegration, which is manifested in what we call problems.

And, if all problems stem from disintegration caused by change, what is the antidote?

Integration!

When a person is in serious trouble, we say she is "falling apart." A family or a country can also fall apart.

When a person is in prime condition, we say, "This guy has it together." We also say that a country "has it together."

When you are integrated, you are "together." But what does being "together" mean? Are modern companies "together"?

Based on many years of experience with companies worldwide, my answer is: No, they are not. And that is why many companies got into trouble when faced with the current financial crisis.

What has "fallen apart"?

Owner/Manager Disintegration

The capitalist system is based on the presumption that capital produces value. You invest money, and your money will work for you. You yourself do not have to labor.

But since you rely on your capital to maintain your well-being, it is normal to want to control what your capital is doing.

At the dawn of capitalism, owners *did* control their capital. Owners were usually the managers of the companies in which their capital was invested.

In modern capitalism, ownership is separated from management. You buy shares of stock, and someone else manages the company for you.

This bifurcation, created by the stock market, is credited with the creation of tremendous wealth. However, it has also produced side effects, including disintegration: Owners have lost control of the companies that use their capital.

So who controls the company—you, the stockholder? No. If you do not like the way the company is being run, you can sell your stock—but that is *all* you can do.

What about the boards of directors? Don't they represent the owners and supervise management?

Granted, boards of directors are *supposed to* represent the owners and *supposed to* supervise management. But do you really think that boards of directors know what is happening in the company? They do not. How can they know what is going on in a company that employs 20,000 people? All they really know is what they can learn by reading the company's financial statements.

But it is not only the board that is detached. Even chief executive officers can be very detached from the day-to-day reality of a company. There is "management by walking around," but just try to walk around a multinational company and meet the employees. It can't be done, can it?

Don't managers and boards know what is going on from the reports they get, from the financial statements? No. Financial statements should and do tell you something about the condition of the company, but by the time you find out there is a problem, it is too late to prevent it.

Do you know what's wrong with managing *by* reports? It is management of outputs rather than inputs.

Allow me to explain, with a joke, why that is a problem.

At an international medical convention when the Soviet Union was under Stalin's regime, the South African representative stood up and said, "We transplanted a heart." There was applause. Then the French representative announced, "We transplanted lungs." Applause. Then the Soviet representative stood up and proudly declared, "We extracted a tooth." Silence. The audience was bewildered. During the break, people asked him, "What do you mean, you extracted a tooth?" The Soviet representative explained: "Oh. You do not understand. It was a major achievement. We extracted a tooth through the rectum, because nobody dares to open his mouth."

Managing by financial reports is managing from the wrong end. What should be managed are not numbers but people and their interactions, which ultimately produce the numbers in those reports.

Management/Worker Disintegration

The first disintegration is ownership from management. But there is another disintegration: Management has become detached from the workers.

When companies were small, owner/managers knew every worker. They had to take care of them because they depended on the workers as much as the workers depended on the owners. Owner/managers also had their names on the door, and took responsibility for and pride in how their companies treated the communities in which they operated.

Now the companies are behemoth, spread all over the globe. Employees are a name on an employment list and a statistic under "labor costs" in the P&L report.

What many do not realize is that employees are an *asset*, not just an expense.

Do you know who knows the company—its problems and uncapitalized opportunities—the best? The employees. They can tell you what is going on in the company better than anybody else.

But does management listen to them? There are suggestion boxes, but they usually collect cigarette butts. There are open-door policies, but how many workers have you seen walk through the open doors of the president's office to talk to her?

So what are we talking about? We are talking about a flat-Earth theory—except in this case the earth is not horizontal; it's vertical. Energy flows only from the top to the bottom, and that is it. It is management by reports. It is management by elitist managers who are not listening to the people they manage.

Management Disintegration

There is disintegration *among* managers, too.

In a typical executive committee session, the lights are dimmed and a PowerPoint presentation appears on the screen. You see a succession of tables and charts. Tables and charts, graphs and tables. And how much open sharing and discussion is there? How much time and energy do managers spend to nurture transparency, openness, and integrity among their subordinates? A very small percentage of their time is spent with that purpose in mind.

Is there teamwork? No. And how easy is it to make changes in a company where the people are interdependent but non-cooperative?

To achieve change, which is essential for successful management of any company, you need an organization that can change easily. For that, the organization needs teamwork: cooperation, and mutual trust and respect. Managers need to talk more, share more, be more open with each other, and support each other more. But management is too busy watching PowerPoint presentations. ...

The Solution

If the cause of all problems is disintegration, it follows that the antidote is integration. We need to manage the integration both horizontally and vertically. We need to manage togetherness.

But we do not teach future business leaders that, do we? Business schools are proud of their computer labs. They teach their students to sit in front of a computer, analyze data, write reports, and know how to present them well. But do they teach people how to work with each other? No! *We are training autistic managers!* Maybe they should call themselves "schools for autistic management."

> Do [business schools] teach people how to work with each other? No! ... Maybe they should call themselves "schools for autistic management."

A manager once said to me, "Dr. Adizes, I like to manage; it is people I can't stand." What did he think he was managing? Oh, yes: the financial reports.

Successful Leadership Training

Management is about working with people. *That* is what we have to teach. Instead, we are training people who will eventually become consultants and investment bankers, people who know how to analyze reports and make presentations. We are not training leaders of change.

Even when we try to teach leadership, what do we teach? To *know* Maslow's hierarchy of needs? That is fine, but it is not even remotely the extent of what our future leaders need to *experience* if they are going to lead.

So how should we train leaders?

Put the students in a room and give them an assignment in which there is a conflict. Teach them how to resolve it. Teach them how a leader *behaves*.

And how *does* a leader behave? He makes his mouth small and his ears big, not the other way around. A leader is a thumb. What does a thumb do? It works with all the *different* fingers to create a hand. A leader knows how to integrate diversity of opinions and styles, how to help people disagree without being disagreeable. A leader is capable of building and nurturing a culture of mutual trust and respect—a culture in which people are not afraid to speak their minds.

Without a thumb, you will not have a hand. Without a leader, there is no teamwork—and without teamwork, the cart will continue to be stuck in the mud.

Let me share with you an excerpt from an article in the August 17, 2009, issue of the *Financial Times*, called "The Capital Gained from Culture":[2]

> Gordon Nixon makes a point of escaping Canada's frigid winter each January for a Caribbean cruise. But the excursion is more work than pleasure for Royal Bank of Canada's chief executive. His 700 fellow passengers are RBC tellers, administrative staff, junior employees, and middle managers who are being rewarded for superior performance.
>
> Mr. Nixon joins the cruises to put into practice the teamwork and mutual respect he has tried to foster among RBC's employees. …
>
> As he sees it, that culture has played a crucial role in RBC's ability—rivaled by only a handful of other large banks—to ride out the storms that have battered the financial services industry during the past two years.

Organizations are like fish tanks. Unless you supply them with oxygen, from the top to the bottom of the tank, the fish will die.

Quo Vadis CEEMAN?

We have to change what and how we teach. When Professor Danica Purg founded CEEMAN, she said to the leading business schools of the West: "Give us the best and keep the rest."

---

[2] "Capital Gained from Culture," by Bernard Simon; *Financial Times*, August 16, 2009.

You have borrowed too much. You have copied the flat-Earth theory of management. That is wrong. Clean the dust off the books on industrial democracy. It is time to revive this old idea. Teach future leadership to listen to the workers and to each other, to manage more by pride of teamwork and less by worshiping numbers. We have to be "together." Integration is the secret of a healthy organization, and that is how we will turn a crisis into an opportunity and succeed in the future, and leave those who are fighting among themselves to catch the cold.

Thank you and God bless.

THE MANY-HEADED HYDRA; OR, THE CRISIS OF 2008-2010[1]

*F*OLLOWING *Dr. Ichak Adizes' keynote speech to the 17th annual CEEMAN Convention, International Management Teachers Academy (IMTA) Managing Director Milenko Gudic spoke with him about the world financial crisis.*

MILENKO GUDIC: *The first sentence of your latest book,* How to Manage in Times of Crisis,[2] *reads: "Right now, in 2009, the world is in a deep financial crisis." The rest of the book, however, offers strong arguments that the crisis is not only financial, but also economic, institutional, social, moral, and ethical. It would be interesting if you could elaborate a bit more on the nature of the current global crisis, particularly its main causes and its repercussions, as well as whether or not this crisis is different from those the world has experienced in the past.*

ICHAK ADIZES: There is more to it than a financial crisis. The financial crisis will pass, but, as I say in my book, since the causes have not been addressed—and cannot be addressed until we change our values—there will be more financial and economic crises in the future. And they will be worse.

Already we have social, ecological, and political crises, too. The cause common to all of them is change. What is feeding the rate of change is technology in the widest sense of the word: hardware, software, and knowledge, as they apply to all disciplines, from medicine to art.

More scientists are alive today than accumulatively throughout the history of mankind. And no one can, or should, stop innovation. But we do

---

[1] This interview was conducted at the 17th annual CEEMAN (Central and East European Management Association) conference in Riga, Latvia, September 24–26, 2009 and was published in CEEMAN News 53 (www.ceeman.org). Reprinted with permission.

[2] Santa Barbara, CA: Adizes Institute Publications, 2009.

not know how to manage constructively, or even survive, when the rate of change is so rapid.

Our values are in a spin: When does life start? When does it end? What do the boundaries of countries mean when TV and radio, as well as air and water pollution, do not respect them? How should we raise children, now that they mature so much faster than past generations?

Because the rate of change is accelerating, the crises are erupting faster and becoming increasingly acute.

The capitalist system needs to be re-engineered, just as it was back in the 1930s. But this time the solution has to be different—not more government or less government. The system needs a paradigm shift in the relationship among government, labor, and capital.

We need to teach future generations how to manage change constructively—starting in kindergarten! Business schools should stop being business schools and become schools of leadership. They should teach students how to lead change successfully, effectively, and efficiently, without causing destructive conflict.

We have not done that.

Q: *As the world changes more and more rapidly, the tendency toward disintegration will match that pace. Consequently, reintegration efforts will need to be made more frequently and more proactively.*

You suggest that each of the four sub-systems[3] be integrated internally, then more or less synchronized with the changing environment and with each other. That's easy to say, much more challenging to do.

What are the main leadership challenges related to achieving integration in each of the four sub-systems and ensuring that the synchronization lasts longer and is more sustainable?

A: There is a major difference between how one behaves on solid land and how one behaves when scuba diving. On solid land you can be inactive and then you can change direction. In contrast, when you are scuba diving, if you stop moving, you will start to sink. You need to make small but nevertheless continuous moves.

---

[3] The four sub-systems referred to here are the teleological (vision and values); the structure of responsibilities; the structure of authority, power, and influence; and the reinforcement sub-system. For more information, see Ichak Adizes, *How to Manage in Times of Crisis (and How to Avoid the Crisis in the First Place)*, (Santa Barbara CA: Adizes Institute Publications, 2009).

I am using this analogy to explain that businesses behave today as if they are on solid land: Every three years or so they introduce a major re-engineering effort. (Those that don't even do that much usually age and die.) But making major strategic changes periodically is disruptive and often prohibitive.

Instead, we need to teach and practice *continuous* change that parallels the continuous change "out there."

What does that mean?

In a company, a person's responsibilities can, and do, change whenever needed. In companies that practice the Adizes methodology, an employee can keep the same title, salary, and fringe benefits, while the structure around him is deliberately fluid: In one phase he may have a supervisor who will become his subordinate in the next phase. And the reporting hierarchy could reverse again as necessary. A fluid structure requires absolute team-work, openness, and transparency; otherwise it will not work.

Integration is continuous because change is continuous. Companies need small, continuous changes. Not big periodic changes.

Q: The current crisis is also a leadership crisis. In the prologue to your book, you quote Albert Einstein saying: "The true crisis is the crisis of incompetence." To what extent are business schools responsible for what seems to have been, in retrospect, incompetent leadership in anticipating the crisis and in acting proactively to prevent it?

> We do not know how to manage constructively, or even survive, when the rate of change is so rapid.

A: My observation is that business schools, or management schools, do not teach management at all. Almost exclusively, they teach sub-system disciplines: accounting, finance, marketing, human resources, operations, etc. General management might as well not exist. Some schools teach strategic planning or organizational behavior and claim that these represent overall management. But, again, they are teaching only a single part of the total field. It is a partial solution claiming to be a total solution.

I have not found any school where integrative disciplines are taught, such as how to manage the totality, how to change without falling apart, without disintegrating.

During Peter Drucker's time, these disciplines were discussed. But academia dismissed him as not being scientific enough. Over time, the research methodologies of the natural sciences have colonized the social sciences, including business schools. As a result, young faculty members can no longer get ahead by writing about the art of management. Nor are there peer review magazines where faculty can publish material that lacks tables, statistics, or mathematical rigor.

We teach the head, but very little about the heart. We do not teach wisdom, the *philosophy* of what it takes to manage. We are training staff people, consultants, to know how to write great reports. But do we teach, experientially, how to lead? We do not.

> Business schools are like museums, telling people what has been done, rather than art studios, where students can explore and push the envelope of knowledge.

Q: *Business schools teach others about managing and leading change, but there is growing criticism that they themselves are rather conservative, adhering to the success factors of the past. How would you describe the current "disintegration" in management education, and what do you think business schools should change and/or innovate within their own sub-systems to make them better synchronized with each other?*

A: Imagine a medical school without an attached hospital in which students could intern and practice. And in this medical school there is no basic research, either. All they do is analyze what is already being practiced in the field. It would be a pretty bad school, right?

But that is what is happening in business schools. The research goal is to find out what the field is actually doing, without developing new protocols and experiences.

To me, business schools are like museums, telling people what has been done, rather than art studios, where students can explore and push the envelope of knowledge.

Show me a business school that has developed a new theory and experience, a new management protocol. There are very, very few, and what they develop is infrequently tested; nevertheless it gets promoted as if it had descended from Mount Sinai with Moses and the tablets.

Our graduates know books and cases by heart but have never experienced the problems of implementing the strategies they learned. They are like doctors who study medicine by learning chemistry, biology, anatomy, and pharmacology from textbooks, but have never touched a patient or had blood on their hands.

Q: *If a crisis is a disaster for the weak, but an opportunity for the strong, how would you position schools in transition and emerging economies, whose experience and tradition lag behind those from established economies? What could be the major sources of their strengths and how would you exploit them?*

A: First, free yourself from feeling inferior to the so-called "leading" schools. They are prisoners of their past.

Skip Harvard. Do not try to copy its success, because it might not apply to you. Develop your own theory and practice. Build a program that makes sense to you. Let them come to study *you* now.

Build a school with an attached consulting center. Require all faculty members to do consulting, thus testing what they preach. Create a journal where they can publish their research, applied and tested by others, as medical journals do.

Walk your talk. Be a leader and not a follower.

And that is just the beginning.

WHEN ARE 'BAD' MANAGERS GOOD, AND VICE VERSA?[1]

I once had a client whose style was very aggressive; I believe that those who study or teach behavioral sciences would have considered it "inhumane."

He fired people left and right for the least transgression, or if their work did not meet his highest standards—which, let me tell you, were exceedingly high.

He demeaned, screamed, and criticized continually. People really feared him.

Another client, this time in Russia, would financially penalize any employee who did not return his calls within fifteen minutes. God forbid that any written rules were violated; all hell would break loose.

I was very unhappy with both their styles and told them so, in unequivocal terms.

But after some time, I checked what was happening to the employees of these companies, and I noticed something interesting that I had not anticipated.

No one had left the company. Those who were not there anymore were the ones who had been fired. Those who stayed worked hard, liked the boss, and would do whatever they were asked to avoid being fired.

STOCKHOLM SYNDROME, OR SOMETHING ELSE?

What was going on?

Was it the Stockholm syndrome, the odd psychological phenomenon in which prisoners identify with and love their captors?

One of these clients told me I simply did not understand that people love to be challenged to do their best, and that those who were fired feel like losers—and *are*, if they do not meet the boss's standards.

[1] Adizes Insights, October 2009.

Huh? I thought.

What happened to treating people with understanding, giving them a chance, being civilized, developing them … ?

Then, while watching some top-notch sports coaches, I had an insight. These coaches are extremely demanding, and if someone repeatedly fails to meet their standards, she is out. Most of them are tough as nails, curse a lot, demean people, shout, and expect the impossible.

But the teams love them, and no one wants to be fired.

It is not toughness that people resent. Rather, they resent when the manager is not fair. To be a tough and unfair manager makes those who are being managed become rebellious. But to be a humane and unfair leader makes people despise you.

We often confuse being fair with being nice. It is not the same at all.

What does it mean to be "fair"?

> It is not toughness that people resent. Rather, they resent when the manager is not fair.

Whatever you do as a leader, whatever decision you make about people, be sure it is a "clean" decision—which means you must get your ego out of the way. Pay attention only to the situation, and respond to the situation. Do not let your personal agenda become involved.

A good coach would be a better coach if she did not scream and yell. But if she does, it must be in order to build a winning team, not to build her own self-confidence and sense of power.

People want to work for a winning team, one whose standards of behavior are high, and they appreciate a leader who imposes such standards.

TOUGH LOVE

Whether a manager is bad or good depends on how fair or unfair she is, not whether her style is rough or soft.

Do we teach managers what "fair" means and that they should make decisions without fear as long as those decisions are fair?

To me, being fair often involves exhibiting tough love, and not all of us like being tough. We do not like being disliked or rejected.

My observation, based on teaching in several graduate schools of business or management and lecturing as a visitor at dozens of others, is that we are developing managers who know how to handle computers, do research, analyze numbers, and make presentations … but how to relate to each other? Not really. We might teach them theory, but do we give them experience? No. And that is like teaching people who are color-blind the chemistry of colors and then expecting them to be painters.

It is not strange, then, that some modern managers spend more time on their computers, BlackBerrys, or similar devices, than talking to their staff.

Most problems in companies are not about the numbers. They are problems with *people*; the numbers are merely the manifestations of the problem.

We are teaching our management students how to deal with manifestations rather the causes.

Do we realize what we are doing? Can we change?

Spirituality Is Missing[1]

O NE of my former clients managed a very successful empire, but continued taking big risks and working harder and harder.

"What for?" I asked him. "You have all the money you may ever need."

"So I can get myself a bigger plane," he said with a smile.

Eventually he owned the biggest, most luxurious private jet. Then he bought an expensive beach compound for the summer, and a lavish, 182-foot yacht, and a compound in the mountains, and began looking for an even bigger mansion with a helicopter pad.

His behavior was typical of thousands of other executives. It also reminded me of women who own hundreds of pairs of shoes and keep buying more. They shop for more and more clothes, more and more jewelry. … What they already have is never enough.

What are they missing?

I suggest that they are missing true meaning in their lives. It is as if they have a hole inside their chests where the heart should be, that they keep trying to fill with material possessions.

When we lack a spiritual center, we try to fill it up with "things." But it never works, because a spiritual hole has no bottom.

When people have spiritual meaning in their lives, their interest in material possessions takes a back seat. For instance, material needs have no meaning whatsoever to those who are candidates for sainthood.

The Meaning of 'Spiritual'

Is being spiritual the same as being religious?

Many people confuse spirituality with religion. Big mistake. Some religions, or the fringes of those religions, have lost their spiritual orientation; they actually preach killing and destruction.

---

[1] Adizes Insights, October 2008.

To me, being spiritual means believing your life has meaning beyond yourself, beyond material goods. It is adhering to moral principles that are absolute and timeless, and wanting to serve in a way that feeds the heart. Not the mind, not the body. The heart.

It is totally intrinsic. You do not care if anyone knows what you did. It is enough that *you* know. It is not conspicuous consumption. It is not in the taking that one gets the pleasure; it is in the giving, without expecting anything in return.

It is pure love. And what is "love"? Love is when the giving is in the taking.

Why do you take your little kids to the circus? So you can write in your diary that you took them and that they'd better take care of you when you get old? God forbid.

There is a Sephardic curse along those lines: "May you expect from your children."

So why *do* you do it?

Because you get your benefit, your reward, in watching your kids giggle and laugh and enjoy the show. The taking is in the giving. That is love.

When you give of yourself rather than giving something material, you also enrich yourself; the more you give, the more you get.

HOW SPIRITUALITY AFFECTS QUALITY CONTROL

Let me give you an example from my consulting experience:

Years ago, I had a client whose company produced respiratory equipment for hospitals. The company had a quality-control problem. The question was how many new quality-control people they should hire.

I suggested an alternative solution: Organize a field trip to the neighborhood hospital for the production staff, to visit with children who have respiratory diseases. Ask them to imagine that those kids are their own sons and daughters. Take photographs of the kids using the equipment the company manufactures, struggling to breathe. Bring those pictures back to the company and hang them up everywhere.

What might that do to the quality of the equipment?

Now imagine a finishing school for young ladies where they are taught to measure their success in life by how many shoes they have and the cost of the clothing and jewelry that fill their closets. You would feel aghast, no?

That is what business schools do. They teach students to measure success exclusively by measuring EBITA, earnings per share, and how much their stockholders' equity has increased.

What I am suggesting is that the executive I described at the beginning of this chapter had no spiritual meaning in his life. He had a "hole," and until he filled up that "hole" with meaning, he would continue building his material empire. But no matter how large his empire might become, he would never feel fulfilled.

We have created a class of rich, unhappy people. To find peace in their lives, they need to develop their spiritual lives independently, because they sure aren't going to get it from business school.

NURTURING THE HEART

We teach our future business leaders numbers, concepts, and theories. We fill their heads, but their hearts might be empty. Schools of management that prepare future powerful leaders nurture the head and neglect the heart. True, these people might donate their accumulated "shoes and jewels" to charity someday, but that is almost like atoning for a wasted life.

I have a suggestion to make: No one should be admitted to a school of business, or get accredited as a professional leader, until he has demonstrated that he cares for the world beyond himself. Today, leading business schools require that an applicant have prior business experience. In the future, I suggest that he must also have community experience.

For instance, he must show that he has worked as a community organizer, or served in the Peace Corps, or volunteered for a not-for-profit organization. And during his management education, he must spend one summer in an internship helping people who need help: Build houses with Habitat for Humanity, or work in poverty-stricken neighborhoods, or raise funds for neighborhood medical centers that provide free care for those who cannot afford medical coverage, etc.

Without spiritual meaning, life is empty. No matter how much we have, we still will not feel complete.

Management and business schools are doing a disservice to their students with their incomplete programs. It is time for schools to train leaders with brain *and* heart, for the sake of society and our own happiness.

THE ADIZES
METHODOLOGY

THE DIFFERENCE BETWEEN ADIZES PRACTICE AND THE TRADITIONAL CONSULTING PROFESSION[1]

A DIZES practice is unique, for many reasons. For one, it is multi-disciplinary. Consulting firms are typically composed of people who specialize in a single area or function; usually they are either content-oriented—IT- or finance-oriented, etc.—or process-oriented, such as those in Human Resources.

Those who are process-oriented are not generally very well versed in the business content. They may be trained as organizational psychologists, for example, or in human behavior and group dynamics. They are specialized by function or sub-system.

A new fad is to use coaches. But an individual cannot change an organization; it takes an organization to change an organization. Sending a coach into an organization to interview a few people, write a report, or offer advice to any individual—even the CEO—will not accomplish organizational change (although it can, and should, achieve some personal growth). It takes a multidisciplinary team working together to provide the critical holistic component to achieve meaningful organizational change.

The real danger of a single-discipline approach to problem-solving lies in the old adage that if the only tool you have is a hammer, every problem looks like a nail. So if a consultant is trained in strategic planning, he will almost certainly tell a company that they must define their goals and strategy before doing anything else. The problem is, that advice is likely to be completely wrong, because the organization cannot yet clearly define its

---

[1] Adizes Insights, January–February 2005.

goals and strategy, and even if it could, it would not be able to implement the necessary changes if its structure does not change first. (More about that later.)

The Adizes Institute includes experienced people from a variety of disciplines: psychologists, economists, attorneys, MBAs, and former business executives. All are very knowledgeable about business and what it takes to lead change successfully. We are both content- *and* process-competent, and we can work together in spite of being trained in different disciplines, because we have a common language—the Adizes methodology for leading accelerated, sustainable change without causing destructive conflict.

As an analogy, think of a company with multiple computers on different operating platforms that cannot communicate with one another. We at Adizes have the "software" that allows all these different operating systems to talk among themselves, to take advantage of their indigenous competitive advantage. As a result, the totality becomes much stronger.

IDENTIFYING AND ADDRESSING PROBLEMS

If companies actually had a clear picture of their problems, it's likely they would have found a solution themselves. Thus, we do not necessarily accept the description of the problem that a client gives us. We utilize the Adizes methodology to define the problem correctly. This methodology has been tested for forty years, among hundreds of companies worldwide, ranging from smaller business units to multinational conglomerates, and including virtually every industry.

Here is the essence of it: Every organization has a lifecycle, and at each stage of its lifecycle, it has problems that are normal and some that are abnormal or even pathological.[2] Understanding this theory enables our clients to determine and better focus on which problems to solve and which to ignore, and then to create a sensible plan of action that works.

Just as a doctor determines the dosage he prescribes depending on her patient's age and size, our prescription—the plan of action—is contingent upon where the organization is on its lifecycle.

Consultants commonly prescribe medicine without regard for an

---

[2] For more information, see Ichak Adizes, *Managing Corporate Lifecycles* (Santa Barbara, CA: Adizes Institute Publications, 2004).

organization's lifecycle positioning. But the right medicine for a mature organization can be life-threatening to an Infant company. For example, clear-cut strategies—planning, in detail, exactly what to do and how to do it—may be appropriate for an organization in or near its Prime. But for a start-up, that practice could be dangerous, because an Infant organization knows only its intentions and dreams. A certain amount of planning is necessary—but not the level of planning certainty that an established company, one that thoroughly knows its market, can employ. An Infant organization has to be very flexible, able to change direction quickly as it explores what works and what doesn't work. By necessity, its planning must be a bit ambiguous.

Another example is when consultants try to discourage or dismantle dictatorial leadership because they believe it is harmful to an organization. While that may be true for a company already in Prime or beyond, it is not true for a start-up; in fact, autocratic leadership in an Infant organization is functional and necessary, because the founder has to protect his creation. It is natural, not abnormal, for the founder to be opinionated and protective of his child.

> Why is the majority of strategic planning never successfully implemented? Because the existing power structures will reject the change unless it suits them—and often those in power prefer to maintain the status quo and not rock the boat.

Yet another example: The consulting prescription of uniting sales and marketing might work for a young company, but it is a disaster for a company beyond Adolescence or approaching Prime. It might age the company, causing it to lose flexibility and its long-term orientation.

We at Adizes examine *all* the relevant factors within an organization—personalities, management style, structure, processes, finances, etc.—so that we are able to identify the true causes of the illness, which may not necessarily be where the client tells us the pain is. Clients, by and large, focus on problem manifestations, not causes.

Addressing the Power Structure

Consultants tend to work within a sequence that says strategy drives structure. That's not so. It may sound correct and it probably *should* be that way, but the reality is that what actually gets implemented is driven, by and large, by the existing organizational power structure at the time.

Why is the majority of strategic planning never successfully implemented? Because the existing power structures will reject the change unless it suits them—and often those in power prefer to maintain the status quo and not rock the boat.

At Adizes, the first thing we do is relax the "engines," making them changeable, more flexible. Once that's accomplished, we can move forward with a strategic plan for the desired direction the boat should take. We do not begin with the strategy, but rather with the power structure that enables the strategy to be designed and implemented.

Most consultants work sequentially. They define the strategy, then recommend the structure that ostensibly will deliver the strategy. That goes nowhere.

For one thing, it is too extreme a change: These consultants write reports describing what the organizational structure *should be* and then expect the change to occur. But when the new organization is announced, there is enormous resistance. It can take years to make the new strategy work because of the resistance to implementation. The result could be partial implementation of the recommendation—which could produce side effects that then need to be treated—and if *that* treatment is also partially implemented, other side effects can appear, creating a chain reaction.

Companies that engage a consulting firm to restructure their organization often run into employee problems, forcing them to call in another consultant to deal with the unions, followed by still another consultant to deal with the financial restructuring caused by the negotiations. All this restructuring could cause misalignment with the strategic advice they received from the original consultant!

I once saw a cartoon in the lobby of a medical building. It listed the names and specialties of the various doctors: a cardiologist, a dermatologist, a urologist, etc. The last was Dr. Goldberg, whose specialty was side effects.

THE STRATEGY/STRUCTURE TRIANGLE

The Adizes methodology, which is a non-linear way of synchronizing the development and implementation of structure and strategy, has been increasingly embraced worldwide by businesses and governments alike.

We work in a more interactive or interchangeable way regarding the strategy and structure. Instead of the typical linear, sequential approach, with strategy coming first and driving structure, we start with an inverted V, or triangle. At the base of one side is "Strategy"; at the other is "Structure."

We start on the strategy side, asking about the mission and nature of the organization. Then we move to the structure side and ask what basic organizational structure template makes sense for that mission. This is not the final chart, only the first draft. It induces the power structure to accommodate the mission. They usually accept the discussion and its conclusions, because as yet, no change has been recommended. It is like administering anesthesia prior to surgery.

We then move back to strategy and start working in more detail, followed by moving back to structure for more details. We continue moving back and forth, much like a person trying to maintain his balance while climbing up two sides of a triangle: one step on one side followed by one step on the other. Eventually, the two sides meet at the top. By then it is clear that the structure has to change if the mission and strategy are to be implemented.

FACILITATING RATHER THAN DICTATING SOLUTIONS

The Adizes Associates are not the ones to develop the strategy, the mission, or the structure. The company's top managers do this by themselves. Our role is merely to lead the discussion, provide the tools for management to deal effectively with the issues, and create a safe environment to prevent the discussion from becoming destructive. We provide both the tools and the process; the client provides the content. That is why we can work in any industry, in any country. And we do.

Because Adizes provides both the tools and the process, we are unique among consultants. It represents a major change in consulting, a paradigm shift in the methodology for leading change effectively.

Other consultants avoid this process, I believe, because it is time-consuming for the client and thus more difficult to sell. And they are afraid—or don't know how—to transform the power structure, to lead this participative process. It is just too much political risk for them to deal with.

But that is exactly the strength of the Adizes methodology: It knows how to handle the power structure constructively. We continuously adjust strategy and structure, fine-tuning each many times in small increments, until they fit together. The beauty of all this is that the organization becomes accustomed to changes, albeit small ones, versus a major upheaval every five or ten years. Continual small changes in process and structure, of course, are far better and more productive than large, traumatic ones. This is one of the principle reasons why Adizes is different: the interdependency between structure and process/strategy, expressed in how we achieve systematic changes in an organization.

Our treatment of an organization is holistic. We diagnose the entire enterprise, and if our treatment requires specialists, we will bring them in, with the agreement of the client, and effectively coordinate their work with ours.

Taking the First Steps

The success of our effort to balance strategy and structure is contingent upon management's acceptance of changing the organizational structure. Resistance can exist in any organization; thus, we do not accept clients until we have first conducted a two-day workshop with them.

Who is included in that workshop? All those who have the authority and power in the company or business unit being diagnosed. This might include several layers of the organizational structure, perhaps twenty or thirty people. The workshop gives us the opportunity to determine whether any managers and/or departments are displaying symptoms of a silo mentality, concentrating on their own specializations or departments without trying to integrate with others—and if so, whether such attitudes can be eliminated.

We provide the tools for self-diagnosis, to determine where the organization is in its corporate lifecycle; once that is determined, we can see which problems are normal and which are abnormal. We can then align the organization's priorities correctly.

Then, we have everyone in the room write down the most pressing problems within the company. They do this anonymously so that they can be completely honest. We don't allow anyone to be mentioned by name.

We also require that the problems be expressed in language that indicates they are controllable by the people in the room. You cannot complain, "It is raining outside"; but you *can* say, "We don't have an umbrella." You cannot say, "Interest rates are unpredictable"; but you *can* say, "We don't have a strategy to respond to unpredictable interest rates."

Then, before I ask to see what problems people have written down, I ask them, "How many of these problems existed last year? Two years ago? Three?" Typically, people will say, "Most of them."

Well, if a problem has existed for the last three years, it's not hard to get people to agree that chances are, that problem will still be around in another three years. And when I ask how many of these problems can be solved by any single individual, including the CEO, people usually say, "None of them."

So even though I don't know what they have written down, their admission that no one person, not even their CEO, can solve the problems alone indicates that if the problems could have been solved, they probably would have been solved by now. But that has not happened, and the reason why is that the organization has its managers each chasing ten problems, instead of having ten managers chasing one problem at a time.

From there, we lead the group discussion to decide which problems they should chase together and which problems should be put on the back burner until the more pressing problems are solved. Their first task, then, is not deciding which problems to solve but rather which problems *not* to solve, for now. This way, the organization can free up resources to jointly work on the top-priority problems. People begin to see that they have been chasing too many problems and that the reason they have been unable to get the cooperation of others is that those people are busy chasing their *own* set of problems. Everyone is running in place, and little is being accomplished.

> *Once organizations realize how their structure is causing their problems, they can see for themselves that they have to deal with the structure first.*

Because no one is mentioned by name, no one is on the hot seat; thus, people are free to open up. They learn to accept that "we" have a problem, not that someone else has a problem. The questions can then relate to what "we" should do, which makes a huge difference in the room's climate. People can join hands to solve problems, instead of pointing fingers at one another.

As the problems are framed in this way, people quickly come to recognize the link between correcting the organizational structure and solving the problems: They have a climate issue, which is causing a structural issue, which is causing an information flow problem, which is causing a strategic problem, which is creating functional problems, which are causing the company to lose market share. There is a sequence to the problems, and after counseling hundreds of companies all over the world for the past forty years, I can assure you that this sequence is universal.

Once organizations realize how their structure is causing their problems, they can see for themselves that they have to deal with the structure first. Unless the structure is repaired, nothing much will change, and the problems will not be solved.

And from that realization, all the steps that follow are perceived as a natural progression.

Transferring the Technology

Another important difference from most traditional consulting firms is that we transfer the technology to the client, so that the organization can continue this process of perpetual change without Adizes necessarily being involved on an ongoing basis. Others give the client advice and, typically, must return later with additional advice, because over time their original recommendations become obsolete.

The "technology" means the management leadership tools I was referring to before: We teach the client what we know and give them the tools so they can continuously apply and adapt them to the changing environment once we leave. We eliminate the need for the client's continued dependency on us. We are actually teachers: We teach the client how to use the tools and self-monitor them as they grow and change.

As an analogy, think of a patient who goes to his doctor with a problem. The doctor, with many years of training, diagnoses the illness and prescribes a treatment that the patient follows but does not have to understand. This relationship represents empowerment of the medical profession and disempowerment of the patient. That is now changing, due to patients' rights, better patient education, and the like. Nevertheless, the established protocol—that the doctor is superior by nature of his knowledge, and the patient is inferior—has been maintained.

At Adizes, we are transforming consulting into a methodology that is therapeutic, using a different protocol. Consider psychotherapists. They do not tell you what to do; rather, they help eliminate barriers or blockages to enable you to do what you realize you should and/or want to do. The same is true of homeopathic medicine: It removes blockages to the flow of energy so that the body can take care of itself.

We do the same thing: We remove the barriers that prevent organizations from healing themselves.

KNOWING WHAT TO ASK

When a traditional consultant—whether it is Peter Drucker or someone else—listens to a client's problems and prescribes a treatment, the answers belong to the consultant, not the client. The client merely has the option of following the advice or not.

The Adizes methodology is the reverse of that. We ask the questions, and the client must come up with the answers. We're like psychotherapists, who do not provide answers but, rather, know what questions to ask and in what sequence to ask them. The process forces clients to come to their own "Aha!" They find their own answers.

We, too, know what questions to ask and in what sequence.[3] We provide the road map and tools to navigate, but they do the "driving" on their own until they reach the light at the end of the tunnel. When we come to a barrier where a client has no answer, we give him the tools to find the answer. If we recommend anything, it is only as a trial balloon.

In this way, clients see and learn how to use the tools we provide. And in this way, the ultimate solution to the problem is their own.

This method has similarities to coaching, in that both methods ask questions. But coaching is neither holistic nor multidisciplinary. Coaches employ psychological tools, versus tools of a business and organizational nature. The questions coaches ask are, by and large, of a psychological nature, and the focus is on the individual being coached. I've seen many coaches actually miss the organizational problem because of their focus on psychodynamics and individual needs. And besides, behind that method is an unsupported assumption: that by changing the individual they can change the organization. But what makes an individual operate better is not necessarily what makes an organization operate better.

By contrast, we work on the *business* of the organization—that is, what makes the organization operate successfully in a changing environment— and help the individual to fit into the organization. Adizes is unique in that

---

[3] For more information, see Ichak Adizes, *Mastering Change* (Santa Barbara, CA: Adizes Institute Publications, 2003).

it recognizes that you must first change the organizational climate before you can change the behavior of the individual.

Talking to the Right People

In addition to asking the right questions, one has to know whom to ask. One of the Adizes principles is, "People who *row* the boat do not *rock* the boat." So when there is a need to change the direction the boat is taking, the first thing we ask is, "Who can rock this boat?" In other words: Who can obstruct the solution, assuming we know what the solution is? What power pieces must be assembled in order to successfully implement a solution?

A lot of consultants rely on what I call the "bypass system": They go into an organization, talk to the people who understand the problem, then write a report and submit it to the people with the authority to decide. Unfortunately, this won't work, because the people in the organization are unable to communicate with one another. That's why they called in the consultant in the first place.

At Adizes, we steer clear of the bypass system. Instead, we gather all the necessary people into a room and provide a methodology that allows them to talk to one another, to jointly determine and agree on the problems they face, and create a road map for a solution.

Here's an analogy: If a husband and wife cannot communicate, they go to a psychotherapist who provides a safe environment for the two to talk to one another. Essentially, this is what we do: provide a safe environment based on some principles and tools that must be followed, so workers and management can communicate with one another.

Barriers to Finding Solutions

In our experience, the solution to an organization's problems generally resides somewhere inside the organization. Often it resides with the employees on the line, or the salespeople, or other workers who are close to what is happening on a daily basis. But that information never flows back to the people who can decide to do something about it.

To avoid that problem, it is vital that you include in the process all the people with the authority to solve the problem.

Organizations typically allocate problems by responsibility, but that's wrong. Having the responsibility to deal with a problem is useless unless you also have the authority to solve it, and in many "sick" companies that is not the case. Problems should be allocated by *authority*, not responsibility.

PARALLEL STRUCTURE IS ESSENTIAL

There is no way to grow and change without a parallel structure that enables the circular flow of energy, up *and* down. The Adizes methodology provides that parallel structure: If you can't get an issue solved at the lower echelons of the organization, you can send a "Potential Improvement Point" (PIP) to a higher-level authority in the parallel structure and move it on to appropriate levels for decision. You have open channels for the PIP to seek the authority that will solve it. Thus, for the problems where the necessary authority is missing, we ascend the organizational hierarchy until we can connect the problem with the authority needed to solve it.

The channels for going up the hierarchy are different from the channels that implement decisions and thus go down, from top to bottom, in the organization. That is what is meant by parallel organizations.

Efforts for change cannot flow through the same channel, i.e., structure, that was designed for efficient implementation of decisions. These "energies" are incompatible. It is normal for managers to be impatient with the need for change and say, "Hey, we have a business to run, sell, and deliver."

But management is about more than selling and delivering. Management, in order to have an effective and efficient organization, needs to lead change as well. However, managing change, while simultaneously managing for effectiveness and efficiency in the short run, are incompatible efforts. Thus, the need for a parallel structure.

BARRIERS TO IMPLEMENTATION

But even authority to make a decision is not enough to solve a problem. Often, the people who make the decisions have the authority but not the power to implement solutions. Who has the power? Those whose coop-eration is needed for effective and efficient implementation. And if those people believe their interests will be threatened by the change, they may not cooperate.

This creates barriers to implementation. It also causes organizational disintegration, because those who have the authority to decide have no power to implement, and those who have the power to make things happen have no authority to decide.

Our strength is in being able to coalesce power, authority, and influence (CAPI). First, we find out who knows how to diagnose the problem and solve it, and we bring them to the table. Next, we bring to the table those who are necessary for implementation of any solution, and we include them in developing that solution. Finally, we bring to the table whoever has the authority to say "yes" and "no" to the developed solution. I do not mean the people who can say "yes" *or* "no," but "yes" *and* "no". This is a critical distinction, one most consultants completely miss. We find that in many organizations, lots of people have the right to say "no," but not to say "yes." It is essential that the people who can say "yes" are included at the table.

There is a specific discipline—a technology—to determine whom to bring to the table and how to get them to start communicating with one another with mutual respect and trust, and with constructive conflict—without fighting. As the discussion advances in diagnosing and solving the problem, the composition of the group at the table might change, because different authority and different people's cooperation might be needed, etc.

This sounds straightforward, but it is not necessarily simple to accomplish. Most consultants never even try. Some consultants never ask the hard questions that determine who within the organization needs to be included. Some are afraid to stipulate that the "yes" people attend. Too often, the group is composed of people who know what should be done but do not have the power or authority to make it happen—although, ironically, some of them may have the power to *undermine* the solution, even without knowing what the solution is supposed to be. Typically, that happens because they are trying to protect their self-interests.

We know how to bring these divergent groups together and get them to jointly begin analyzing the problem, come to a conclusion as to what the problem is, why it is necessary to reach a solution, and, at the end of the day, to jointly conclude that they should cooperate to get things moving forward. In this way, the whole company moves ahead toward the solution, because we have united the knowledge, power, and authority.

If for some reason the knowledge does not already reside within the company, then it must be imported using outside consultants. However, I have only seen that occur twice in forty years! The solution is almost always resident within the organization. The art is in helping the company uncover, examine, discuss, and implement the solution in an environment of mutual trust and respect. Seeing the solutions implemented as a result of our efforts is wonderfully rewarding.

On Participative Management

The re-engineering fad in America today has replaced hierarchies with "teamwork," "network management," and other trendy words and ideas. But during the many years of my professional life, I have seen the pendulum swing from side to side. Years ago, the trend was toward hierarchies, spans of control, units of direction. Next, the trend was to eliminate them; that package was called participative management.

But wherever organizations have tried to re-engineer down hierarchies, the result has only been more questions: "Who is accountable?" or, "How do we find out what's going on?" I give that kind of change five years, and then I predict the pendulum will swing back. You cannot have only muscles. You also need bones. You need hierarchy.

I often sit back during deliberations at a meeting and wonder, "Why do we always think in terms of 'either/or'? Why can't it be 'and'?"

> American culture wants easy solutions, and it is suffering from easy solutions.

Life, after all, is not "either/or." Instead, one often has to integrate two opposing factors, which is difficult. An "either/or" argument is easy. Unfortunately, American culture wants easy solutions, and it is suffering from easy solutions.

Managers will be making a mistake if they reject hierarchies and go into team management exclusively. They will end up with management by committee and will not be able to get accountability. While decision-*making* should be by the team, decision-*taking*—i.e., finalizing a decision—should be done by an accountable hierarchy.

Companies today, with all the trendy phrases competing for their attention, have to be wary of switching horses. The result is continual confusion. The system has to have teamwork *and* hierarchy.

Adizes is a holistic, systemic, structural, participative methodology whereby we bring in all the participants necessary for finding a solution. I believe that's unique in the consulting profession. Others may use pieces of what we do, but they may not be systemic. Those who are systemic are not structural. Some are structural but not multidisciplinary. TQM, for example, doesn't have parallel entrepreneur and integrator structures (EI) to deal with change. It does not have the methodology to get the information up the corporate hierarchy from the lower ranks where the issues are generated. Nor does the TQM methodology coalesce a group of people who have the needed coalesced authority, power, and influence (CAPI) to make decisions and implement them.

DOING WHAT WORKS

Most important, the Adizes methodology works, as demonstrated by our remarkable success rate of almost 100 percent implementing organizational strategic changes with hundreds of companies in more than fifty countries.

One of our clients grew from $150 million to $1.5 billion in sales in ten years, without stumbling, and continued to grow into a $4 billion company without any dilution of ownership, just pure organic growth.

We provided the tools and the process to enable a military electronics company to move into consumer and medical electronics, something they had been trying to do for years. With our tools and process, they succeeded in just months.

We helped Bank of America convert itself from being just a bank—and mostly retail—into a financial services institution.

We helped Salinas Group Mexico grow from $250 million capitalization to $3.5 billion capitalization.

These tools have also been used on a macro level. We helped organize the Cabinet structure for Vicente Fox, the President of Mexico.

Other examples can be seen in the numerous testimonials, from CEOs around the world, that we have collected on our website, www.adizes.com.

WHO IS QUALIFIED TO APPLY THE ADIZES METHODOLOGY?

Our training is rigorous. It takes about three years to become fully trained and qualified, even if the trainee was a CEO before joining us. All our Associates undergo comprehensive training and must pass written exams before they are qualified to practice. They then practice under supervision, similar to an internship. If they do well, they must pass an oral exam in front of all the certified Associates who attend the annual Adizes international convention. They are then certified.

To maintain certification, they must take at least one course a year at the Adizes Graduate School, which is licensed to grant both masters and doctoral degrees in the methodology. Today, we have offices with trained and certified Associates in ten countries. Worldwide, there are about fifty Adizes Associates, some of whom have been practicing for more than twenty years.

Does It Always Work?

Our success is not guaranteed, of course. It will not work, for example, if the CEO is not committed to making changes along with his people, or if he makes decisions with outside consultants and then brings the "solution" into the company, only to end up with a disempowered management team. It is unusual, but we have stopped working with clients where we felt the CEOs expected a solution to be handed to them or who refused to participate in the change.

We do all the planning and implementation of the changes with the people involved, and that requires a confident CEO who is not afraid to hear and even learn from people lower in the organization. It requires a CEO willing to invest the time, both his own and that of the appointed team, to deal with the problems.

ABOUT THE ADIZES INSTITUTE

FOR the past 35 years, the Adizes Institute has been committed to equipping visionary leaders, management teams, and agents of change to become champions of their industries and markets. These leaders have successfully established a collaborative organizational culture by using Adizes' pragmatic tools and concepts to achieve peak performance.

Adizes specializes in guiding leaders of organizations (CEOs, top management teams, boards, owners) to quickly and effectively resolve such issues as:

- Difficulties in executing good decisions.
- Making the transition from entrepreneurship to professional management.
- Difficulties in aligning the structure of the organization to achieve its strategic intent.
- "Bureaucratizing": the organization is getting out of touch with its markets and beginning to lose entrepreneurial vitality.
- Conflicts among founders, owners, board members, partners, and family members.
- Internal management team conflicts and "politics" severe enough to inhibit the success of the business.
- Growing pains.
- Culture clashes between companies undergoing mergers or acquisitions.

Adizes also offers comprehensive training and certification for change leaders who wish to incorporate into their practice the Adizes methodologies for managing change.

Adizes is the primary sponsor of the Adizes Graduate School, a non-profit teaching organization that offers Master's and Ph.D. programs for the Study of Leadership and Change.

For more information about these and other programs, please visit www.adizes.com.